FAIR HOUSING

A Guidebook for
Owners and Managers
of Apartments

Fair Housing

A Guidebook for Owners and Managers of Apartments

Published in Washington, D.C. 20005 by
The Compass Group, LLC

Manufactured in the
United States of America.

Author, Title, Subtitle
The Compass Group,
Fair Housing
A Guidebook for Owners and Managers of Apartments, Second Edition

ISBN
978-0-615-2291-4

Portions of this book have appeared previously in The NAHMA Fair Housing Guidebook
for Owners and Managers of Housing Receiving Federal Financial Aid, Third Edition.

Publication Information

Fair Housing: A Guidebook for Owners and Managers of Apartments

A question and answer guidebook covering nondiscrimination laws as they apply to the rental of apartments.

Second Edition
October, 2008

Published by:
The Compass Group, LLC
927 15th Street, N.W., Suite 600
Washington, DC 20005
www.compassgroup.net

Copyright

Disclaimer

This publication is designed to provide accurate and authoritative information in regard to the subject matter covered. It is sold with the understanding that the information herein is of a general nature. If legal or other expert assistance is required, the services of a competent professional should be sought.

The information contained herein is based on sources believed to be accurate and reliable. However, no representation or warranty is made as to such accuracy. Readers should refer to primary sources whenever appropriate, and should make certain that information has not been affected by recent developments.

This guidebook is an introduction to certain important issues involved in fair housing for the rental of apartments in the United States. It is not exhaustive of the issues and requirements. It reflects the authors' professional experience, research and opinions, which may or may not agree with those of other commentators or experts in the field. The reader must appreciate that the correct course of action will turn on particular facts and circumstances that surround a particular property, its geographic location, and the evolution of case law.

Acknowledgements

The first edition of this Guidebook represented a significant enhancement of material previously published in the NAHMA Fair Housing Guidebook – 3rd Edition. The first edition of this Guidebook was possible thanks to the efforts of so many. The primary authors of that effort were Anker Heegaard, Charlie Wilkins and Tracy Barnes of the Compass Group. NAHMA contributors were primarily Terry Ross, Mike Goodwin, Gwen Volk and Roxie Munn. Their contributions, in particular, went beyond the call of duty. Additional and helpful guidance was provided by Chris Hanback, Kathy Coughlin, Peter Burkett, and Fred Wood. Invaluable assistance was also provided by Beverly Heegaard, who stayed the course of this work during its reconstruction, and Shiela Salmon, whose comments helped to loosen the knots.

This second edition reflects substantial additions and revisions to the previously published material. The principal authors have been Anker Heegaard and Charlie Wilkins. A continuing partnership with the National Affordable Housing Management Association has provided invaluable commentary on draft material and special thanks go to NAHMA members Arthera Burgess, Brian Carnahan, Carole Glodney, Allan Pinter, Greg Proctor, Scott Reithel, Melanie Shapiro, Gwen Volk and Kathi Williams. And to Kris Cook on whose handshake this renewed venture is based. The authors also wish to acknowledge the input and contributions of Jeff Lubell, an early contributor to this edition, and Michael Allen, whose comments concerning the rights and needs of people with disabilities have improved this edition. Lastly, special thanks to Abhisek Mitra, whose committed efforts toward this edition are deeply appreciated.

Additional Copies

Discounts are available based upon NAHMA membership and purchase volume. Please visit us at www.compassgroup.net for more information on ordering this publication. See the last page of this book for ordering information.

Other Publications

The Compass Group has published other books of interest to housing professionals: "Shelter from the Storm: Successful Market Conversions of Regulated Housing", "Managing Housing Credit Apartments, A Question and Answer Handbook", and "Managing Occupancy: A Companion Guide to HUD's Occupancy Handbook".

The Compass Group, LLC

The Compass Group is a consulting partnership that specializes in affordable housing policy, management and finance. Its two principal partners are:

Charles S. Wilkins, Jr.

cwilkins@compassgroup.net

and

Anker Heegaard

anker@compassgroup.net

Introduction

As Americans, we enjoy some of the best housing in the world. And as Americans, we usually take for granted our ability to choose suitable housing based on our preferences, our ability to pay, and our housing and credit history.

However, it was not always so: the landmark Fair Housing Act dates only to 1968. Federal protections for persons with disabilities, and for families with children, are even more recent, having been added to the Fair Housing Act in 1988.

Yet, today, anyone who attends housing industry meetings will find that the principles of fair housing are thoroughly ingrained in the thoughts and actions of professional owners and managers. Everyone agrees that residents and applicants are entitled to be treated consistently and on the basis of their individual situations. Similarly, everyone believes that it is not only illegal but immoral to base our treatment of residents and applicants on our own stereotypes, myths, or fears.

So, if everyone agrees on general principles, what is the need for a guidebook like this, why does it cover so many topics, and why does it go into such detail? Here are a few of the answers:

- As we implement fair housing, the relatively simple principles of fair housing begin to interact with a bewilderingly complex array of housing markets, properties, residents and applicants, an environment in which nothing is simple.
- The principles of fair housing sometimes contradict, or seem to contradict, other strongly held American values, and it is not always easy to determine what is legal, let alone to determine what is right and moral.
- There are a variety of fair housing laws (federal, state and local) with differing applicability to different apartment properties.
- Many aspects of fair housing practice stem from laws and regulations that, although simple and definitive in the abstract, are subject to varying interpretations in the real world. This means that case law becomes relatively more important than in most other areas of apartment ownership and management. It also means that the cutting edge of fair housing practice is always changing.

The purpose of this guidebook is to help apartment owners and managers translate their support of fair housing in principle, into the consistent day to day reality of fair housing in the properties they own and manage.

This process begins with an understanding of the various fair housing laws. Next is an assessment of each property for potential fair housing challenges. We suggest policy approaches that will provide a firm foundation for each property's fair housing efforts. The guidebook also presents a wide range of fair housing issues, including issues at the cutting edge of fair housing practice.

We also include citations for landmark cases, plus a variety of appendices containing useful information that is sometimes not easy to find. Finally, the guidebook includes insights from expert owners and managers who have faced these issues and developed particularly effective approaches.

We hope that this guidebook will contribute to the continuing advancement of fair housing principles and practice in the apartment industry.

A Note on the Second Edition

First published in 2000, this Guidebook helped to fill a need in the apartment industry. By 2008 the call for a revision was clear and we began scoping out the changes that would characterize this edition. Most importantly, we have added a number of new Questions which we believe are timely. These include:

Question 14. . . . What Fair Housing Considerations Apply to Victims of Domestic Violence?

Question 15. . . . What Does the Violence Against Women Act Require for Federally-Assisted Properties?

Question 19. . . . What Are the Most Common Non-Federally Protected Classes?

Question 20. . . . In What Ways do the Fair Housing Act and State and Local Laws Overlap?

Question 33. . . . What Constitutes Sexual Harassment?

Question 34. . . . What Fair Housing Considerations Apply to Non-Citizens?

Question 35. . . . May I Designate a Property, or Portions of a Property, "Smoke-Free"?

Question 36. . . . What Constitutes a Reasonable Accommodation in Response to Complaints Regarding Second-Hand Smoke?

Question 37. . . . What is 'Linguistic Profiling'?

Question 38. . . . Am I Responsible for Intervening When an Applicant or Resident Is Harassed by Another Person?

Question 46. . . . What are Best Practices for Recordkeeping?

Question 60. . . . May an Owner Adopt a Resident Selection Policy That Excludes Voucher Holders?

Question 61. . . . What Are the Fair Housing Considerations Related to Students?

Question 83. . . . Could a Reasonable Accommodation Request for a Unit Transfer Include a Request that the Landlord Pay the Resident's Moving Costs?

Question 95. . . . Service Animals in Projects for the Elderly or People with Disabilities

Readers should be aware of a major development affecting the ADA (and fair housing generally). In June 2008, the U.S. House of Representatives passed legislation entitled 'The ADA Amendments Act of 2008'. In September, the Senate passed similar legislation. The bills are expected to be reconciled before the end of the term, and if so the law (in its reconciled form) will be effective as of January 1, 2009. The Act articulates the intent of Congress regarding protections for people with disabilities and repudiates a number of legal precedents which Congress felt were inconsistent with "a clear and comprehensive national mandate for the elimination of discrimination."

The effect of the Act will be to broaden the population covered by the ADA. Fundamental aspects include:

- A less restrictive standard for defining the term 'substantially limits';

- Any determination about whether a disability substantially limits a major life activity must be made without regard to whether the effects of the disability can be addressed with mitigating measures; and,

- A disability does not need to be ongoing: courts may not consider whether a disability is 'episodic, latent or in remission'.

TABLE OF CONTENTS

Note: References are to Question Numbers

Chapter Four: Introduction to Fair Housing Enforcement

Chapter Five: Fair Housing Marketing and Advertising Requirements

Note: References are to Question Numbers

Note: References are to Question Numbers

Note: References are to Question Numbers

Chapter Thirteen: Admissions and Eviction Issues for People With Disabilities

Chapter Fourteen: Fair Housing Issues for Specific Disabilities

Note: References are to Question Numbers

Note: References are to Question Numbers

Chapter Seventeen: Accessibility and Federally-Assisted Properties

Chapter Eighteen: Occupancy, People With Disabilities, and Federally-Assisted Housing

Note: References are to Question Numbers

Chapter Nineteen: Fair Housing Marketing and Admissions Issues for Federally-Assisted Properties

Chapter Twenty: Familial Status Issues in Federally-Assisted Housing

Note: References are to Question Numbers

Chapter Twenty-One: "Mixed Population" Issues in Federally-Assisted Elderly Properties

Index

About Us and Our Publications

Chapter One: Fair Housing Laws and Regulations

1 What Is Fair Housing?

Fair housing refers to the prohibition against discrimination in any activity relating to the sale or rental of dwellings, in the availability of financing or other real estate related transactions, or in the provision of housing-related services.

Regulations under the Fair Housing Act provide that:

"No person shall be subjected to discrimination because of race, color, religion, sex, handicap, familial status or national origin in the sale, rental or advertising of dwellings, in the provision of brokerage services or in the availability of residential real estate-related transactions." [1]

Technically, only the Fair Housing Act (Title VIII of the Civil Rights Act of 1968, as amended by the Fair Housing Amendments Act of 1988) is a "fair housing" law. However, there are other federal, state and local laws that also prohibit discriminatory conduct in housing-related activities, although these non-discrimination laws sometimes have a broader application than housing. For purposes of this guidebook the term "fair housing" will refer to the entire collection of federal, state and local requirements governing non-discrimination in housing.

This guide addresses fair housing issues applicable to multi-family rental housing. Readers should be aware, however, that significant fair housing requirements apply to for-sale housing, real estate brokerage, and other areas of residential real estate practice.

For guidance on how fair housing laws apply to small properties, see question 3.

Additionally, for purposes of this guidebook, multifamily housing is defined as buildings with five or more rental apartments. Some laws apply to small rental housing properties of one to four apartments.

---

1. *24CFR, §100.5*

2 Who Must Obey the Fair Housing Act?

- Persons engaged in the real estate profession (such as owners, managers, sellers or financiers) who have been involved in three or more sales or rentals in the prior 12 months.

- Owners of buildings that contain two or more dwelling units.

See question 18. Housing providers should also determine whether applicable state and local laws may impose additional requirements beyond those of the Fair Housing Act.

3 I Have a Small Rental Property. Do the Federal Fair Housing Laws Apply to Me?

Concerning small properties, the following rules apply:[2]

- The rental of single-family homes is exempt from federal fair housing laws, unless (1) the owner has an interest in more than three single-family homes, or (2) a broker or agent is in any way involved in the transaction. See the last two bullets for exceptions.

- The owner of a property with fewer than five dwelling units is exempt *only if* the owner actually resides in one of the units. See the last two bullets on this page for exceptions.

- Owners of buildings with two or more rental units, where the owner is not a resident of one of the units, must adhere to all federal fair housing requirements.

- Owners of buildings with five or more rental units, regardless of the occupancy of the owner, must adhere to all federal fair housing requirements.

2.Note that the federal fair housing law discussed above applies to the total number of units, not the actual occupancy. Additionally, state and local fair housing laws, as well as federal, state or local civil rights laws may apply,

- Prohibitions against discriminatory advertising, statements and notices apply to all rental properties, regardless of the number of apartments. Therefore, even single-family rentals must abide by certain fair housing requirements.

- Any person engaged in three or more rental transactions in the last twelve months must abide by fair housing laws.

Exceptions for Small Properties

The owner of a duplex resides in the downstairs unit, and offers the upstairs unit for rent. A woman and her five-year-old child apply and are rejected by the owner who says, "I don't want any children here." While the owner of this small (and otherwise exempt) building is free to reject the woman and child on any grounds, including their familial status, the owner's verbal statement was discriminatory and is not exempt.*

* HUD Administrative Law Judge, 02-98-0276-9, HUD v. Schmid

4 Which Federal Laws and Regulations Govern Fair Housing for Apartments?

For greater detail on the Fair Housing Act, see question 5 and question 6.

Title VIII of the Civil Rights Act of 1968 (the "Fair Housing Act") provides protection from discriminatory housing practices based upon race, color, religion, and national origin. In 1974, sex was added to the list of protected classes. The Fair Housing Amendments Act, discussed below, added two additional protected classes and also provided for the award of monetary damages for discriminatory housing practices.

For greater detail on the Fair Housing Amendments Act, see question 6.

The Fair Housing Amendments Act of 1988 ("The Amendments Act") expanded the scope of protection under the Fair Housing Act to prohibit discrimination against people with disabilities and against families with children. The Amendments Act also significantly enhanced HUD's ability to investigate complaints under, and enforce, the Fair Housing Act. This book uses the term 'Fair Housing Act' to refer to the protections against discrimination afforded by both the Civil Rights Act of 1968, and the Fair Housing Amendments Act of 1988.

For greater detail on the ADA, see question 13.

The Americans With Disabilities Act (the "ADA") requires accessibility for people with disabilities, and prohibits discrimination against people with disabilities, in employment, governmental activities and commercial activities.

For greater detail on Section 504, see question 125 and question 126, and Chapter 15 and Chapter 16.

Section 504 of The Rehabilitation Act of 1973 ("Section 504") requires accessibility for people with disabilities, and prohibits discrimination against people with disabilities, in housing and other programs that receive federal financial assistance.

Title VI of the Civil Rights Act of 1964 ("Title VI") prohibits discrimination on the basis of race, color or national origin in all HUD-assisted programs. Title VI covers all HUD housing programs except for its mortgage insurance and loan guarantee programs.

The Age Discrimination Act of 1975 prohibits discrimination on the basis of age in programs and activities receiving federal financial assistance.

See question 18; also see question 125 for laws and regulations specifically affecting federally assisted properties.

Note that in addition to the Federal Fair Housing laws listed above, many states and localities have issued their own laws, some of which accord protection from discrimination to additional classes of people.

5   Who Is Protected by Federal Fair Housing Laws?

Protected Classes

With respect to rental housing, providers may not discriminate in any activity relating to the rental of dwellings, or in the provision of services or facilities, on the basis of:

- Race
- Color
- Religion
- Sex
- National origin
- Handicap or disability[3]

See question 3 and Chapter 8.

Note that many states and localities have issued their own laws, some of which accord protection from discrimination to additional classes of people. see question 19.

- Familial status (generally, the presence of children under 18 in a household)

The above seven categories, known as the 'protected classes,' are the only groups explicitly protected by the federal fair housing laws.

The terms 'race', 'color' and 'national origin' are sometimes used interchangeably, and the differences can be subtle:

- Race refers to any group of people identified on the basis of their genetically transmitted physical characteristics, taking into account social and cultural characteristics, as well as ancestry.

- Color discrimination occurs when preferences or unequal treatment are based on skin color.

- National origin discrimination is based on the country from which a person or a person's family has come.

In addition to the direct protection against discrimination afforded by membership in a protected class, applicants and tenants are protected from discrimination based on the protected status of their guests or associates.[4]

Persons are Protected from Discrimination Based on their Guests

Resident Alfred enjoys frequent visits from his mother, who has a mental disability. The owner of the property attempts to evict Alfred, fearing that his mother will cause some harm. Alfred is protected from eviction and from interference with his enjoyment of the dwelling on the basis of his mother's disability.*

* 24 CFR §100.60(b)(5) and 24 CFR §100.400

---

3. *The preferred term in this book is 'disability', however, some laws and regulations governing Fair Housing use the term 'handicap' and that term will be used in the context of those laws and regulations.*
4. *See U.S. v. Thomas Nail, CASE NO. 3:00-CV-659-J-HTS*

Persons are Protected from Discrimination Based on their Guests

Applicant Gerry is a white woman. She appears at the leasing office of an apartment property to submit a rental application accompanied by her friend Harry, an African American. Her rental application is declined. The property is liable for discrimination against Gerry if its refusal to rent to her is based on her association with Harry, even though the discrimination is not based on Gerry's race.

Exclusions and Exceptions

See question 72 for exemptions from familial status requirements under the Fair Housing Act.

There are a few specific exclusions to the protected classes listed at the beginning of this question:

- Although familial status is a protected class, certain properties reserved for seniors are exempt, and may deny applications based on the inclusion of children in the tenant's household.

- Although religion is a protected class, housing provided by religious organizations for non-commercial purposes may give preference based on religion, unless membership in that religion is restricted by race, color or national origin. For example, housing provided rent-free by a religious organization to members of a religious order (a non-commercial purpose) could be selective on the basis of religion, whereas housing provided by a religious organization to the public (a commercial purpose) could not discriminate on the basis of religion.

See questions 108 through 113.

- Although drug addicts are protected, those currently using illegal, controlled substances are not. Additionally, anyone convicted of the illegal manufacture or distribution of a controlled substance is not protected.[5]

See question 121 for further information on mental illness as a disability.

- Although mental illness is protected, HUD's fair housing regulations make a specific exception for transvestism, which is not protected. Note however that a transvestite may have other mental disorders that would provide for protected status.

---

5. *24CFR, §100.10(a)(4)*

6   What Is the Fair Housing Amendments Act of 1988?

The Fair Housing Amendments Act of 1988 extended to people with disabilities and to families with children the same protection from discrimination in housing which was provided in Title VIII of the Civil Rights Act of 1968 to individuals based on race, color, religion, sex and national origin.

The Amendments Act was passed 20 years ago. Despite this, discrimination against people with disabilities is the single most prevalent bias. HUD indicates that of the 10,000 housing discrimination complaints filed in 2007, 43% were on behalf of people with disabilities.

Disability-Related Requirements

A disability is an impairment which substantially limits a major life activity. Persons who have a "record of" such an impairment, or are "regarded as" having such an impairment are also considered to have disabilities. The Fair Housing Act requires that rental housing providers permit residents with disabilities to make reasonable modifications to existing premises if necessary to enable them to take full advantage of rental housing opportunities. Housing providers must make reasonable accommodations in rules, policies, practices and services to accommodate the disabilities of residents and applicants.

Key Areas of Concern Related to Disability

With respect to people with disabilities, housing providers and people with disabilities have expressed the following key areas of concern:

See question 31.

- How to respect the rights (or, accommodate the needs) of people with disabilities in the applicant screening process;

- How to balance the obligation to provide accessibility against other obligations of the property, in the context of a limited budget; and

- How to balance the rights of people with disabilities with the rights of other residents and applicants.

Requirements Related to Familial Status

Familial status protections of the Fair Housing Act prohibit providers from discriminating against households with individuals who are under 18 years of age, pregnant women and households seeking custody of an individual under 18 years of age. In addition, providers may not:

- Limit the use of facilities or services by such households

- Impose special charges for such households

- Inappropriately influence the household's choice of a dwelling unit

Key Areas of Concern Related to Familial Status

With respect to families with children, housing providers and families with children have expressed the following key areas of concern:

- Occupancy limits for apartments which may serve to exclude families

- The imposition of additional charges or fees on families

- The imposition of rules and regulations which limit families' full enjoyment of housing facilities

See question 72 for definitions of these properties.

Note that there are a few apartment properties that are reserved exclusively for the elderly and as such are exempted from the prohibition against familial discrimination.

The Fair Housing Amendments Act[6] also gave the Department of Housing and Urban Development the power to administer and enforce the Act including the power to make regulations that interpret and implement the Act.

7   Who Is Responsible for Enforcing Fair Housing Laws?

Congress has charged HUD with the principal enforcement responsibilities under the law, including the development of regulations, initiation and investigation of complaints, conciliation between parties, and referral of complaints for judicial action.

---

6. *FHA regulations are found at 24 Code of Federal Regulations, Sections 100-105.*

See question 41 for further information on the referral of complaints to agencies of states or localities that have substantially equivalent laws.

States and localities may be authorized by HUD to assume some of these responsibilities if they adopt fair housing laws which are 'substantially equivalent' to the federal act. Under most circumstances, if a state or local law is substantially equivalent, a complaint filed with HUD may be referred for investigation to the state or local agency charged with enforcing the substantially equivalent law.

8 What Are Examples of Prohibited Conduct Under the Fair Housing Laws?

Prohibited conduct under the Fair Housing Act includes not only an outright refusal to rent or sell housing to a member of a protected class, but more subtle forms of discrimination in advertising, applicant screening, resident selection, occupancy requirements and eviction. While this book addresses only rental housing, housing providers should be aware that there are similar fair housing requirements for housing for sale.

Examples of Prohibited Rental Housing Practices

A number of practices are prohibited by the Fair Housing Act. These include, but are not limited to:

- Refusing to rent after a bona fide offer has been made, or to negotiate the rental of a dwelling, based on membership in a protected class

- Establishing requirements for admission which operate to exclude protected groups

See Chapter 6.

- Using different lease or contract provisions to discriminate against a person with disabilities, a family with children or another protected class.

Chapter 7 for occupancy issues

- Employing any form of quota system to limit occupancy by protected individuals

See question 68 and question 77 for examples of discriminatory conduct.

- Limiting the use of facilities or services by a protected individual, or providing a lower quality of sermvice to such a person

- Providing false or misleading information about a housing opportunity

- Discouraging applications or inappropriately influencing the choice of a dwelling through 'steering', threats or intimidation; (steering is any attempt on the part of the leasing agent to direct an applicant to or away from a particular unit or area)

See questions 31, 48 and 49.

- Having advertising or on-site marketing activities that indicate any preference, limitation, or discrimination based on membership in a protected class

See questions 119 and 120.

- Failing to provide equally effective communications to individuals with disabilities

See questions 78, 91 and Chapter 10 and Chapter 12.

- With respect to people with disabilities, refusing to make reasonable changes in rules, policies, services or practices to permit full use and enjoyment of the housing by such persons;

See questions 87, 88, 84 and Chapter 10-12.

- Failing to allow reasonable modifications to dwellings and common areas to permit accessibility by people with disabilities

See question 84.

- In the case of new construction, constructing buildings and apartments that are inaccessible to people with disabilities

See questions 71 and 114.

- Employing different eviction standards for a member of a protected class, or in any way enforcing lease provisions based on membership in a protected class

See questions 11 and 12.

- Taking any action against an employee of a real estate organization for refusing to violate fair housing laws, or refusing to hire an employee to a real estate organization based on membership in a protected class

The above examples are are only an illustrative listing of the ways in which a housing provider can violate Fair Housing laws.

Unintended Discrimination

Discrimination complaints are based not only on intentional discrimination, but also on the perception of discrimination by the applicant or resident. Thus, even "good faith" actions may result in the filing of a discrimination complaint.

Example of 'Unintended Discrimination'

A leasing agent may feel that a family wants to be closer to the playground, which is in the back of the property. The family is only shown apartments in the back of the property and is not informed of the availability of other apartments closer to the front of the property. The agent may have done this with "good intentions;" the family however perceives that they are not offered the same options as other applicants and calls the local fair housing council to file a complaint. The leasing agent in this case should have shown the family a list of all available apartments for which they qualified; it is up to the applicant to decide which apartments are suitable, not the leasing agent.

See question 78 for more on 'reasonable accommodation'.

Most housing providers are aware that intentional discrimination against protected classes is prohibited. In addition to intentional discrimination, acts with an unintended but discriminatory effect are also prohibited. For example, a policy that all rental payments must be made at the rental office without exception fails to consider that someone with a disability may not be able to physically come to the office but could instead mail their rent payments. If you do not reasonably accommodate the needs of people with disabilities, you could be faced with a discrimination complaint.

9   What Is "Disparate Impact"?

Disparate impact discrimination occurs when a housing provider implements an apparently neutral policy or procedure (i.e. one that on its face applies to all persons equally and is not overtly discriminatory) yet can be shown to have a disproportionately negative effect upon members of a protected class.

* HUD v. George and Mary Ross; HUDALJ 01-92-0466-8
** Gilligan et al v. Jamco Development Corporation et al, case number 95-56290, US Court of Appeals, 9th Circuit, (a final resolution of this case is pending).
† Also see Achtenberg Memo dated Dec. 17, 1993.

Example of Disparate Impact

In two cases, housing providers had a policy of refusing to accept as tenants persons who received Aid to Families with Dependent Children (AFDC). Source of income is not a protected class under the federal Fair Housing Act and therefore this policy did not, on its face, violate the Act. However, in the first case* evidence was tendered to prove that the overwhelming percentage of AFDC recipients in the relevant County were women. The policy therefore had an indirect but palpable impact on women and as such the housing providers were held to have discriminated against women on the basis of their sex. In the second case** the court ruled that a prima facie case of discrimination under the Fair Housing Act was established against a housing provider that had a policy of not renting to any recipients of AFDC benefits. Since only families with children are entitled to receive AFDC it was alleged by the Plaintiffs that the policy had a disparate impact on that protected class (i.e. families with minor children).†

Where there is a finding that an apparently neutral policy disproportionately affects members of a protected class, the housing provider must demonstrate that the policy has a solid business justification.

10 What Are the Consequences to Owners and Managers Who Violate Fair Housing Laws?

In general, anyone engaging in activities related to the rental of apartments who is found to have engaged in a prohibited practice can be subject to serious penalties of law. Managers should be concerned not just about a "finding" of discrimination but also about "filing" of discrimination complaints.

In Meyer v. Holley,[7] a Supreme Court case decided unanimously in January 2003, the Court held while the Fair Housing Act holds a corporation liable for the illegal acts of its employees, it does not hold an officer of the corporation personally liable for the acts of an employee.

---

7. *See Meyer v. Holley, 537 U.S. 280 (2003).*

11 What If My Employer Asks Me to Violate Fair Housing Laws?

It is unlawful to discharge or take any adverse action against an employee for refusing to participate in a discriminatory housing practice.

See questions 2 and 10.

An employee cannot be required by an employer to take actions that are in violation of the law, or that would expose the employee to personal liability for housing discrimination.

12 Do Federal Fair Housing Laws Address Discrimination in Hiring Practices?

The federal fair housing laws do not address discrimination in hiring or employment, as these are practices prohibited by existing employment laws. However, it is a violation to "impose different standards or criteria for membership in a real estate sales or rental organization because of race, color, religion, sex, handicap, familial status or national origin."[8] The term 'membership' refers to associations or other non-employment based affiliations.

13 What Is the Americans With Disabilities Act?

The Americans With Disabilities Act was passed in 1990. Subsequently, Congress passed the ADA Amendments Act of 2008.[9] The ADA Amendments Act clarifies protections for people with disabilities and asserts the ADA's objectives of providing 'a clear and comprehensive national mandate for the elimination of discrimination' and 'clear, strong, consistent, enforceable standards addressing discrimination' by reinstating a broad scope of protection to be available under the ADA.

The ADA, as amended, extends protection to people with disabilities, in the following contexts:

---

8. *24CFR, §100.50(7)*
9. *Passed as HR 3195 on September 17, 2005, and not enacted into law as of the publication of this revised edition of the Guidebook.*

Employment (Title I)	Title I of the ADA requires employers with more than 15 employees to make reasonable accommodations and reasonable modifications for employees with disabilities, and applicants for employment with disabilities, so that they can perform essential job functions. Technically, this Title is not a fair housing issue, and so it is not covered in this Guidebook. However, many of the general principles regarding accessibility are relevant to Title I.
Activities of State and Local Governments (Title II)	Title II of the ADA prohibits discrimination against qualified individuals with disabilities in all programs, activities and services of public entities. It applies to all State and local governments and their departments and agencies. A state or local government must eliminate any eligibility criteria for participation in programs, activities and services that screen out or tend to screen out people with disabilities (whether intentionally or not), unless it can establish that the requirements are necessary for the provision of the service program or activity. Included in this requirement is a requirement that a public entity must ensure that individuals with disabilities are not excluded from services, programs and activities because existing buildings are inaccessible.
Public Accommodations, Accessed by the General Public, but Operated by Private Entities (Title III)	A public accommodation is a private entity that owns, operates, leases, or leases to, a place open to the general public. Title III prohibits discrimination against people with disabilities in the use and enjoyment of goods, services and facilities of any place of public accommodation. Places of public accommodation include a wide range of entities, such as restaurants, hotels, theaters, retail stores, museums, libraries and parks. It also includes, however, parts of private residential facilities to which members of the public are entitled to have access, for example rental offices. With respect to rental offices and other common areas (for example laundry rooms), as long as the rental office or common area is open to the public, it is subject to the ADA.
	With respect to apartment properties, the ADA has the following general applicability:
Governmental Activities	The ADA's Title II covers 'activities of state and local government'. Some properties are owned by governmental entities,

which would bring all of property operations under Title II. Properties that are bond-financed are discussed under State/ local bond financing below.

State or local government programs that operate on property premises (such as Head Start, public school programs, Meals on Wheels, etc.) will be subject to ADA Title II. Expert managers advise that the property and the sponsoring government agency should determine who will bear the responsibility for ADA compliance with respect to the program and the on-site environment in which it operates.

Business Locations

In general, apartments are not covered under Title III of the ADA; however, the property's rental office is covered (and thus must be made accessible). Thus, the ADA may require reasonable changes to structures, policies and procedures so that people with disabilities can access the rental office and its business services. These modifications might include removing structural barriers or relocating offices to accessible locations, or adding technological aids such as intercoms or doorbells in parking areas.

See also question 28.

Businesses that operate on property premises (such as day care centers) may be subject to ADA Title III. The housing provider and the independent business should determine who will bear the responsibility for ADA compliance with respect to the business and the on-site environment in which it operates. Typically, these sorts of non-housing activities will be subject to written agreements with the third party service providers. For existing agreements, that do not discuss ADA compliance issues, there may be provisions stating who has the responsibility for maintenance of the premises, who is responsible for ensuring that the physical facility is in compliance with governmental requirements, and so forth. These existing provisions may give an indication of which party should bear the responsibility for any physical modifications necessary for ADA compliance.

There are two areas where expert opinion is divided as to whether or not the ADA applies:

Short-Term Furnished Rentals

Some apartment properties offer furnished apartments for temporary stays of 30 days or more. Because hotel operations are covered under the ADA's Title III, and because the services offered by these apartment properties are in some ways comparable to those provided by hotels, expert opinion is divided as to whether these activities are covered by the ADA. Currently, the weight of opinion seems to be that stays of 30 days or more do not fall under the ADA "transient housing" definition, and thus the ADA does not cover this type of activity. Check with your attorney for an up-to-date expert opinion.

Note that ADA Title III covers places of public accommodation, including homeless shelters and 'social service center establishments'. As such, these facilities are covered by the ADA, regardless of the transience of their occupants.

State / local Bond Financing

Some apartment properties were financed by taxable or tax-exempt bonds issued by state or local governments. Because the ADA's Title II covers activities of state and local governments, expert opinion is divided as to whether these properties are subject to the ADA. Currently, the weight of opinion seems to be that, unless the housing is actually owned or managed by state or local government, Title II of the ADA is not applicable. Again, check with your attorney for an up-to-date opinion.

Properties subject to Section 504 should refer to questions 129, 141 and 151.

The ADA may require physical modifications to a property to allow access. Properties or portions of properties that are subject to Title III of the ADA must make changes that are "readily achievable without too much difficulty or expense."

14   What Fair Housing Considerations Apply to Victims of Domestic Violence?

Increasingly, state and local laws pertaining to rental housing have been implemented to protect victims of domestic violence. Housing providers should determine whether any of the following types of laws are applicable to their projects:

- Provision of Housing — Prohibiting owners from denying housing on the basis of the applicant or tenant's status as a victim of domestic violence.

- Calling Police — Ensuring that tenants' rights to call the police are not interfered with by landlords.

- Right to Early Lease Termination — Permitting victims of domestic violence to terminate a lease prematurely. The requirements differ in each state.

- Eviction Defense — Protection from eviction for tenants who are victims of domestic violence.

- Lease Bifurcation — Permitting the landlord to amend the lease and evict the perpetrator of domestic violence while retaining the victim as a tenant. Under some of these laws, the evicted perpetrator may continue to be held financially liable for the rent.

- Lock Changes — Requiring lock changes by the landlord, or requiring the landlord to permit the tenant to change the locks, when the tenant is a victim of domestic violence.

Owners and managers are strongly advised to rely on local counsel when addressing domestic violence issues.

Because victims of domestic violence are predominantly women, some advocates have taken the position that discrimination against victims of domestic violence has a disparate impact on women and thus is prohibited by the Fair Housing Act.

Domestic violence is an important housing issue in part because domestic violence is strongly associated with homelessness: A Ford Foundation study found that 50% of homeless women and children were fleeing abuse.[10] According to a 1998 study, 22% of homeless mothers had left their last place of residence because of domestic violence.[11] And, half of the cities surveyed by the U.S. Conference of Mayors in 2005 identified domestic violence as a primary cause of homelessness.

---

10. *Woman Battering: A Major Cause Of Homelessness by J. Zorza, Clearinghouse Review 25(4), 421-427 (1991) (7 pages)*

11. *"Hidden Migration" Report, Institute for Children and Poverty, April, 2002*

15   What Does the Violence Against Women Act Require for Federally-Assisted Properties?

Note: The Violence Against Women Act covers existing residents, new admissions, and requests to add new household members. HUD issued implementing guidance on September 30, 2008, as Notice H 08-07.

The Violence Against Women and Department of Justice Reauthorization Act of 2005 (VAWA) became effective January 5th, 2006 and applies to any admission decision or termination of occupancy or assistance after that date. The law provides certain protections to tenants of assisted housing, and applies to all HUD programs as well as properties with federal low-income housing tax credits. Properties governed by these programs may not terminate the occupancy or assistance of a resident on the basis that he or she was a victim of (actual or threatened) abuse, including domestic violence, dating violence or stalking. Domestic violence constitutes criminal activity, which is generally grounds for denial of admission or termination; however, managers may not deny admission or evict certain members of a household on the basis that "...the tenant or an immediate member of the tenant's family is the victim or threatened victim of that abuse." In addition, the law specifically prohibits eviction of victims of abuse for 'other good cause' (it also prevents termination of assistance for 'other good cause' in these situations)., and you may not rely on this lease clause as a basis for terminating assistance. In practice, this means that the owner can evict a member of the household who commits abuse, but must retain the remaining members of the household. Similarly, the owner may admit the victim of abuse, but may reject for admission the perpetrator of the abuse.

Bifurcation of Leases

This refers to the removal of the perpetrator, while retaining the victim as a tenant. HUD permits 'bifurcation' of a lease in cases of domestic abuse, in order to protect the rights of the victim of that abuse. A lease may be bifurcated, even if the lease does not expressly permit it—the authority granted by VAWA to evict a single member of the household for committing an act of domestic violence supersedes any local, state or federal law to the contrary. However, the termination of the abusive tenant must be carried out (i.e., its process must be) according to federal, state and local law. The abusive tenant may be a signatory to the lease, or may be a member of the household who has not signed the lease.

Certification

In order to establish whether members of a household are entitled to these rights, managers may request certification from the resident who claims to be a victim of domestic violence. PHAs and managers of properties which accept tenant-based vouchers may use Form HUD-50066. Managers of properties with project-based assistance may use Form HUD-90066.[12] These self-certification forms are optional and the tenant may instead provide either a police or court record, or a signed statement from an attorney, domestic violence service provider, or medical professional who has provided assistance to the victim (guidelines for these statements are provided on the self-certification form). If the resident or applicant fails to provide the requested certification or documentation within 14 business days of the request (or a longer period if permitted by the manager), the manager may terminate assistance to the household for activity that may be related to such abuse.

Any certification must be treated as confidential. HUD cautions that the certification form should be provided confidentially and discretely, so as not to put the victim at risk in the event it is discovered by the abuser.

When You May Evict

Although victims of abuse have some protection, managers may terminate these households when:

The household member has not provided certification (within 14 days of being requested to do so by the manager) and has consequently not established his or her rights under VAWA.

The cause for eviction is not based upon or related to the domestic violence.

The domestic violence poses an imminent threat to other tenants or property employees.

---

12. *Issued as HUD Notice H 08-07 on September 30, 2008.*

Notification of
Residents, and
Your Tenant
Selection Plan

VAWA requires that public housing authorities advise applicants and residents, as well as owners and managers of housing which accept Section 8 vouchers, of their rights and
responsibilities under the law. HUD issued Notice H 08-07 on
September 30, 2008, implementing the law.

We recommend owners of affected housing programs to revise
property tenant selection plans to conform to the requirements
of this law. Consult with your attorney when implementing
these new requirements into your tenant selection plan, evic-
tions policy, and application materials.

16   What Is the Architectural Barriers Act?

Publicly owned residential properties including properties
that were financed wholly or partially with federal funds are
subject to the provisions of the Architectural Barriers Act and
regulations made under that Act. These regulations provide
that residential structures shall be designed, constructed or
altered to ensure that physically handicapped persons have
access to and use of those structures. It is also provided that
this requirement is satisfied by using the specifications contained in the Uniform Federal Accessibility Standards (UFAS).

17   May an Owner Adopt New Screening Guidelines to Enhance Security in Light of the Events of September 11, 2001?

In December 2002 HUD published a three-page guidance entitled, "Response to Concerns About Housing Security Following September 11, 2001: Rights and Responsibilities of
Landlords and Residents in Preventing Housing Discrimination Based on Race, Religion, or National Origin in the Wake of
the Events of September 11, 2001".[13] This guidance does not
change any existing policies, but it does provide HUD's view
on a number of issues at the intersection of security and fair
housing:

---

13. As revised January 6, 2003

The Fair Housing Act does not prohibit discrimination based *solely* on a person's citizenship status (that is, whether someone is a citizen or not); it is legal to base housing decisions on citizenship status. Housing providers may ask applicants to provide documentation of their citizenship or immigration status during the admissions process. Such procedures must be uniformly applied and carried out in a nondiscriminatory fashion (that is, it is not permissible to make citizenship inquiries for some applicants but not for others).

See question 34.

The treatment of applicants and tenants (and their guests) must be without regard to their race, religion or national origin. For example, it is not permissible to have different policies for applicants of Middle Eastern descent.

Chapter Two: States and Localities

18   Do States and Localities Have Fair Housing Laws?

Many states have enacted fair housing laws that are "substantially equivalent" to the federal Fair Housing Act. Some state laws go beyond the federal requirements.

Some state and local laws add new classes of applicants and residents who receive protection against discrimination. Such examples of additional protected classes may include:

- Source of income (e.g., recipients of public assistance)

- Marital status

- Sexual orientation

See Chapter 6.   Other state and local laws create firm standards in areas where federal laws are less specific, for example in the area of occupancy standards.

See question 7.   Know that state and local fair housing laws may exist and may apply to you. In addition, a large percentage of Fair Housing cases are processed at the state and local level.

19   What Are the Most Common Non-Federally Protected Classes?

Federal fair housing laws protect seven specific classes of people. These protected classes are race, color, national origin, sex, religion, disability, and familial status. In many cases, states and localities have passed laws modifying or enhancing the definitions of the seven federally protected classes.[1] State and local governments can increase (but never diminish) the federal fair housing laws. As a result, an act which might not violate the federal fair housing law might violate a state or local law which applies different standards.

Going beyond the federally protected classes, numerous states and localities have established additional protected classes. Housing operating in these areas is therefore subject to fair

---

1. *This Guidebook intentionally does not provide a specific listing of state and local laws, as changes would inevitably render the material here obsolete and incorrect.*

housing requirements—at the state or local level—that extend to additional classes of people, beyond the seven which are protected under the federal law. Because state and local laws are continuously evolving, this Guidebook provides a general overview of the types of additional protected classes:

- Age—Age is not a federally protected class, except that families with children under 18 may not be discriminated against.[2] Certain states have added 'age' as a protected class, making it illegal under those state laws to discriminate against a tenant or prospective tenant on the basis of age. However, most such laws create an exception that allows age discrimination in some, but not all, housing established to serve senior citizens. And, regardless of an applicant's age, it is reasonable to require they be old enough to enter into a contract (such as a lease) under State law.

- Ancestry—where this is a protected class, you may not discriminate based on the identity of a person's ancestors. For example, you could not refuse to rent an apartment to someone because of his Armenian ancestry.

- Marital Status—this protected class prohibits any practice which would treat someone differently based on whether they are married, For example, in states with this protected class, you cannot charge a higher rent, require a higher income, or impose different policies to unmarried households and married households. Additionally, if married households are allowed to combine their incomes to qualify then unmarried households must have the same opportunity.

- Military (or Veteran) Status—discrimination may occur against a military households when a housing provider has concerns about a future deployment, and effect this might have on the likelihood of the service member to serve out a lease term. Additionally, depending on the

---

2. *However, the Age Discrimination Act of 1975 prohibits age discrimination by federally-assisted properties.*

law, it may be illegal to consider the nature of a service member's discharge in your selection criteria.

- Sexual Orientation—discrimination against a person based on his or her sexual orientation (gay, lesbian, etc.). A few states also protect transsexual or transgender persons.

- Source of Income—often, these protections address discrimination on the basis of legal, verifiable income paid directly to the tenant or his or her representative (such as a payee). Some examples of income types are Social Security, Supplemental Security Income (SSI), Temporary Assistance to Needy Families (TANF), unemployment insurance, veteran's benefits, pensions, and wages.

See question 14.
- Victim of Domestic Abuse—many states have enacted laws to ensure that victims of domestic violence have certain protections against housing discrimination.

While the listing above reflects commonly protected classes at the State level (some appear in as many as 20 states), there are others which are used less frequently. These include, 'place of current residence', 'matriculation' (that is, whether someone is a student), 'political affiliation', 'personal appearance', 'gender identification', and 'HIV/AIDS'. California has included as a protected class 'arbitrary characteristics' prohibiting any practice which discriminates based on a personal characteristic which is not relevant to a person's ability to abide by the terms of the lease.

20 In What Ways do the Fair Housing Act and State and Local Laws Overlap?

The Fair Housing Act allows states to establish 'substantially equivalent' laws that mirror the federal requirements, and it allows states to establish additional laws that extend the protections of the Fair Housing Act to additional protected classes, or to broader definitions of the seven federally protected classes. The Fair Housing Act also prohibits states and localities from establishing laws which would in any way lessen the protections it provides.[3]

When a state or locality establishes 'substantially equivalent' protections, an act which violates the Fair Housing Act simultaneously violates the substantially equivalent state or local law. As a result, remedies can be sought under both the Fair Housing Act as well as under the state or local law.

States and localities which have established 'substantially equivalent' laws can be certified by HUD, receiving funding and the authority to process federal fair housing complaints locally.

---

3. *See 42 USC § 3615.*

Chapter Three: Basic Fair Housing Compliance for Apartments

21   How Do I Avoid Fair Housing Complaints?

See question 8,
'unintended
discrimination.'

Avoiding fair housing complaints often means going beyond the level of technical compliance with fair housing requirements. Many complaints originate because an innocently intended action or remark is interpreted as discriminatory. Expert owners and managers recommend the following guidelines to help create an environment in which complaints are less likely to be generated.

Signal that the Property is Fair Housing Sensitive

When applicants visit the property for the first time, do they see accessible parking spaces? Are fair housing posters prominently displayed? Does the property sign have the Equal Housing Opportunity symbol and slogan? Are all housing applicants and residents greeted in a courteous and professional way? Note also that under the Fair Housing Act failure to display the Fair Housing Poster is considered to be evidence of a discriminatory housing practice in a complaint of discrimination.

Avoid Words that May Be Misunderstood

Certain terms used in advertising or leasing may have a discriminatory effect, by discouraging applications from persons who are members of a protected class. For example, many real estate professionals may use the word "exclusive" to describe a desirable community, but to a member of a protected class this same word may indicate an intention to "exclude people like me." In particular, advertisements, brochures, and rental applications should be reviewed carefully to make sure that they don't inadvertently create a perception of discriminatory intent. The entire basis of a racial discrimination case brought against a housing provider was that over a three-year period all its advertisements (billboards, newspaper advertisements and brochures) featured only White human models.[1] This was regarded by a number of fair housing advocacy groups as an expression of a preference for housing that racial group to the exclusion of other racial groups—an impermissible practice under the Fair Housing Act.

---

1. *Anthony Tyus et al v. Urban Search Management et al, US Court of Appeals for the Seventh Circuit, Nos. 95-3793 and 95-3932*

Give Consistent Answers

Management staff, especially front line staff, will repeatedly be asked the same very basic questions by a great many potential applicants: "Do you have any two bedroom apartments?;" "How much are your two bedroom apartments?;" "Can I look at a two bedroom apartment?" If all members of staff answer these questions the same way to every applicant each day, the property will remove one common cause of fair housing complaints: the giving of inconsistent or inaccurate information. At the beginning of each day, make sure all management staff know which apartments are available, at what prices, which residents have given notice of intent to vacate, and so forth.

Do Consistent Screening

See question 55 on the use of informally obtained information, and Chapter 6 for recommended practices and policies in applicant screening and selection.

A property may have a very experienced manager who has a very well-developed ability to interpret nuances of body language and subtle differences in tone of voice and to make judgments about a person's character based on such factors. This manager may believe that he or she can "just tell" which applicants to accept and which to decline, short-cutting the normal resident screening and selection process. This type of "intuitive" screening should be discouraged. In the litigious environment in which housing providers currently operate, decisions to reject applications for housing will frequently be challenged and must be justified on the basis of discernible and objective facts. Trying to defend a decision to reject an application on the ground that the manager "had a feeling" that the applicant would not comply with the requirements of the lease is not going to find favor with a court of law. The professional and prudent approach therefore is to (a) follow the standard process with all applicants and (b) make decisions based on the facts and according to established criteria.

Training

Expert owners and managers advise making fair housing education a part of every employee's orientation process, and providing ongoing fair housing training and support. Maintain proof of fair housing training in each employee's personnel file. In the event that a fair housing complaint is filed against a property a court may give favorable consideration to the fact that employees at the property received fair housing training.

Fair Housing Policy

Experienced management companies develop—and display prominently—a clear policy statement that commits the company to provide equal housing opportunity. For example:

"XYZ Apartments is Fully Committed to Equal Housing Opportunity." This is a simple example of the articulation of broad policy that demonstrates the moral and legal commitment to meet both the spirit and the letter of the law. If backed by real policy measures, the establishment of clearly understood principles will provide the framework for decisions which employees must make every day. Have each employee sign this policy statement, and place a copy in the personnel file

Many fair housing complaints arise from perceptions of staff insensitivity, and from careless staff remarks that inadvertently give the impression that the property is not concerned about fair housing. By developing the proper atmosphere at your property you will avoid most complaints. HUD has stated that, in evaluating discrimination complaints, the manner in which fair housing responsibilities are carried out, or the "pattern of behavior," will be heavily weighed.

22   What Are the Basics of Fair Housing Compliance?

Appearing below are some suggested steps that you may wish take in order to help your property's operations comply with the requirements of the Fair Housing Act, the Americans with Disabilities Act, or Section 504 of the Rehabilitation Act (if applicable):

*   Review your existing policies to identify any potential for fair housing misunderstanding. HUD has stated that, for enforcement purposes, it will not only look at your actual standards and practices but at whether, as implemented, they limit housing opportunities for protected households. Although your present policies may be intended to be fair, all policies should be reviewed carefully to determine if there may be unintended adverse effects on protected classes of applicants or residents. For example, house rules that, in trying to protect the property or the rights of other residents, are unusually harsh on children may be viewed as unfair to families. Or, having applications and leases available only in written form may be viewed as discriminatory against persons with visual impairments.

- Collect and study regulatory information concerning applicable fair housing requirements.

See question 13.
- Determine the extent to which your operations are covered by provisions of the Americans With Disabilities Act (ADA).

See questions 126 and 128.
- Determine whether the property receives "federal financial assistance" and thus is subject to Section 504 of the Rehabilitation Act.

See Chapter 21.
- For federally assisted seniors properties: determine if each property falls within the mixed populations provisions of the 1992 Housing and Community Development Act and, if it does, decide whether you want to implement those provisions.

See question 18.
- Determine whether your operations are subject to state and local fair housing laws whose provisions may be more extensive than those in federal fair housing laws. For example many States have extended their protected classes beyond the provisions of the Fair Housing Act by prohibiting discrimination in housing on the basis of age, marital status, sexual orientation, ancestry, source of income, or other criteria.

- Meet with a local disability-oriented organization with accessibility expertise (for example, a local Independent Living Center) to gain insight into the experiences and expectations of people with disabilities and to better understand how to accommodate people with various disabilities.

See question 28.
- Perform an Accessibility Review for the property. This encompasses a "self-evaluation" of existing barriers to accessibility (structural and procedural), plus a "transition plan" setting forth the steps for completing any needed changes.

See question 32 for detail on familial status reviews, and Chapter 7 on occupancy standards.
- Perform a Familial Status Review to identify and eliminate any unintended adverse impacts that your property rules and regulations or occupancy standards may have on families with children. For example, you may find that your occupancy standards (governing assignment of unit types

or sizes based on household size and composition) need to be changed because they unduly restrict opportunities for families with children to live at your property.

- Hold a series of meetings with key management staff to develop a framework for analyzing fair housing issues. At these meetings, assist management staff in making proper judgments about the range of fair housing decisions involved in advertising, resident selection, accessibility modifications and accommodations, and occupancy and eviction standards.

- Have your management staff attend training in fair housing compliance issues, particularly those employees who routinely interact with applicants or residents. Consider developing in-house training, if appropriate.

See question 50 for further information on the use of the non-discrimination statement, logo and slogan.

- Develop improved policies and procedures. For instance, your advertising and marketing plan should specify how you will use the nondiscrimination logo, statement and/or slogan. You should also address questions such as, how will people with hearing or vision impairments communicate with you?

- Make needed physical and procedural modifications, so that mobility impaired persons can visit the property and submit rental applications.

See question 72.

- For seniors' properties: determine if each property meets the criteria for an exemption from the familial status provisions of the Fair Housing Act.

The above list is not exhaustive nor is it necessary that you undertake all of these recommendations. When you have completed those steps applicable to your property, you will be well on the way to a comprehensive compliance program. Be aware, however, that compliance is an ongoing process that requires your continuing attention.

23 How Should I Refer to People With Disabilities?

As a general rule, the term "disability" is preferable to "handicap." "Person with disabilities" (or "person with a disability") is preferable to "handicapped person." "People with disabilities" is preferable to "persons with disabilities." "Wheelchair user" is preferable to "wheelchair-bound".

Experienced housing providers suggest that you ask the persons with whom you develop your self-evaluation and transition plan to comment on this question, because in some localities there may be a preference for different terminology.

In this book, because of legal context, the term "handicap" is sometimes used because that is the term used in the particular law or regulation being discussed.

24 What Does "Accessible" Mean Under the Fair Housing Act and the ADA?

Federally assisted properties should refer additionally to Chapter 17.

Regulations under the Fair Housing Act define "accessible" to mean that the public or common use areas of a building can be approached, entered and used by individuals with physical handicaps. Under the ADA the definition is a little wider: "Readily accessible to and usable by individuals with disabilities" means that a facility can be approached, entered and used by individuals with disabilities (including mobility, sensory and cognitive impairments) easily and conveniently. The ADA accessibility requirements therefore require that account be taken of other impairments besides physical handicaps.

Owners and managers should remember that 'accessibility' can mean more than wheelchair ramps and counter heights. For people with cognitive impairments and mental disabilities, accessibility is also critically important. For these populations, your housing is accessible if it makes reasonable accommodations to ensure their equal access and enjoyment.

25 What Are the Accessibility Requirements for New Construction, Under the Fair Housing Act?

See question 84 and Chapter 11 generally for further information on the accessibility requirements of the Fair Housing Act. Federally assisted properties should refer additionally to question 153.

Regulations under the Fair Housing Act[2] require that covered multifamily dwellings constructed for first occupancy after March 13, 1991 must contain certain accessibility features; for example, at least one building entrance must be on an accessible route. In the case of dwellings constructed for first occupancy prior to March 13, 1991, the Fair Housing Act requires that residents be permitted to make "reasonable modifications" to their premises if this is necessary "to afford the handicapped person full enjoyment of the premises of a dwelling."[3]

26 What are the Accessibility Requirements for New Construction, Under the ADA?

See question 13 for a discussion on the applicability of the ADA; see Chapter 11 for questions on physical modifications for accessibility.

The ADA[4] requires that all newly constructed properties that are subject to Title II of the Act must be constructed in accordance with either the Americans With Disabilities Act Accessibility Guidelines (ADAAG) or the Uniform Federal Accessibility Standards (UFAS). Properties subject to Title III must follow ADAAG. New construction requirements apply to any facility first occupied after January 26, 1993. In addition, alterations that were begun after January 26, 1992 must be accessible to individuals with disabilities in accordance with ADAAG or UFAS to the maximum extent feasible. In the case of existing facilities, the ADA Title III requires that physical barriers to entering and using facilities must be removed when "readily achievable." "Readily achievable" means "easily accomplished and able to be carried out without much difficulty or expense."[5] If removal of physical barriers is not "readily achievable" alternative steps must be taken to provide accessibility. Title II, however, requires a public entity to make its programs accessible in all cases except where to do so

---

2. *24 CFR Subtitle B, Chapter 1, Section 100.205*
3. *24 CFR, Section 100.203(a)*
4. *28 CFR, Section 35.151 and 28 CFR, Section 36.401*
5. *ADA Title III, Section 36.304*

would result in a fundamental alteration in the nature of the program or in undue financial and administrative burdens.

27 What Accessibility Requirements Apply to a Property That Is Subject to More Than One Law?

Generally, where a property is subject to the accessibility requirements of more than one law—for example the Fair Housing Act and the ADA—it should observe the more stringent standard. The more stringent standard would provide for greater accessibility. This also applies where a property is subject to any state or local requirements, which may go beyond federal requirements.

28 What Is an Accessibility Review?

Physical Accessibility Reviews are recommended for all properties that may be subject to accessibility requirements of the Fair Housing Act, the Architectural Barriers Act, Section 504 of the Rehabilitation Act or Title II and Title III of the ADA.

Experts recommend in particular that anyone acquiring a property completed for first occupancy after March 13, 1991, should conduct an accessibility review because the accessibility requirements of the Fair Housing Act apply to those properties. The accessibility review should comprise the following elements:

- Reviews to determine which federal accessibility requirements apply to the property. This should include the following:

See questions 125, 126 and 128.

- An analysis to determine whether accessibility requirements imposed by Section 504 of the Rehabilitation Act of 1973 apply to the property. If the property receives federal financial assistance, the Section 504 requirements will apply.

See question 16.

- A determination whether the property is subject to the requirements of the Architectural Barriers Act.

- A determination whether the requirements of Title II of the Americans With Disabilities Act apply. Properties owned by a state or local government entity are affected by this title of the ADA, requiring that all new buildings (i.e. completed for first occupancy after January 26, 1993) constructed by State or local governments be accessible to people with disabilities and that pre-existing buildings must undertake structural changes to achieve accessibility by January 26, 1995.

- A determination whether the requirements of Title III of the Americans With Disabilities Act apply. Title III prohibits discrimination against people with disabilities in places of public accommodation. Residential facilities are not considered places of public accommodation and are therefore not subject to Title III of the ADA and this applies also to amenities provided for the exclusive use of residents and their guests. However, rental offices and sales offices for residential housing, as well as meeting rooms, recreational areas and retail space, are open to the public and as such are places of public accommodation and therefore they must comply with ADA accessibility requirements.

- In addition, all apartment properties are subject to the Fair Housing Act, which, in addition to the design and construction requirements also requires all owners to allow residents with disabilities to make reasonable structural modifications to individual dwelling units and common areas as needed to provide or improve accessibility.

- Using the Uniform Federal Accessibility Standards (UFAS) Accessibility Checklist or similar instrument, inspect the exteriors and common areas of the property to determine if there are any physical barriers which prevent mobility-impaired persons from having full access.

- Determine if any of the units are accessible to wheelchair users, or can be modified to be accessible. "Accessible" includes an accessible route to the unit, plus interior accessibility features as well. Even if there is no current requirement to modify any units, it may prove useful to have developed a plan for use if and when a resident or applicant proposes such modifications in the future.

- An analysis of the physical characteristics of the property including both the exterior and interior, common areas and individual dwelling units, to determine whether there are structural barriers or impediments to accessibility for persons with handicaps and how the property must respond based upon the various laws and regulations that address accessibility.

See question 29 for more on reviewing policies and procedures that may serve as barriers to accessibility; see question 30 for more on transition plans.

- If barriers can be removed through nonstructural changes, such as reasonable accommodations in procedures and practices, the necessary changes should be implemented immediately. If structural modifications are required, a "transition plan" for accomplishing the modifications should be prepared.

29   What Is a Self-Evaluation?

Federally assisted properties should refer additionally to questions 126 and 128.

The self-evaluation is similar to an accessibility review. However, in addition to focusing on barriers to physical mobility, a self-evaluation is also an assessment of services, policies, procedures, rules and practices to see whether they facilitate or hinder accessibility. Although a self-evaluation is a good practice for any property, those that are subject to Section 504 were required to conduct a self-evaluation by July 11, 1989 and all relevant properties that have not yet undertaken this evaluation should do so. Properties that are subject to Title II of the ADA were also required to do self-evaluations by January 26, 1993. Self-evaluations may be useful to properties that are not legally required to undertake one as a means of identifying and correcting problems before they result in a fair housing complaint.

Organizations required to conduct these evaluations, which have more than fifty employees, must retain copies for at least three years. Smaller organizations were encouraged, but not required, to have kept these documents. A thorough self-evaluation involves the following steps:

- Evaluate current policies and practices to see whether they are reasonable, whether they truly afford equal housing opportunity, or instead have the unintended effect of limiting housing opportunities for certain types of households. To avoid unnecessary and costly legal challenges, housing standards and practices should also appear to be fair in addition to meeting the letter of the law.

See question 32.
- Conduct a Familial Status Review.

- Identify the policies and practices needed in order to accommodate applicants and residents with disabilities. Failure to implement such policies and practices can be costly if this failure amounts to a breach of the Fair Housing Act.

Failure to Reasonably Accommodate People With Disabilities Can Be Costly.

The resident of a unit at a cooperative used a wheelchair because he had an illness that caused progressive deterioration of his neuro-muscular system. His illness prevented him from traveling to an office and he therefore worked from home. He requested a reasonable accommodation to the property's policy that prohibited residents from working from their apartments. This request was refused. A lawsuit was filed against the property but the applicant died before the date of the trial. The case was, however, settled with the property agreeing, among other things, to pay the applicant's estate $180,000 and to institute a reasonable accommodation and reasonable modification policy for residents with disabilities.*

---

* *Palmour & The Fair Housing Council of Greater Washington v. The Cathedral Avenue Cooperative.*

- The self-evaluation will include a discussion of the number and mix of units that are accessible to wheelchair users, to persons with hearing impairments, and to persons with vision impairments.

See question 106.
- You should remove references to "independent living," and you should carefully review any references to disability conditions.

See question 100.
- Determine if any of the units have accessible fire alarm systems or other features for the vision- or hearing-

impaired, or can be modified to include such features. Again, consideration should be given to developing a plan for future modifications.

- Consider reviewing all of the above with a local disability organization and individuals with disabilities.

See question 30.   • Develop a Transition Plan.

30   What Is a Transition Plan?

If structural modifications are required, you should also prepare a transition plan. The following considerations should be addressed in the plan:

- The transition plan will discuss how the property will respond if there is a present (or future) need for additional units which are accessible to these populations. All properties should plan ahead for the time when a resident proposes to make accessibility modifications (under the Fair Housing Act) at his or her own expense. The property must permit these modifications but may impose reasonable requirements about the design of the modifications and how the work is done.

- A plan of action for accomplishing structural changes needed to provide accessibility to the rental office, and to any other common areas covered under the ADA.

See question 126.   • A plan of action for accomplishing structural changes currently required in order to provide accessibility to the apartments. For example, apartments must be made accessible immediately in properties subject to Section 504, to the extent needed by existing residents.

- The transition plan should include a schedule for implementation. Some modifications will be complex and will require significant architectural review. Other modifications may be costly, and require time because of resource constraints—both Section 504 and the ADA provide exceptions for particularly costly modifications.

- The transition plan should include, in appropriate detail, the construction or rehabilitation methods to be used to provide accessibility.

- The transition plan should discuss how funding will be sought, if present property resources are inadequate.

- The transition plan should identify the person who will be responsible for implementation of the plan.

- The transition plan should identify the persons or groups who assisted with the Accessibility Review. Experienced housing providers advise that this participative process is valuable in developing a high quality approach to accessibility. In most areas, local disability-oriented organizations (such as Independent Living Centers) are available to participate in the Accessibility Review.

31   How Can My Property Become Disability Aware?

Fair Housing has opened vast new opportunities to the several million Americans who have a disability. As a judge wrote in a 1990 legal decision against a Public Housing Authority:

"For over 200 years our Country has prospered under the principle that all men and women should have an equal opportunity to enjoy 'life, liberty and the pursuit of happiness.' There was a time when the disabled did not have the same opportunities and were relegated to a kind of second class status in employment, housing and transportation. That circumstance was caused more by the community's misinformation and thoughtlessness than by the individual's actual disabling condition. Much has been done to eliminate this situation but it would be simplistic to believe that problems do not remain. Public agencies must be especially vigilant to protect the disabled from all forms of discrimination—intentional as well as benign discrimination caused by the public's perception of what is 'best' for the disabled." [6]

---

6. *Cason v. Rochester Housing Authority; 748 F. Supp. 1002; 1990 US Dist.; Lexis 14229; FHFL 15, 643*

Here are some general principles and practical suggestions to guide you in meeting fair housing obligations toward applicants with disabilities. These should not be viewed as requirements, but as guides to best practice.

Become a Disability-Aware Person

Your first step is to examine your personal attitudes toward various physical and mental impairments, and to strengthen your own awareness of people with disabilities.

- Be respectful. Avoid being overly intrusive or patronizing when assisting people with disabilities. Take care that in assisting someone, you do not make assumptions about their abilities or disabilities.

- In deciding how to treat a person with disabilities, think about how you would treat a TANF (Temporary Assistance to Needy Families) recipient or Hispanic single parent or involuntarily displaced person. This is not a perfect approach, but it will get you started in the right direction. You will then regard the applicant as someone deserving of especially considerate treatment, and as someone who may have a history, or expectations, of being discriminated against.

- Evaluate your assumptions about how to treat people with disabilities. Imagine that a wheelchair user visits your property, followed by an otherwise similar person who does not use a wheelchair. Would you treat these two people differently? How? As you study this guidebook, decide whether each example of different treatment is a good idea. Often, you will find that different treatment will not be welcomed by a person with disabilities. Further, different treatment will sometimes violate Fair Housing requirements.

- Set aside your personal opinions about disability conditions. You are a housing provider, not a medical expert. Your own opinions regarding disability conditions, no matter how well informed, are your worst enemies in your battle to avoid discrimination based on disability status. Your applicants and residents with disabilities are individuals, each with different needs and abilities. Treat them as individuals without making hasty judgments about what they can and cannot do.

- Set aside your personal opinions about the riskiness of accepting applicants with disabilities. Some housing providers may have the perception that people with disabilities are high-risk applicants by comparison to persons without disabilities. If you share this attitude, we recommend that you discard it, because the facts do not support it (and because this attitude may lead you to take unprofessional and illegal actions in your job).

Become a Disability-Aware Property

There are a number of actions each property can take to create a disability aware atmosphere. Properties that take these actions are less likely to suffer fair housing complaints. In addition to ensuring that your property is disability-aware, it is also important to convey to the public that you place importance upon your disability-awareness.

- Review all materials that are shared with applicants. Your property's Rental Application, your Resident Selection Plan, your newsletter, your advertisements, your brochures and the memos on your bulletin board can easily give the impression that you are not interested in housing people with disabilities. Are you displaying the Fair Housing poster?

- Complete your self-evaluation and transition plan activities. For a typical property, this would include instituting procedural changes to accommodate persons with visual or hearing impairments, and structural changes to accommodate persons with mobility impairments.

- Pay special attention to unit availability questions. Large numbers of fair housing complaints arise when properties give different households different answers to the same question, especially the most frequently asked question: "Do you have any apartments available?" For properties with several staff members who deal with applicants, start each day with a briefing of exactly which apartments are available. For properties with waiting lists, develop a written explanation of how the waiting list works, and how long the wait is likely to be.

Develop Disability-Aware Application Procedures	Your application materials and your Resident Selection Plan need to be reviewed for disability awareness.

- Process each applicant as if he or she were fully able. Even if you are aware of a disability condition, ignore disability status right up to the point of accepting or declining the application. If a person with a disability can qualify without special treatment, so much the better. More importantly, you must not allow your personal ideas about disabilities to cause you to treat the applicant differently, at least not at this stage. (See the discussion below on declining applications).

Develop Disability-Aware Screening Procedures	Your procedures for resident selection should be examined to ensure that they focus only on lease compliance issues.

- Ask about lease compliance matters, not about lifestyle. As housing providers, you should care whether applicants can and will comply with the lease. Will they pay the rent on time? Will they respect the rights of other residents? Will they take reasonably good care of the apartment? Those are the things you should care about, not what medicine they take, how often they bathe, how they purchase and prepare their meals, or how they meet their transportation needs.

- Documentation, not guesswork. Much past discrimination against people with disabilities has been caused by the public's often-incorrect assumptions about what these people could and could not do. Rely on each individual's prior rental history, not on your own ideas of what a particular individual can and cannot do.

- Follow normal screening practices consistently. If your policy is that neutral or favorable references from the current landlord and one prior landlord, assuming both are unrelated to the applicant, are sufficient to establish the applicant's ability and willingness to comply with the lease then follow this policy! If you have enough information to satisfy this criterion look no further; if you keep "digging," you run the risk of a discrimination complaint if the applicant turns out to have a disability and you ultimately refuse the application.

Fair Housing Requires Neutral Screening Criteria, Applied Consistently

A case of discrimination was brought against a co-op board by an applicant who suffered from a mental disability and whose application to sublet a unit at the co-op was refused by the board. Several reasons were offered for the board's refusal including that it did not want to participate in the Section 8 program. Because, however, the board had questioned the applicant about his medication and this was the first sublet request ever denied by the board, without ruling on the merits of the case the court held that a reasonable jury could find that the board's decision to deny the sublet was actually due to discrimination, despite the apparently neutral reasons they offered for their actions. Consequently the board's application to dismiss the case was denied and the court ordered that the case proceed to trial. [*]

[*] *Milligan v. Lakeland Owner's Corp.; US District Court for New York; FH-FL Reporter 16, 291, No, 96-CV-1091*

See question 106.

- We recommend that you remove "independent living" from your vocabulary. If you mention this phrase to five applicants with disabilities, you will get at least one fair housing complaint, no matter what you meant by the phrase, and no matter how well you explained it.

- Whether residents comply with the lease is your business; how they comply is their business. A resident who personally does housekeeping tasks, one whose grandchild comes over once a week to do housekeeping, and one who hires a chore service to do housekeeping are all the same to you as the housing provider, both for resident selection purposes and for lease enforcement purposes. If the housekeeping isn't being done at all, then you should be concerned.

- You can have special screening procedures for applicants who do not have a rental history. For example: find or ask the applicant to provide an objective, qualified third party who is familiar with the applicant, and ask that person the same types of questions you ask landlords (in other words, questions relating directly to lease compliance issues).

See question 9 for a discussion of disparate impact.

- You cannot have special screening procedures for applicants with disabilities. This also holds for applicants for one bedroom apartments, single person households, or other categories which may be viewed as intending to target a protected class. If applicants with disabilities apply disproportionately for one-bedroom apartments, screening procedures that apply only to applicants for such units would not be permissible because of the "disparate impact" such a policy would have on people with disabilities—in other words, a set of special policies for one-bedroom or single applicants could be perceived as a way to indirectly discriminate against people with disabilities.

Decline Applications in a Disability-Aware Manner

The point at which the housing provider indicates that the application for housing may not be approved is the point in the admissions process where applicants with disabilities are most likely to exercise their right to request a reasonable accommodation. Experienced housing providers suggest the following steps when declining an application from a person with disabilities:

- Before declining the application of a person with known disabilities, get a second opinion. You are most vulnerable to a discrimination charge when you are actually aware of a disability condition during the applicant selection process. Before declining the application, review your decision with someone whose judgment you trust.

- Before declining the application of a person with a known disability, offer an informal meeting. Prior to issuing a rejection letter, offer (in writing, with written response required) to meet with the applicant to discuss whether a reasonable accommodation would make the application acceptable. Your letter should explain the reasons why the application, as it presently stands, is unacceptable. Without this information applicants will not be able to address the issue of whether a reasonable accommodation would enable them to meet the admissions criteria.

- Whenever you decline an application, reach out to people with disabilities. Although it is the applicant's responsibility to make an initial request for a reasonable accommodation, your standard rejection letter may foster requests and indicate your openness to them. For example, your standard rejection letter could state: "If you are a person with disabilities, and you feel that a reasonable accommodation by us would allow you to meet our admissions standards, contact us and we will hold a follow-up interview with you to discuss your application." Again, give the specific reasons for declining the application: reasonable accommodations cannot be discussed in a vacuum, rather, they must relate to some particular conduct, behavior or procedure. In the follow-up interview, ask the applicant to suggest reasonable accommodations. It is important to preserve the applicant's dignity and privacy during the "reasonable accommodation" discussion. The best approach is to allow the applicant to lead the discussion; you should discuss only information that the applicant volunteers.

Remember That Screening Has Its Limitations

In the rental housing business, we take a good deal of risk on all applicants, any of whom might turn out to be an undesirable resident no matter how good the application appears. We depend on the law of averages to keep us from having more than a few non-lease-compliant residents. A judge pointed this out to a Housing Authority, which had special "independent living" screening only for elderly and disabled applicants:

"In renting to a non-handicapped person, the Authority takes a similar, and perhaps in some cases, a greater risk that some harm will come to the property or to other tenants. Yet such applicant's ability to live independently is never questioned, and they are not required to disclose their medical history. It would thus seem that the Authority is content to rely upon information of a less intrusive and personal nature to assess the threat posed by these non-handicapped tenants. Without any objective evidence to indicate otherwise, it appears that the difference in treatment of the handicapped stems from unsubstantiated prejudices and fears regarding those with mental and physical disabilities. This is precisely the sort of situation that the fair housing laws were designed to prohibit."[7]

An Ounce of
Prevention...

Once again: in fair housing it is just as important to avoid the appearance of discrimination as it is to avoid actual discrimination. If you have created a fair housing compliant atmosphere at your property, you are much less likely to suffer complaints, and you are much more likely to receive the benefit of the doubt if a complaint is actually filed.

32   What Is Included in a Familial Status Review?

See question 72 for qualifying properties.

Unless your property is a certain type of "seniors only" property the Fair Housing Act provisions against discrimination on the basis of familial status will apply to your property.

- Examine any restrictions that are specifically geared towards either resident children or households that include minor children to see whether they are reasonably necessary either for the health and safety of the children or the protection of the property. If they are not, they should be removed.

- Examine your occupancy standards (see below) for conformity to HUD regulations as well as any applicable local and/or State laws.

- Examine your advertising materials: do they suggest a preference (whether overtly or implicitly) for applicants without children?

See Chapter 8 and question 69 for further information on this issue.

- Consider whether all aspects of your property, internally and externally, are safe for children. If there are safety hazards at your property it is advisable that you take action to correct them since it is not permissible to discourage applicants with children from living at your property on the ground that it is unsafe for children.

See Chapter 7.

- Occupancy standards. This is a term that refers to your policy regarding the largest household ("maximum occupancy standard") or smallest household ("minimum occupancy standard") that can occupy a given unit type. For example your occupancy standard may provide that no

---

7. *Cason v. Rochester Housing Authority; 748 F. Supp. 1002; 1990 US Dist.; Lexis 14229; FHFL 15, 643*

more than four people can occupy a two-bedroom dwelling. Minimum occupancy standards are more commonly found in public or assisted housing where there is a shortage of available units.

See question 70.

- House rules. Your present house rules might (in violation of the Fair Housing Act) include rules that apply only to families with children. For example, based on the belief that households with children cause greater wear and tear within dwellings, your rules may wrongly require that such households must pay larger security deposits than childless households. This is not permissible as it amounts to discrimination on the basis of familial status under the Fair Housing Act. If you have house rules like this, you will want to modify or remove them to be compliant with the Fair Housing Act.

- Some experts recommend you remove all references to children from your lease, house rules, occupancy standards, and other property documents.

33 What Constitutes Sexual Harassment?

Fair Housing Act regulations prohibit "denying or limiting services or facilities in connection with the sale or rental of a dwelling because a person failed or refused to provide sexual favors."[8] Although the Fair Housing Act itself does not address 'sexual harassment' explicitly,[9] courts have treated it as a form of discrimination on the basis of sex, and have found that sexual harassment does constitute a violation of Fair Housing laws. Management companies have been held liable for failure to prevent acts of sexual discrimination by their employees, under the Fair Housing Act.[10] There have been at least two settlements in excess of $1M for sexual harassment.[11]

---

8. *See §100.65(b)(5)*
9. *42 U.S.C. § 3604(a-c)*
10. *See U.S. v. Ersil James, et al, Civil Action No. 5:06-cv-06044-DW (April, 2008); and U.S. v. Richard Mills, et al, Civil Action No.: 1:00-cv-00276-SM (November, 2001)*
11. *U.S. v. James G. Mitchell and Land Baron Enterprises, LLC, Civil Action No. 1:07-cv-00150-SJD, and U.S. v. Bobby Veal and Jewel Veal, 02-0720-CV-W-DW*

34 What Fair Housing Considerations Apply to Non-Citizens?

The Fair Housing Act prohibits discrimination on the basis of national origin (that is, the country someone comes from), but does not prohibit discrimination on the basis of citizenship (that is, whether someone is a citizen, legal non-citizen, or illegal non-citizen). It would be a violation of the Act if citizenship requirements discriminated against applicants on the basis of their national origin.[12] For example, if a policy appears to be directed to all illegal aliens, but in reality it is applied only to illegal aliens from South America, the housing provider would be violating the Fair Housing Act. Additionally, because legal non-citizens generally have the same rights and responsibilities as citizens, a property's policies should, at a minimum, treat citizens and legal non-citizens equally.

See question 34. Various federal and state housing programs impose requirements related to citizenship (that is, whether an applicant or resident is a citizen, or a legal non-citizen, or an illegal non-citizen, etc.) .

35 May I Designate a Property, or Portions of a Property, "Smoke-Free"?

Smokers are not a protected class and HUD has stated that restrictions on smokers do not violate fair housing laws.[13] Additionally, property owners may have a compelling business rationale for restricting smoking. As a result, an increasing number of multifamily properties have instituted smoking restrictions. Some are focused on common areas, while others extend into the residential units themselves. If you decide to implement smoking restrictions in the units, professional apartment owners and managers recommend that rules restricting smoking in rental housing be reasonable and express a legitimate concern for the safety of residents and the

---

12. See, e.g., Espinoza v Hillwood Square Mut. Asso., 522 F. Supp. 559 (D. Va. 1981).

13. HUD General Counsel Letter, July, 2003

condition of individual apartment units and the property generally. Provide adequate notification to existing residents, and implement any restrictions after the expiration of existing residents' lease terms. Federally assisted properties that are required to use the HUD model lease must obtain prior approval of a smoke-free lease amendment.

36 What Constitutes a Reasonable Accommodation in Response to Complaints Regarding Second-Hand Smoke?

The following discussion from the Department of Justice indicates that it is possible for a person's sensitivity to second-hand smoke to be severe enough to constitute a disability, and accordingly in such situations a request to institute a smoking ban would need to be considered in the same manner as any other request for reasonable accommodation from a person with a disability. These reasonable accommodations might include transfers, establishing smoke-free policies, setting aside select buildings as smoke-free or other changes. If, however, the person's sensitivity to second-hand smoke does not constitute a disability, then the owner would not be obligated to consider or grant reasonable accommodations. According to the Department of Justice:[14]

> "The ADA prohibits discrimination on the basis of disability. The ADA clearly permits a ban on smoking, but it only requires covered entities to make reasonable modifications in their policies and practices that are necessary to enable individuals with disabilities to participate in their programs and activities.

> "The Department of Justice has declined to state categorically that sensitivity to cigarette smoke is a disability because the degree of impairment varies among individuals. To be legally recognized as a disability, a physical or mental impairment must substantially limit one or more

---

14. *DOJ Letter, Isabelle Katz Pinzler, Acting Assistant Attorney General, Civil Rights Division, June 13, 1997*

major life activities of an affected individual. Thus, the determination as to whether sensitivity to smoke is a covered disability must be made using the same case-by-case analysis that is applied to all other physical or mental impairments.

"In some cases, an individual's respiratory or neurological functioning may be so severely affected by sensitivity to cigarette smoke that he or she will be considered disabled. Such an individual would be entitled to all of the protections afforded by the ADA. These protections may include a ban on smoking in a specific covered facility if such a ban can be imposed without fundamentally altering the nature of the business or program. In other cases, however, an individual's sensitivity to smoke will not constitute a disability because the individual's major life activity of breathing is affected, but not substantially impaired. In this situation, an individual would not be entitled to claim ADA protection.

"After a determination is reached that a person is an individual with a disability who is entitled to claim the protection of the ADA, it is necessary to determine if a requested modification, such as a ban on smoking, is "reasonable." This determination involves a fact-specific, case-by-case inquiry that considers, among other factors, the effectiveness of the modification in light of the nature of the disability in question and its effect on the organization that would implement it. Staron v. McDonalds Corp., 51 F.3d 353 (2d Cir. 1995)...Because of the case-by-case nature of these determinations, the ADA regulations do not require an absolute ban on smoking."

The guidance from the Department of Justice reinforces that a person's reaction to cigarette smoke must be severe and 'substantially impair a major life activity' in order to require a reasonable accommodation under the ADA. Similarly, the Fair Housing Act protects tenants with disabilities, and requires reasonable accommodations be made when necessary to afford disabled tenants equal right to enjoy and use the premises.

37 What is 'Linguistic Profiling'?

The phrase "linguistic profiling" refers to the illegal practice of discrimination which occurs when the housing provider guesses at the race (or national origin) of an applicant based on his or her accent or voice. For example, when a telephone caller asks whether apartments are available, it is not permissible to give a different answer depending on the caller's accent or voice. Because so many fair housing complaints are related to questions about whether apartments are available, experienced owners and managers advise creating a reliable system to track unit availability, and procedures to ensure that all callers are provided the same information from this common source. Similarly, it is important that all staff who answer apartment-availability questions have access to and answer questions exclusively based upon this common source of information.

Inconsistent information regarding unit availability is commonly cited in fair housing complaints. Fair housing groups, which have traditionally relied on visits by testers, may have testers with different linguistic profiles call and inquire about apartment availability.

38 Am I Responsible for Intervening When an Applicant or Resident Is Harassed by Another Person?

If an applicant or resident is harassed in a manner that interferes with his or her fair housing rights, the harassment is illegal, and the person committing the harassment has broken the law. When the person committing the harassment has a business relationship with the landlord, it is possible that a court or fair housing enforcement agency may hold the landlord responsible. If, for example, the harassment is committed by the landlord's employee or agent, the landlord should expect to be held responsible.

If the harassment is committed by a vendor, a contractor, or another resident, the outcome is less clear. This is an evolving area of fair housing law and practice. The Department of Justice web site reports a number of settlement agreements in which landlords have accepted responsibility. Accordingly, to be accused in this sort of harassment situation likely would be expensive simply in terms of legal costs and might result in a finding of liability. Accordingly, it would be prudent for owners and managers to establish clear guidelines for vendors, contractors and residents, and to respond when harassment is reported.

Chapter Four: Introduction to Fair Housing Enforcement

39 Who Are the Parties to a Fair Housing Complaint?

The parties to a fair housing complaint are: (i) the aggrieved person; (ii) the complainant; and, (iii) the respondent.

- The *aggrieved person* is the person who actually experienced the discriminatory conduct and who provides the initial information for the filing of the complaint.

- The *complainant* is the person or entity in whose name the complaint is formally brought. In some instances the aggrieved person may also be the complainant, but HUD and fair housing organizations representing the aggrieved person may also be complainants.

- The *respondent* is the person or other entity accused in a complaint of a discriminatory housing practice. This may include the housing provider, the property manager and/or leasing agent.

40 Who May File a Fair Housing Complaint?

Complaints may be filed by anyone who believes he or she has received discriminatory treatment from a housing provider. The Fair Housing Act regulations refer to such persons as "aggrieved persons." This includes anyone, whether a member of a protected class or not, who has been injured in any way as a result of discriminatory conduct—even if this conduct was not directed towards them. The standard for determining whether a party has standing to sue or file a complaint is that the plaintiff must allege that: (1) he or she has suffered a "distinct and palpable" injury; and (2) that injury is "fairly traceable" to the defendant's discriminatory conduct.[1]

---

1. *Havens Realty Corp. V Coleman, 455 US 363 (1982) at 376 (1) and (6); Sullivan v. Little Hunting Park, Inc., 396 U.S. 229 (1969) (5); Trafficante v. Metropolitan Life Insurance Co., 409 U.S. 205 (1972)(2)*

Persons, Who Are Not Themselves Members of a Protected Class, May File a Fair Housing Complaint

Owners of a condominium successfully sued the condominium association for discrimination on the basis of familial status even though they had no minor children, because the association's unlawful policy of prohibiting sales of units to purchasers with minor children significantly hindered the owners in selling their own unit. In another case it was held that white residents have standing under the Fair Housing Act to challenge racial discrimination directed against African-Americans in their neighborhood.† Similarly, the Supreme Court upheld the standing of a white plaintiff to sue who had been expelled from membership in a community recreational organization because he had rented property and assigned his membership rights to an African-American‡. So, the right to file a fair housing complaint extends beyond actual membership of a protected class*

---

* *Simovits v. The Chanticleer Condominium Association, 933 F.Supp. 1394 (N.D. ILL 1996)(3)*

† *Gladstone Realtors v. Village of Bellwood, 441 US 91 (1979)(4)*

‡ *Sullivan v. Little Hunting Park Inc. 396 US 229 (1969)*

See question 43 for further information on the role of testers in fair housing complaints.

Complaints may also be filed by fair housing advocates or other representatives of the aggrieved person. This includes "testers" employed by Fair Housing Enforcement Agencies on behalf of persons they believe were discriminated against.[2] Additionally, courts have held that if testers are given false or misleading information they are also eligible to sue or file a complaint on their own behalf. The person or entity filing the complaint is referred to in the Fair Housing Act regulations as the "complainant."

---

2. *Havens Realty Corp. V Coleman, 455 U.S. 363 (1982)*

41 What Is the Fair Housing Enforcement Process?

See also question 7.

The Fair Housing Act provides two alternatives for its enforcement:

- Complaints of violations of the Act may be filed with HUD or with state or local fair housing enforcement agencies. These complaints may culminate in an administrative hearing of the complaint before an Administrative Law Judge; or,

- Civil actions may be instituted in district, state or federal courts by persons alleging violations of the Act.

Similarly, enforcement of the ADA and Section 504 of the Rehabilitation Act may also be achieved either by the filing of civil suits in the appropriate federal court or by administrative action by the agency responsible for administering the relevant law (the Department of Justice in the case of the ADA) or the relevant program under which the property operates (HUD in the case of Title II of the ADA and Section 504).

HUD's Administrative Procedure

The process begins with a *complaint*. Complaints filed with HUD under the Fair Housing Act must be filed within one year after the occurrence or termination of an alleged discriminatory housing practice. If the complaint is filed with HUD but there is a "substantially equivalent" state or local fair housing enforcement agency in the area where the acts complained of occurred, the complaint will be referred by HUD to that agency for investigation. (See "Referral" below).

The procedures described in this question are applicable only to enforcement of the Fair Housing Act. Enforcement of the ADA and Section 504 are covered more extensively in questions 42 and 127.

HUD or the state or local agency then *investigates* the complaint. The investigation may result in *conciliation* (a negotiated resolution), or in a *finding* (a determination by the enforcement agency). If the terms of the conciliation are not observed by the *"respondent"* the enforcement agency can turn the conciliation into a finding. The following flow chart shows the resolution process.

The Resolution Process

Action	By Whom	When
Complaint filed with HUD or equivalent agency	Aggrieved person	Within one year of the act of discrimination
Respondent notified of complaint	HUD or equivalent agency	Within ten days of filing of complaint
Answer to complaint filed	Respondent	Within ten days of notification of complaint
Commencement of investigation	HUD or equivalent agency	No time specified for HUD; equivalent agency must commence investigation within 30 days.
If no conciliation, then investigation completed by a finding of reasonable cause (charge issued) or no reasonable cause (charge dismissed)	Conciliation is handled by HUD or the equivalent agency. Findings are the reponsibility of the Assistant Secretary for Fair Housing.	Within 100 days of filing of complaint
Charge filed and served on respondent	Assistant Secretary for Fair Housing	Within three days of issuing charge.
Election of civil proceedings	Complainant, Respondent or Aggrieved Person	Within 20 days of service of charge
No election for civil trial, administrative hearing begins	Administrative Law Judge	Within 120 day of issuing charge.
Initial decision on case	Adminsistrative Law Judge	Within 60 days after completion of hearing

The Resolution Process

Action	By Whom	When
Petition for review of initial decision	Complainant, Respondent or Aggrieved Person	Within 15 days of initial decision
Final decision issued	HUD Secretary	Within 30 days of initial decision
Petition filed with Court of Appeal for review of final decision	Party adversely affected by decision	Within 30 days of final decision

Referral of Complaints

Complaints are handled by the appropriate enforcement agency. In many states, HUD is the appropriate enforcement agency. In other states with *"substantially equivalent"* fair housing laws, state and/or local agencies are responsible for handling enforcement. If there is an equivalent agency in the jurisdiction where the alleged discriminatory action took place, HUD may refer the complaint to that agency. Upon receipt of the complaint, the enforcing agency notifies the respondent by providing him or her with a copy of the complaint. Notification of complaints filed under the Fair Housing Act must be given to respondents within ten days of the filing of the complaint. If the "substantially equivalent" state or local agency fails to commence proceedings with respect to the complaint within 30 days from the date when the complaint was referred, HUD may revoke the referral and assume responsibility for investigating the complaint.

Investigation

The enforcing agency reviews the complaint, interviews the person who filed the complaint, and interviews the respondent. Typically, the investigator will review a variety of files and documents. The investigation sometimes also includes a visit to the property and may often include sending testers to the property.

See question 43 for further information on the use of testers and question 45 for more on questions that investigators may ask.

The Fair Housing Act states that investigations should be completed within 100 days of the filing of the complaint, but they often take longer. If the investigation is not completed in the 100-day period the enforcement agency must give written reasons to the complainant and respondent why they failed to do so.

Conciliation

HUD's enforcement regulations require the enforcement agency, after investigating the complaint, to attempt a negotiated resolution of the complaint. This negotiated resolution process is called *conciliation*. If the complaining party and the respondent are able to reach agreement on the terms of the conciliation, the enforcement process stops. HUD will terminate the conciliation process if a civil action has been filed with respect to the alleged discriminatory housing practice, and the trial in the action has commenced. HUD may periodically review compliance with the terms of the conciliation agreement. If HUD has a good reason to believe that the conciliation agreement has not been followed, HUD must refer the case to the Justice Department (Attorney General) and recommend that a civil action be brought against the respondent to enforce the terms of the conciliation agreement.

Findings and Appeal

If the complaint is not successfully conciliated, the enforcement agency issues one of two possible findings based on the evidence that has been collected during the course of the investigation:

- A *finding of reasonable cause to believe that a discriminatory housing practice has occurred or is about to occur* in which case the enforcement agency will issue "a charge" against the respondent. The charge will be heard by an Administrative Law Judge unless either the complainant, the aggrieved person on whose behalf the complaint was filed or the respondent elects to have the charge decided in a civil action.

- A *finding of no reasonable cause to believe that a discriminatory housing practice has occurred or is about to occur* in which case the complaint will be dismissed.

Findings of "Reasonable Cause" or "No Reasonable Cause" cannot be appealed by any of the parties to the proceedings.[3]

The Court Process

Civil actions under the Fair Housing Act may also be brought by aggrieved persons in an appropriate district or state court. These actions must be brought not later than two years after the occurrence or termination of the alleged discriminatory housing practice. If a complaint about the discriminatory housing practice had been filed with HUD, the computation of this two-year period would exclude any time during which the complaint is pending with HUD. Many lawsuits (whether related to fair housing or not) are *settled* by the parties before or during trial. A trial, if pursued to completion, will result either in *dismissal* of the complaint or an *order* for such relief as may be appropriate against the respondent. Such an *order* may include the assessment of a financial penalty.

Potential Remedial Actions

Typically in conciliation agreements or when a court rules against the respondent, the respondent agrees, or is ordered, to modify any procedures or practices that are determined to be in violation of fair housing laws. The respondent may incur financial penalties as well, in the form of fines and/or payments of damages to the complaining party. Often, the respondent agrees or is ordered to reverse the action that led to the complaint (e.g., accepting rather than declining the household's application, terminating an eviction action, agreeing to, rather than refusing to, make a reasonable accommodation or modification).

42 What Is the Enforcement Process for the Americans With Disabilities Act?

Federally assisted properties subject to Section 504 should refer to question 127 for the 504 enforcement process.

Remember, complaints of discriminatory housing practices may be brought under various laws, including the Fair Housing Act and the ADA. The procedures outlined in the previous question are applicable to complaints under the Fair Housing Act. The ADA has its own procedures, an outline of which appears below.

---

3. *Marinoff V U.S. Department of Housing & Urban Development 892 F. Supp. 493; aff'd and adopted 78 F. 3d 64 (2nd Circuit 1996)*

Complaint and Investigative Procedures for ADA Title II

Any individual who believes that he or she is a victim of discrimination prohibited by Title II may file a complaint. Individuals wishing to file Title II complaints may either file:

- An administrative complaint with an appropriate federal agency; or,

- A lawsuit in federal district court.

The following additional provisions apply to Title II complaints:

- Complaints must be filed within 180 days of the date of the alleged act(s) of discrimination.

- HUD is the "appropriate federal agency" for filing complaints involving programs, services and/or regulatory activities relating to State and local public housing. However, complaints may also be filed with the Department of Justice (DOJ), but that department will refer the complaint to the appropriate federal agency for handling.

- HUD processes Title II complaints under the same procedure as it processes complaints under Section 504.

- Cases may be referred for resolution to a mediation program sponsored by the DOJ.

- If the complaint does disclose non-compliance with the ADA, HUD will, in the first instance, try to obtain voluntary compliance by the housing provider. If this cannot be achieved, the law will be enforced either by the termination of federal funding following an administrative hearing or by a referral to the the Department of Justice ("DOJ") for judicial enforcement.

Complaint and Investigative Procedures for ADA Title III

Title III complaints may be filed either with:

- The Department of Justice; or,

- In a U.S. District Court

Complaints filed with DOJ will be investigated, with a view to determining whether or not there is an ADA violation. If the DOJ believes that there is a pattern or practice of discrimination, or if the complaint raises an issue of general public importance it may attempt to negotiate a settlement of the matter. If negotiations to settle the matter are unsuccessful then suit may be filed against the offending party in US District Court. The following provisions also apply to complaints under Title III:

- When private parties bring lawsuits to stop discrimination no monetary damages are available in such suits.

- In suits brought by the Attorney General monetary damages (not including punitive damages) and civil penalties may be awarded.

- Civil penalties may not exceed $50,000 for a first violation and $100,000 for any subsequent violation.

43   What Are "Testers"?

Testers are individuals who, without an intent to rent or purchase a home or apartment, pose as renters or purchasers for the purpose of collecting evidence of discriminatory practices.

Fair housing enforcement organizations sometimes employ testers as a way of determining whether an owner or manager is engaging in discriminatory conduct. For example, an applicant is denied housing and believes that the denial is discriminatory. The applicant may then complain to the local fair housing advocacy group, which may employ a paid "tester" with similar rental qualifications but who is not a member of the same protected class as the applicant. The tester will apply for housing at the property that denied admission to the original applicant. If the tester receives the same treatment or information as the original applicant, that is an indication that the housing manager's conduct was not based on the applicant's protected status; however, if the tester is treated more favorably than the original applicant, that is instead an indication that the housing manager may have violated fair housing non-discrimination requirements.

See question 53 for a discussion on the importance of consistency in leasing practices.

Another variation on the use of testers may involve two testers with similar rental qualifications being sent to the property. One tester will be a member of the same protected class as the original applicant while the other is not. Again, if both testers receive the same information and treatment this would tend to suggest that the original applicant had not been discriminated against. However, if the tester who is not a member of the relevant protected class receives more favorable treatment or information than the other tester this would support a conclusion that discriminatory conduct had occurred.

An example of the use of testers can be seen in a case of housing discrimination filed with HUD by the Fair Housing Council of Greater Washington.

An Example of the Use of Fair Housing "Testers"

An apartment property was tested as part of a project by the Fair Housing Council of Greater Washington to assess the incidence of racial discrimination in apartment rental in Northern Virginia and not as a result of an actual complaint. In the first instance the Council sent a black tester to the property who was given information on only one available apartment style that rented for $775 per month. A white tester was then sent to the property and received information on two apartment types ranging from $705 to $775. There were also discrepancies in the availability dates on the units shown to each tester. On a subsequent visit to the property the black tester was told that no one-bedroom apartments were available until May 15 and was instead encouraged to rent a two-bedroom unit while the white tester was told of a one-bedroom availability upcoming on May 10 and was invited to place a deposit on that unit. This unequal treatment of the two testers led to the filing of the complaint with HUD. Resolution of the complaint is pending.

The Supreme Court has ruled that testing is often the only way to determine whether discrimination occurred. Additionally, courts have held that testers who are given false or misleading information are also eligible to sue on their own behalf.[4]

A housing provider may also be ordered to pay damages to the organization that employed the testers. For example, the organization would be entitled to recover damages for economic losses stemming from the time and resources it devoted to investigating the complaint.

4. *See Smith v. Pac.Props. & Dev. Corp., 358 F.3d 1097, 1104 (9th Cir. 2004)*

44   How Do I Respond to a Fair Housing Complaint?

Experienced housing providers give the following advice:

- *Designate a fair housing coordinator* – Have a central person in your organization who will be notified immediately if anyone in the organization receives a fair housing complaint.

- *Resolve it* – Many fair housing issues involve unclear areas of the law. Most fair housing issues involve expenses that are relatively small, by comparison to the costs of defending (or pursuing) a lawsuit. Accordingly, both parties typically have strong motivations to negotiate a solution quickly, rather than to pursue a lengthy legal process.

- *Seek expert advice* – Build business relationships with attorneys and other experts who are familiar with the range of fair housing issues you are likely to encounter. When a complaint occurs, consult your expert advisors before taking any other action.

- *Respond appropriately* – After seeking the advice of your experts, respond completely to requests for information.

- *Respond timely* – When an investigator requests information, respond promptly. More importantly, note and adhere to any deadlines imposed for responding or providing information. For example, answers to complaints under the Fair Housing Act must be filed within ten days of receiving notification of the complaint.

45   What Questions Do Investigators Ask?

Investigators can ask a wide variety of questions. Some of the more typical are:

- *Similar situations* – What information do you have about other applicants with similar characteristics to the rejected applicant? What were the results of their applications? For example, if the complaint was from a mobility-impaired applicant whose application was denied, the investigator will want to establish if there is a pattern of similar actions by the housing provider.

- *Resident profile* – Do other members of the relevant protected class live in the property? If no other members of that protected class reside at the property, then it is possible that there have been prior discriminatory acts. On the other hand, if there are a number of residents representing that particular protected class, then it is less likely that the housing provider discriminated in denying the application of the particular complainant.

- *Similar units* – If the complaint relates to choice of unit offered to the complainant, the investigator will want to know where similar units are located within the property. The investigator will want information pertaining to vacancies and rent readiness of similar units at the time of the alleged discrimination.

- *Similar households* – The locations of similar households within the property may establish if there has been a process of steering those households to specific locations within the property.

- *Policies and procedures* – The investigator will want to review your resident selection policy, your lease and house rules, your lease enforcement policy, and other policies that have to do with fair housing or with the action (or alleged action) that led to the complaint. Good policies are not by themselves enough to provide protection from charges. You may have to demonstrate that you have followed the policies. Good record keeping is critical. Other things being equal, the investigator is likely to respond favorably if management has good policies and procedures, good records indicating compliance with the policies and procedures, and good records documenting interactions with applicants and residents.

46   What are Best Practices for Recordkeeping?

Good recordkeeping is critical. Management should have sound policies and procedures, good records indicating compliance with the policies and procedures, and organized and complete records documenting interactions with applicants and residents.

Tracking Unit Availability

A significant number of Fair Housing complaints originate when one applicant (a member of a protected class) is told there are no units available, and a subsequent applicant (who is not a member of a protected class) is shown and rented an available unit. Unfortunately, in many cases this is outright discrimination. In other cases, the complaint originates because the housing provider is disorganized and provides inconsistent information unnecessarily. Experienced owners and managers strongly recommend that housing providers rely on a system for tracking unit availability (such as a whiteboard in the office) and that all inquiries receive answers based on the same source of information.

Foundation for Addressing Residents' Issues

When addressing or responding to residents, it is a good practice to cite the relevant written policy, lease provision, law, or regulatory requirement. For example, rather than notifying a resident that he 'cannot hang laundry out of his window', refer to the various restrictions in place.

Documenting Requests for Reasonable Accommodation

To ensure your ability to document and keep records on important communications with residents related to fair housing, establish a policy requiring that all requests for reasonable accommodation be submitted in writing. Keep in mind, however, that you may have to make reasonable accommodations to this policy. Your response to the request should also be in writing. Ensure that these communications are incorporated into resident files.

Daily Communications

A detailed record of communications with tenants can be very effective in demonstrating your professionalism and competence—not only in a fair housing related proceeding, but in other legal contexts. Track all communications with tenants in a log. Expert owners and managers recommend having a separate log for each tenant as part of their file. When a resident contacts the housing provider for any reason, the communications log in the resident's file should be annotated with the time, date, and nature of the call.

Chapter Five: Fair Housing Marketing and Advertising Requirements

47   Does the Fair Housing Act Impose Requirements on Marketing?

The goal of professional marketing is to reach the maximum number of potential customers in the most cost-effective way with the most effective messages. Professional apartment marketing must also be non-discriminatory. Under the Fair Housing Act it is illegal to:

"make, print, or publish, or cause to be made, printed, or published any notice, statement, or advertisement with respect to the rental or sale of a dwelling that indicates any preference, limitation or discrimination because of race, color, religion, sex, handicap, familial status or national origin, or an intention to make any such preference, limitation or discrimination."[1]

Even if there is no evidence of discrimination in your admissions policies and practices, you could still be faced with a fair housing complaint based solely on the way in which your property is marketed. To avoid this possibility, you should:

See question 48.   •   Be inclusive rather than exclusive in your marketing;

See question 49.   •   Avoid 'red flag' words;

See question 50.   •   Ensure proper use of the "Equal Housing Opportunity" logo, slogan and statement;

See question 51.   •   Depict diverse individuals when using human models in your advertising; and,

See question 52.   •   Display the Fair Housing Poster.

At the very least, review your entire marketing campaign to ensure that persons who are members of a protected class do not feel unwelcome.

There are no federal requirements, other than the general prohibition outlined above, that apply to advertising. At this point, HUD's advertising guidelines exist in two forms:

---

1. *24 CFR Section 100.75(a)*

- The Code of Federal Regulations (24 CFR Part 109) contained guidelines on advertising and fair housing. This part of the Code was removed (effective May 1, 1996) in a Federal Register notice dated April 1, 1996.

- Memo from Roberta Achtenberg (then Assistant Secretary for Fair Housing and Equal Opportunity) dated January 9, 1995 and titled, "Guidance Regarding Advertisements under 804(c) of the Fair Housing Act."

The Fair Housing Poster is required, however, of all properties; see question 52. Federally regulated properties face additional requirements, addressed in Chapter 19.

Neither (the removed) Part 109 of the Code of Federal Regulations, nor the Achtenberg Memorandum are legally binding, and neither require any specific action regarding use of models, language, or the EHO logo. HUD refers to both documents as "guidance" and considers whether a housing provider has followed these guidelines in determining whether advertising is discriminatory. Courts of law, outside of HUD's jurisdiction, also consider whether this guidance has been followed in determining whether advertising is discriminatory.

Internet Advertising

HUD has asserted that advertisements placed on the Internet must comply with all fair housing requirements. Postings which advertise apartments should be written carefully to avoid the use of 'red flag' terminology (See question 49).

48 What Are the Basic Fair Housing Considerations in Apartment Marketing?

See question 53 for leasing considerations.

Fair housing marketing should be inclusive rather than exclusive. Look at your complete marketing campaign and ask yourself these questions.

- Are we using a variety of media outlets that reach diverse groups in the community?

- Does our advertising campaign reach people who would want to live here and could afford the rent, regardless of their status as a member of a protected class? In practice, this generally means people who either live or work within a reasonable proximity of the property.

- Convey awareness of fair housing issues.

Before finalizing signs, brochures, flyers and advertisements, review design and content to determine if members of protected classes might take offense at something you might or might not say or imply. There are words and messages that are advisable to avoid in your marketing materials. Some subtle examples:

Examples of Discrimination in Advertising and Marketing

A property feels its competitive strength is in its fitness-related amenities and wants to market its exercise equipment, jogging trails, sauna and pool. It reasonably concludes that these amenities should be illustrated in the property's brochure. The result includes pictures of young adults running, swimming, jogging, and exercising happily. Although the models in the brochure are racially diverse, there are no children (families are a protected class), and no people with disabilities (also protected). Some readers of the brochure will notice that certain classes of people are not represented, and may conclude that their absence is an intentional message that they are not welcome. The property should show that its fitness activities are available to all and in some manner accessible to all.

Another property finds that many of its residents attend the Catholic church across the street. The manager concludes that this proximity to the church has marketing value, and decides to give prominence to the church in the new brochure. The church is a backdrop in one of the photos, and the location of the property is billed as being, "across the street from the Catholic church." Because of the prominence given to the church, some readers might conclude that other faiths are not welcome (or as welcome) at the property. Discrimination on the basis of religion is prohibited under the Fair Housing Act and this property could face fair housing complaints.

Consistency

To the extent that your staff follow consistent procedures, give consistent answers, and present the property in consistent ways to all applicants, you are less likely to receive fair housing complaints. Perfect consistency is neither possible nor appropriate (after all, good leasing technique involves responding to each applicant's particular needs and interests), but reasonable consistency is achievable and advisable. It is recommended that non-leasing staff, such as maintenance or groundskeeping crews, either be equally well informed about the current operations of the property or be instructed to direct all questions to the appropriate leasing staff. Your best efforts at being consistent can be defeated if the maintenance technician incorrectly informs a prospective housing applicant that there are one-bedroom units available and the leasing staff correctly informs the applicant that no one-bedroom units are available.

49   Fair Housing Considerations for Advertising

Avoid "Red Flag" Words or Phrases

Managers always attempt to portray the property in ways that will appeal to prospective residents. Sometimes, managers choose wording that, although innocently intended, raises fair housing concerns. Here are some examples:

- *"An exclusive community"* – Meaning to convey that the property is desirable and preferred, uses a word ("exclusive") that literally means excluding those who are not wanted.

- *"Close to churches"* – Raising concerns that the property is not interested in renting to people who are not religiously observant, or to people whose religions don't involve "churches."

- *"Ideal for seniors"* – Raises concerns that the property isn't interested in renting to families with children. An exception would be for properties that are permitted to operate specifically as housing for seniors and that would then be marketed as such.

- *"For the active lifestyle"* – Intending to market fitness amenities, the property sends a different message to some people with disabilities.

- *"Quiet, peaceful, restful community"* – This may raise concerns that the property is attempting to discourage applications from families with children.

- *"Latino neighborhood"* – This would raise concerns that the property is specifically for Latinos, to the exclusion of others.

Individual words descriptive of protected classes that may convey discriminatory intent are:

- Race specific references such as black, African-American, white, Hispanic, Asian or Asian-American;

- Color specific references such as white or black;

- Specific references to national origin such as Mexican-American or Russian;

- Specific references to religion such as Protestant or Christian. Note however that advertisements that use the legal name of the property (e.g. Concord Catholic Home) or that advertise services on the property such as "provides Kosher meals" or use of certain non-secular terms like "Merry Christmas" are allowable.

- Indicators of gender are not permitted. For example, it would be inappropriate to advertise that an apartment is "perfect for a bachelor." However, words that are traditionally descriptive of apartment features, such as master-bedroom or mother-in-law suite, are allowable.

- A phrase such as "no wheelchairs" is not permitted; but terms like "walk-up," "jogging trails," or "great view" are. The general rule is that you may describe features of the apartments, but you should avoid referring to who would benefit from those features.

- References to resident characteristics such as adults, retired, singles or couples are not permitted as they may discourage families with children from applying. However, terms like "family room" are allowable.

Media Selection   Although it is important to ensure that your advertising doesn't contain any discriminatory statements or messages, it is also important to ensure that you communicate broadly and inclusively. Certain media outlets may be perceived as being associated with particular racial or ethnic groups. If you select media outlets that cater to specific segments of the population, you should have as part of your larger advertising campaign similar advertising that is directed to other groups and/or directed to a wider population. If you are uncertain whether the audience you will reach through a newspaper advertisement or radio commercial is sufficiently broad, ask for readership or listenership demographics before making your media selection. Your entire marketing campaign should be addressed towards and attractive to people who would want to live there and who are capable of affording the rent.

Media Selection Should be Broad and Inclusive

The Dunes Apartments is advertising solely in general-circulation media (consisting of the main local paper and the local apartment guide). It has experienced increased traffic and leases from the Russian immigrant community and based on this, it wants to do some targeted marketing to the Russian community. The Dunes may undertake this targeted marketing, but only if it also undertakes targeted marketing to other groups so that its entire marketing approach is sufficiently broad and inclusive. To market exclusively to this community on a regular basis would demonstrate a preference for this group over others.

Special Requirements for Federally Regulated Properties

If your property is required to prepare an Affirmative Fair Housing Marketing Plan (AFHMP) and the segment of the population that you are trying to reach is a heavily under-served population, the HUD approved plan may include marketing that is targeted to that specific group (to the exclusion of others).[2] See question 179.

50 When and How Do You Use the EHO Logo, Statement or Slogan?

HUD guidelines require[3] that all advertising for the sale, rental or financing (whether existing or planned new constructed) of residential housing contain an equal housing opportunity (EHO) logotype, statement or slogan.

EHO information should be included in all written or verbal advertisement including phone book ads, realtor signs, business cards, flyers, brochures, radio or television commercials,

---

2. *HUD Directive 8025.1, rev-2, 3-5, 3-8 and 3-12.*

3. *The Guidelines "require" use of the logo as a best practice: When reviewing a case against a housing provider, the Department will consider whether its marketing activities are discriminatory, and the standard it will use in its consideration will be the extent to which those activities are consistent with HUD's Guidelines on advertising, see question 36.*

print advertisements (including newspapers and apartment shoppers guides) and the Internet.

Definitions and Examples

- The EHO Slogan reads: "Equal Housing Opportunity" or "EHO," depending on space available.

- The EHO Logo shows the graphic Fair Housing symbol:

- The EHO Statement reads:

EQUAL HOUSING
OPPORTUNITY

"We are pledged to the letter and spirit of U.S. policy for the achievement of

equal housing opportunity throughout the nation. We encourage and support

an affirmative advertising and marketing program in which there are no

barriers to obtaining housing because of race, color, religion, sex, handicap,

familial status, or national origin."

See question 18.

You can change the language of the Statement to reflect additional protected classes in your area.

When to Use the EHO Slogan, Logo or Statement

In general, large ads, brochures and signs should use either the Statement or Logo, and smaller ads may use the Slogan. The size of the logo varies according to the size of the ad or sign, but it should be proportionally sized.

The HUD guidelines for the content and size of EHO Statements and Logos are as follows:

- Advertising of 4 column inches[4] or less should include the Equal Housing Opportunity Slogan or a Statement that the housing advertised is available to all without regard to race, color, religion, sex, handicap, familial status or national origin. Check to see if there are additional local protected classes.

- All other print advertising may include either an Equal Housing Opportunity Statement or an Equal Housing Opportunity Logo. Verbal advertising (voicemail recordings, radio commercials, etc.) should include the Statement.

---

4. *A "column inch" is the width of a standard newspaper column one inch long.*

- The site sign is advertising, and as such must include the Logo or Slogan.

Size and Placement of EHO Slogan, Logo or Statement

If the Statement is chosen, it should be clearly visible and in print size comparable to that used in the rest of the advertisement.

If the Logo is chosen, HUD provides the following size standards:

Size Standards for Use of the EHO Logo

Size of Ad	Size of Logo
½ page or larger	2" x 2"
⅛ page to ½ page	1" by 1"
4 column inches to ⅛ page	½" by ½"
Less than 4 column inches	Slogan not logo

If these sizes are not relevant (for example, for a small pamphlet, brochure or other advertisement), the EHO Logo should be of a size at least equal to other logotypes in the ad. If there are no other logos, the EHO Logo should be in bold display face that is clearly visible. If an EHO Statement is used instead, it should take up 3 to 5 percent of the ad.

Using the Slogan, Logo or Statement consistently may be instrumental in demonstrating to HUD or a court that your marketing campaign is not discriminatory. For this reason, experts recommend that you establish a company policy, or standard practice of using the EHO Slogan, Logo and Statement. Of course, these do not, by themselves, constitute a comprehensive fair housing marketing plan. In addition, as discussed above, your advertising campaign should make appropriate media selections, avoid 'red flag' wording, and if you use human models they should reflect appropriate diversity.

51   The Use of Human Models in Advertisements

The use of human models (generally, pictures or visual representations of people in any element of your marketing) can be a complex issue. Some housing providers have opted to discontinue the use of human models in marketing materials, while others seek legal guidance as a matter of practice.

See question 47.

The goal in proper use of human models is to ensure that you fairly represent different groups; thereby communicating that your property does not have a preference for one group over another.

When the courts and HUD receive a complaint based on advertising that is claimed to infer a preference for one group over another (protected) group they typically evaluate each individual advertisement in the advertising campaign, the overall advertising campaign for a particular property over a period of time, and the company's overall advertising campaign for all properties over a period of time. They will attempt to ascertain from this examination whether the campaign shows a "pattern" of discriminatory conduct. As stated in a legal case on the matter[5],

"The discriminatory character of an advertising campaign is often not self-evident, and the law does not automatically make every ad showing persons of only one race actionable. Only when enough ads have run to allow a pattern to emerge is a violation likely to become apparent."

In evaluating whether advertising materials violate the Fair Housing Act, determine whether the ad suggests to an ordinary reader that a particular group is preferred or discouraged from the housing in question; would the ad discourage an ordinary reader of a particular (protected) group from answering it? These questions should be considered when you decide upon a particular format for your advertising. There are a number of other considerations when you evaluate your overall advertising campaign:

---

5. *Tyus et al v. Urban Search Management*

85

- Are the human models in your ads fairly diverse or are they skewed to a particular group?

- Are the models in ads for your up-scale suburban property mainly white adults and the models in ads for your moderately priced urban property mostly minority families?

- Are you representing not only different races, but different age groups?

- Are you portraying families with children?

- Are people portrayed in equal social settings? It may not be perceived as an equal social setting if the residents are of one race and the service workers are of another.

How Extensive Should Diversity of Representation Be?

Managers need to take into consideration the demographic make-up of the geographic area in which the advertisement is to be placed and should be careful to ensure that the groups represented are reflective of that population and include members of protected classes.

Some state and local jurisdictions have additional laws on the type and placement of advertising. Become familiar with this information for all localities in which you market your properties.

52   What Is the Fair Housing Poster, and How Am I Required to Display It?

All multifamily rental properties must display the required Fair Housing poster[6]. This poster states the basic requirements of the law, and informs the public about where they may file a complaint.

The poster must be "prominently displayed so as to be readily apparent to all persons seeking housing accommodations..."[7] Generally, the poster is displayed in both the rental and leasing offices. The poster is available from regional and area offices of the U.S. Department of Housing and Urban Development.

---

6. *24 CFR, Part 110*
7. *24 CFR Section 110.15*

The required poster is 11 by 14 inches, and appears below:

U.S. Department of Housing and Urban Development

**EQUAL HOUSING
OPPORTUNITY**

We Do Business in Accordance With the Federal Fair Housing Law

(The Fair Housing Amendments Act of 1988)

It is Illegal to Discriminate Against Any Person Because of Race, Color, Religion, Sex, Handicap, Familial Status, or National Origin

---

In the sale or rental of housing or residential lots

In advertising the sale or rental of housing

In the financing of housing

In the provision of real estate brokerage services

In the appraisal of housing

Blockbusting is also illegal

Anyone who feels he or she has been discriminated against may file a complaint of housing discrimination:
    1-800-669-9777 (Toll Free)
    1-800-927-9275 (TDD)

**U.S. Department of Housing and Urban Development
Assistant Secretary for Fair Housing and Equal Opportunity
Washington, D.C. 20410**

Previous editions are obsolete

form HUD-928.1A(8-93)

Chapter Six: Applicant Screening and Selection

53　Fair Housing Considerations for Apartment Leasing

There are two primary practices that should be followed to ensure compliance with the Fair Housing Act in your apartment leasing policies: consistency and accommodation.

Consistency

Consistent application of your leasing policies will minimize the risk that an applicant or resident will perceive illegal discrimination.

If a member of a protected class receives information that deters them from leasing an apartment at your property and this information is in fact incorrect, there may be a perception that the information was deliberately misleading in order to discourage the application.

In many instances inaccurate information is provided to applicants for discriminatory reasons—precisely the type of activity that the Fair Housing Act was intended to address. Inaccurate information is also given to applicants when a rental office is not operated in a professional or organized way; for example:

- *The office is disorganized and information is in disarray.* Pricing information is not clear, even to employees who are trying to provide the right information. As a consequence, different applicants receive different information.

- *Too many employees are involved in providing information.* Even with good systems and accessible information, when too many people are providing information, it is inevitable that information will not be consistent.

- *Don't overlook the role of your maintenance staff.* They should either be kept as regularly informed as your leasing staff or should be instructed to direct all inquiries concerning the leasing of apartments to the leasing staff.

See question 43 for more on testers. See question 48 for additional information on the importance of consistency in leasing.

When a fair housing agency investigates a complaint by sending testers, and each tester receives different information on apartment availability, or different treatment in general, it is likely that a claim of discrimination will be filed with HUD, regardless of whether the discrimination was intended, or was the result of disorganized management operations.

Accommodation
You are obligated to make reasonable accommodations to enable applicants with disabilities to have equal opportunity to apply and be considered for leasing an apartment. You can't inquire into the nature or severity of a disability, but once an applicant has requested that you accommodate his or her disability, you do have the right to verify the existence of the disability and that the disability would be addressed effectively by the proposed reasonable accommodation.

Reasonable accommodations during the preliminary leasing process might include:

- Offering to read materials that normally are provided in written form (for visually impaired applicants);

- Offering to provide in written form materials that are normally provided orally (for hearing impaired applicants);

For other examples of accommodations, see Chapter 12.
- Allowing the applicant to take the application home and return it later (for applicants with disabilities that affect their ability to read, write or understand) even though your normal policy is that applicants have to complete the application during the initial interview.

The obligation to make reasonable accommodations exists throughout all stages of the leasing process, from the initial contact with an applicant to their continuing occupancy as a resident of your property.

See questions 78 and 79.
Expert managers advise communicating your commitment to accessibility in a way that encourages applicants and residents with disabilities to request the accommodations they need.

54 Fair Housing Considerations for Applicant Screening

Neutrality. Consistency. Reasonable Accommodation.

All aspects of your resident selection criteria should be geared towards assessing the likelihood that the applicant will (1) pay the rent on time and in full; and (2) adhere to the other terms of the lease. These generally include: respecting the rights of neighbors, avoiding undue wear and tear on the apartment, maintaining it in good condition and refraining from criminal activity. A manager may reject an applicant for either a history of prior non-payment or a history of prior lease violations as long as he or she does not discriminate on the basis of race, color, religion, sex, familial status, national origin, disability or locally protected classes, if any.

Neutrality

Make certain that your criteria are neutral and do not affect an applicant by virtue of membership in a protected class. Once you've ensured that your criteria are neutral, then take steps to ensure that they are applied consistently.

Consistency

Your screening process should use the same set of criteria for all applicants. These criteria should be applied consistently. By reviewing each application against the same criteria, all applicants receive equal consideration. If you do more thorough background checks on the housekeeping histories of families with children (vs. single applicants), your practices are discriminatory.

See question 9 for the definition of disparate impact.

However, special screening procedures may be permissible for certain categories of applicants who are not members of a protected class. For example, you may have additional screening for students, provided students do not disproportionately represent members of a protected class. While age is not a federally protected class, requiring home visits on elderly applicants might be viewed as discriminatory to people with disabilities, since elderly persons have a higher rate of mobility impairments than the general population.

Expert managers have learned that certain practices are more likely to result in consistency, for example:

- *Have all screening done by one person.* This prevents inconsistencies that might occur as a result of different interpretations and applications of established criteria.

- *Use standard forms whenever possible.* Using standard forms will increase the likelihood that each applicant receives the same consideration. Further, used properly they will document the fairness of your own practices, should you ever need to prove this.

- *Use objective criteria whenever possible.* If you remove opinion and subjectivity, you are more likely to treat all applicants equally.

- *Follow written standards for processing applications.*

Reasonable Accommodation

Provide reasonable accommodations in screening. Make certain that your screening requirements, including the procedures for actually submitting an application, do not discriminate against people with disabilities.

An Example of Reasonable Accommodation in Screening

Your screening criteria require applicants to have a history of timely rent payment. An applicant appears who has a rental history marked by frequent late rent payments. The applicant requests, as a reasonable accommodation, that you consider mitigating circumstances. This applicant previously lived in a place where rent had to be paid in person, at an office that was not accessible and therefore the applicant had to rely on another person to take the check to the rental office. Hence, it tended to be late. Your rent is to be paid at an office that is accessible (or you'll accept the check by mail) so this will no longer be a problem.

Requiring Additional Information

In some cases, you may require additional information from an applicant to determine eligibility because the applicant may have an unconventional credit or rental history. In most cases, it is best to establish this procedure directly on your rental application. For instance, ask, "If you don't have at least X years rental history please describe where you have lived for the last X years and what, if any, financial arrangements you had while living there."

Generally, your screening criteria should allow for the pursuit of additional information by (1) specifically determining when additional information may be sought, (2) how it should be obtained, and (3) how it should be factored into the determination of eligibility. As with other aspects of screening, however, you must be certain that any requirements for additional information are applied consistently, and are neutral (i.e., do not have a specific impact on any member of a protected class). For example, you have a (written) screening policy that allows you to accept personal references in lieu of landlord references, *if* the applicant has insufficient rental history.

When your screening criteria stipulate that you should request additional information, make certain that these requirements are related to the issues of the individual applicant's likelihood of (1) paying the rent and (2) abiding by the lease terms. Make certain that requirements for additional information are not triggered merely because the applicant is a member of a protected class. Make certain that any additional requirements are applied consistently.

The Application Process

The purpose of the application process is to screen out unqualified applicants (i.e., those unlikely to abide by the terms of the lease and pay the rent). No aspect of your application process should have the effect of either discouraging a qualified applicant from pursuing the application or rejecting an applicant who is qualified.

The type of information requested during the applicant screening process must, of course, be consistent and neutral to membership in a protected class. Similarly, the application process must also be consistent and neutral. However, variations from your standard procedure (reasonable accommodations) may be required in order to accommodate a candidate with disabilities.

55 Can Informally Obtained Information Be Used in the Screening Process?

The short, definitive answer is NO. Many properties repeatedly run into this problem. It may seem like "common sense" for a manager to consider information obtained from informal sources in an attempt to more fully screen applicants. However, the use of any information not obtained through the normal screening process opens a hornet's nest of potential fair housing issues. Your screening process has to be designed so as to maximize your ability to get the truest and most complete information about the applicant, which is relevant to the application. One purpose of a well-designed screening process is to keep the decision making process fair and nondiscriminatory. Gossip or other inside information, no matter how reliable it seems, is most likely discriminatory because it is not obtained equally for all applicants. For example, a person who has resided in a community for some time would most likely have an informal reputation, which could be used against him or her, but a newcomer to the area would not.

Professional managers are very careful to ensure that only information obtained through the normal screening process is relied upon when deciding to accept or reject an application.

56 Can a History of Non-Lease-Compliant Behavior Be a Cause for Rejection (or Eviction) Even If the Conduct Is a Manifestation of a Disability?

Different considerations may apply depending on whether the case involves an application for housing or the continuation of an existing tenancy.

Prior Misconduct by an Applicant

In many cases it may be difficult, if not impossible, for a leasing agent to determine whether the prior misconduct of the applicant with a known disability (1) occurred because of the applicant's disability and, if it did (2) is something that is likely to continue and, if so (3) can be addressed through a reasonable accommodation by the property.

The prohibition against probing into the nature and extent of an applicant's disability makes it difficult to determine if prior violations are a product of a disability, and whether they are likely to recur.

Considerations in Rejecting An Applicant With a History of Disruptive Conduct

Suppose the applicant's previous lease was terminated because the applicant frequently engaged in disruptive behavior that interfered with the ability of other residents to quietly enjoy the property. This behavior may have resulted from the applicant's mental disability, but a leasing agent may not know this when reviewing the application.

In addition, the agent should be aware that accepting this application, despite the previous misconduct, might impose a responsibility on the housing provider to take steps to ensure that the applicant does not again interfere with the rights of other residents to quietly enjoyment of the property.

Considerations in Rejecting An Applicant With a History of Disruptive Conduct

In these circumstances, if nothing more is known than that the applicant has a history of disruptive behavior, it should be safe to reject the application on the ground that all the information that can be legitimately obtained strongly suggests that the applicant will not observe the requirements of the lease.

See question 107.

On the other hand, suppose the applicant voluntarily discloses information about the circumstances surrounding the misconduct, revealing for example (1) the existence of a disability, (2) that the medication he was taking at the time was not effective in controlling the disruptive behavior; and (3) that he has now switched medications and there are no more behavioral problems. Furthermore, he produces credible written medical evidence that confirms these facts. To reject the applicant because of the prior misconduct in those circumstances could conceivably lead to a charge of discrimination on the basis of disability.

HUD regulated properties should also see question 172.

Some experts recommend notifying applicants in the rejection notice of their right to request a reasonable accommodation (though this is not required under the Fair Housing Act). If an applicant then requests an accommodation, he or she will likely reveal the details of the situation.

Misconduct by an Existing Occupant

The case of misconduct by an existing occupant with a known disability is more clear-cut. There are several legal decisions stating that if the lease non-compliance is due to the resident's disability, there is a duty to try to accommodate the disability before taking eviction action. The housing provider is required to take steps to accommodate the non-compliant behavior, as soon as it is known to be a manifestation of the resident's disability.

57 May an Owner Deny Occupancy to a Member of a Protected Class Based Upon the Fact That No One in the Household Is of "Legal Age"?

If an applicant is not of legal age to enter into a binding contract (such as a Lease Agreement), occupancy may be refused on that basis, regardless of the applicant's status as a member of a protected class. "Age" is not a protected class under the Fair Housing Act (though it is under some state's fair housing laws).

Providers must be aware of, and consistently adhere to, the precise provisions of applicable state or local law as regards age limitations for engaging in certain types of activity. In some localities housing may be refused on the basis of the applicant's age, without any qualification. In others, there may be significant qualifications; for instance, a person under "legal age" who is married, who is enlisted in the Armed Forces, or who has obtained a court order declaring him or her to be an "emancipated individual" may be able to enter into a legally binding contract, despite being "under age."

Consistent adherence to state or local laws or customs with respect to contracts for the rental of housing would not be assumed to be in violation of the Fair Housing Act or federal regulations.

58   Fair Housing Considerations for the Use of Criminal Background Checks

See question 54 for general applicant screening considerations. Federally regulated properties should also see question 183 for additional considerations when conducting criminal background checks.

If you are using, or considering using, criminal background checks as part of your resident screening procedures, expert managers recommend that these checks be applied consistently to all applicants at a property. They caution against applying the checks selectively, even if you suspect that a particular applicant has a checkered past, or as an additional screening criteria. Note, however, that some managers recommend an alternative strategy. They advocate placing a question on your application that asks whether the applicant or other adult household member has any criminal convictions. Considerations to include in the use of background checks are:

- Managers must get written consent from an applicant before undertaking a criminal background check. Even where such checks are required (for example in public housing) the applicant must give his or her signed consent for this information to be released.

- If you run criminal background checks, you should do so on all adult members of each household. Otherwise, a household might list the member without such a record as the head of household.

- Be extremely careful about using criminal background checks at only some properties in your portfolio. The level of existing criminal activity at a particular property or in a particular neighborhood may be a reasonable justification. However, if you perform criminal background checks at a single property due to the level of crime there, be sure that all other properties in your portfolio with an equivalent level of crime also use the same background checks.

- Use criminal background checks as a part of your screening process only after you have established clear procedures for their use. Apply them consistently to all applicants.

- Use written standards when reviewing the results of criminal background checks. The type of crime and how long ago it was committed may be taken into consideration in your decision making process.

- Written screening criteria for criminal background checks should focus on the terms of your lease and whether the applicant's criminal history would cause a reasonable person to doubt the applicant will adhere to the lease. For example, convictions of most violent crimes, especially if committed recently, would lead you to reject based on a lease clause that prohibits any activity that interferes with the peaceful enjoyment of the premises by other residents. Similarly, drug-related convictions would raise the issue of observance of a lease clause prohibiting drug-related activity. Expert managers advise that any rejection for past criminal behavior should be related to the lease terms, and these decisions are more likely to be upheld by the courts.

- If you can't make a reasonable connection between the offense and the requirements for residing at your property, then you should probably not reject. For example, there is no logical connection between having been convicted of driving under the influence of alcohol and being unable or unwilling to abide by the terms of a residential lease. To reject an applicant because of such a conviction could lead to a charge of illegal discrimination if the applicant is a member of a protected class. The goal always is to avoid the perception that the reason given for rejection is really based on membership of a protected class rather than the past criminal conviction.

- Owners and managers should not assume that courts will uphold rejection decisions that are based on information on arrests and pending charges.

- Consistency of rejections is also important. Make certain that you do not reject one applicant for a criminal record, and then fail to reject another applicant with a similar record. Keep a log of rejections, and review each one against your own history of rejections.

59 How Should Applicants Without Rental/Credit Histories Be Processed?

The purpose of investigating an applicant's rental and credit history is to provide you with some indication of the applicant's ability to (1) pay the rent in full and on time, and (2) adhere to the other terms of the lease. These include respecting the rights of the neighbors, avoiding undue wear and tear on the apartment and refraining from criminal activity. Some members of protected classes may not have a traditional rental history. Examples could be an individual who was hospitalized because of chronic mental illness or someone who has been in a residential drug/alcohol rehabilitation facility. If your application form asks a question about gaps in a rental history and asks what the housing arrangements were during that time you should have enough additional information to assess and process the application

Other means of assessing an application where information is not consistently available might include considering employment history or references, the applicant's involvement in civic activities, or statements from neutral, credible professionals who are knowledgeable about the applicant.

Experience has shown that higher risks of lease violations are posed by:

- Applicants who have never had primary responsibility for their housing, and

- Applicants whose current and prior housing situation is different from your apartment environment.

With those applicants there is greater uncertainty in predicting whether the applicant will abide by all the terms of the lease. When assessing an application, housing providers may take into account the differences between the applicant's previous housing history and the rental environment offered by your property.

60   May an Owner Adopt a Resident Selection Policy That Excludes Voucher Holders?

Generally, participation by a landlord in the Section 8 Housing Choice Voucher program is voluntary. However, once a landlord accepts one resident who is a voucher holder, the landlord cannot refuse future applicants simply because they are voucher holders.

However, there are situations in which owners may not discriminate based on status as a voucher holder. These situations include:

- Properties receiving Low Income Housing Tax Credits.

- Properties financed with 501(c)(3) tax-exempt bonds.

- Properties receiving HOME program funds.

- Properties subject to HUD Mark-to-Market restructuring plans.[1]

- HUD Rental Rehab and HODAG projects.[2]

---

1. *42 U.S.C.A. § 514(e)(9), § 1437f note, and 24 C.F.R. §401.483*

See Chapter 2.

- Properties purchased from HUD.[3]

- Properties located in areas where applicable State or local law prohibits such discrimination

With respect to certain other federal and state multifamily programs, however, the answer is less clear. The discussion that follows is a brief summary of a very complex and difficult area of law and regulation. Owners and managers are advised to consult their legal advisors for more information.

Federal Prohibitions of Discrimination Against Voucher-Holders

HUD is required[4] to ensure that owners of most subsidized properties (including project-based Section 8 developments, Section 202 developments, properties that receive enhanced vouchers and others) "...not interfere with the efforts of tenants to obtain rent subsidies or other public assistance." This would not appear to prohibit discrimination against voucher-holders by much of the balance of federally-assisted properties.

An old HUD regulation[5] appears to allow properties with HUD-insured mortgages to refuse to enter into housing voucher contracts. However, it is not clear to what extent this regulation is consistent with current statutory requirements and applicable laws.

In areas where voucher-holders are more likely to be minority than non-voucher holders, a separate issue arises as to whether discrimination against voucher-holders has a discriminatory impact on minorities in violation of the Fair Housing Act. Court opinions on this topic differ.[6]

Finally, the HUD handbook 4350.3 states that "owners may not discriminate against segments of the population (e.g., welfare recipients, single-parent households)." Although not explicitly

---

2. *42 U.S.C.A. § 1437o note, §§ 1437o(c)(2)(G)(i) & (d)(4)(D)(i), and 24 C.F.R. § 511.11(d)(III) & § 850.151.(c)*

3. *Handbook 4350.3 Rev-1, 3-21.D. See also 12 U.S.C.A § 1701z-12 and 24 C.F.R. §§ 290.19 and 290.39.*

4. *12 U.S.C.A. § 1715z-1b(b)(2)*

5. *24 C.F.R. § 245.205(c)*

6. *Compare Bronson v. Crestwood Lake Holding Section 1 Holding Corp., 724 F. Supp. 148 (S.D.N.Y. 1989) with Knapp v. Eagle Property Management Corp. 54-F.3d 1272 (7th Cir. 1995)*

stated, it is possible this could be read to prohibit discrimination against voucher-holders even for those properties not clearly covered by other prohibitions.

State and Local Anti-Discrimination Provisions

A number of States and local laws prohibit discrimination based on a family's source of income. Such laws generally act to prohibit discrimination against voucher holders.

Other Considerations

A prohibition on discrimination against voucher-holders does not obligate an owner to accept every family with a voucher. It just means that the owner cannot refuse to accept families on the grounds that the families participate in the voucher program. The owner can still refuse to rent to any particular family that does not satisfy the property's eligibility and tenant selection criteria. Similarly, owners are not obligated to accept vouchers with the PHA payment standard is insufficient to pay the market rent charged to other households.

Due to the prohibition on families receiving multiple subsidies, families with vouchers must give up their vouchers before receiving assistance under any of the following programs: Project-based Section 8, RAP, Rent Supplement, Section 202 PAC, or Section 202 and Section 811 PRAC. Families do not need to give up their vouchers if they are admitted to an unassisted unit in a partially-assisted property, or to a unit developed through one of the following programs: Section 236, Section 221(d)(3) BMIR, or Section 202 (without assistance contracts)

61 What Are the Fair Housing Considerations Related to Students?

See question 20.

Students are not a federally protected class, except under certain state and local laws.[7] However, for federally-assisted properties there are extensive requirements related to student housing. These requirements are not primarily based on Fair Housing principles, and are not covered in this Guidebook.

---

7. *In the District of Columbia, for instance, students are protected from discrimination in housing as a class, known as 'matriculation'.*

Chapter Seven: Occupancy Standards

62   Owner's Right to Set Occupancy Limits

Federally assisted properties should also refer to Chapter 18 for questions that address the occupancy requirements of these properties.

Property managers and owners may set reasonable limits on the number of persons that may occupy a rental dwelling covered by the Fair Housing Act. Nothing contained in the Act limits the applicability of any reasonable local, state or federal restrictions regarding the maximum number of occupants permitted to occupy a dwelling.[1] The question of what constitutes a "reasonable" maximum occupancy standard is, however, one on which tenant advocates and housing providers have not yet reached consensus. This is a complex and rapidly evolving area of fair housing practice. Because the imposition of maximum occupancy standards often has the effect of excluding families of a certain size from renting dwellings, housing providers are advised to obtain the advice of counsel regarding decisions on such standards in order to reduce the likelihood that these standards will be found to be discriminatory.

See question 68 for additional information on the relationship between occupancy standards and discrimination on the basis of familial status.

Owners and managers may adopt reasonable occupancy requirements for each unit-type based upon factors such as the size and number of sleeping areas, and the overall size of the dwelling relative to household size. Such requirements must be applied to all households and may not unreasonably limit or exclude opportunities to obtain rental housing by families with children. Because families with children are most likely to be adversely affected by the imposition of occupancy standards, challenges to those standards usually arise from claims of discrimination on the basis of familial status. Many of these challenges stem from restrictive maximum occupancy standards that have the effect of excluding families with children from the property. It may be held in such cases that the occupancy standard is not reasonable and is in reality a device to discriminate against families with children.

In addition to restricting families with children, certain occupancy requirements may discriminate against other protected classes.[2] A consent decree was entered against a City which

---

1.   42 USC 3607 Section 807 (1)
2.   See U.S. v. City of Waukegan, CIVIL ACTION No. 96-C-4996.

had established a zoning ordinance that restricted the number of people 'unrelated by blood or marriage'. The Department of Justice pursued this as discrimination on the basis of national origin in violation of the Fair Housing Act.

See Appendix B.

A March 20, 1991 Memorandum from HUD's General Counsel (known generally as the Keating Memorandum) contains the most widely accepted guidance on acceptable occupancy standards. HUD indicated in that Memorandum that, in general, a standard of two persons per bedroom may be considered reasonable, depending upon the size of the dwelling and the number and type of rooms it contains, and taking into account a number of additional factors. On December 18, 1998 HUD adopted this Memo[3] as its official policy for use in resolving fair housing complaints in which occupancy standards are called unreasonable and therefore discriminatory. Housing providers should note, however, that in many areas, state and local agencies handle fair housing enforcement, and these agencies are not required to follow HUD's policy on occupancy standards. In these cases, following the Keating Memorandum guideline may not render an occupancy standard immune from challenge on the ground that it discriminates against families with children.

Many apartment units are of modest size, with relatively small sleeping areas, and do not include dens. For these units, a maximum occupancy standard of two persons per bedroom should satisfy the Fair Housing Act test of "reasonableness" and would be consistent with HUD guidelines and practices. For some of these units, a more restrictive occupancy standard might be appropriate, based on other relevant property-specific conditions (for instance, health and safety issues that are affected by the property's infrastructure such as the capacity of utility systems and considerations of the residents' comfort based on the size of recreational facilities, adequacy of parking, and other factors). For units that are larger, have larger sleeping areas, or include dens, a less restrictive standard might be appropriate.

---

3.   *Federal Register, December 18, 1998, at 63 FR 70256-70257*

Experienced housing providers advise that, to reduce the likelihood of a challenge on the ground of familial status discrimination, occupancy standards should refer to the number of persons permitted to occupy a dwelling, not to the number of adults versus children.

63 Occupancy Guidelines

The following questions should help you to establish the appropriate occupancy standards for your property:

- Do any state, county or city laws regulate occupancy standards?

- What are the building codes for your state, county and city?

- What are the laws established by your state, county or city health department regarding occupancy standards, if any?

When you have this information, you should be able to develop a chart with the apartment sizes your property has, with assignments of the maximum number of occupants for each apartment type. Review this with your legal counsel before adopting it as your policy.

64 Owner's Occupancy Limits vs. Local Law

Some states and localities have adopted various codes that govern the maximum number of persons who may occupy a dwelling unit.

In general, a housing provider's occupancy standards should not permit *greater* occupancy than the local codes, as this would place the property in violation of the local code. You may, however, provide for *lower* levels of occupancy than the local codes, but in doing so there may be a greater risk of having the standard declared "unreasonable" by a court, should it be challenged.[4] Courts consider a variety of factors in deciding whether or not an occupancy standard is reasonable, including a comparison between the owner's standard and the standard set by any applicable law or code. If the owner's standard is more restrictive then it may be more difficult to prove that that standard is reasonable and therefore not discriminatory towards families with children.

An Example of Occupancy Standards and Discrimination on the Basis of Familial Status

In one case* a property owner adopted more restrictive occupancy standards than the applicable local and state laws. He refused to rent his three-bedroom townhouse to a married couple and their four children on the ground that he would not allow more than four people to occupy the unit. Despite the fact that he subsequently rented the unit to a married couple and their two children (suggesting that he was neither "anti-family" nor "anti-children") the judge held that this occupancy policy was unreasonable and was discriminatory in that it denied a rental unit based on familial status and also applied differential terms and conditions based on familial status. The judge also noted that the existence of more liberal local or state occupancy laws would tend to undermine an argument that a landlord's more restrictive occupancy standards are in fact reasonable. This suggests that if a landlord intends to adopt a more restrictive occupancy standard he or she will need to provide very compelling evidence to justify it.

---

* *HUD v Ineichen HUDALJ 05-93-0143-1*

See question 62.

It is likely that a maximum occupancy standard that conforms to the HUD Keating Memorandum would not be successfully challenged. However, make certain that your standard is appropriate to your own property.

Each lease agreement should specify the maximum number of occupants permitted in the particular unit so that if the number is exceeded after the commencement of the lease, appropriate eviction or relocation action can be taken.

Consistency in the application of your occupancy standards is also critical. Once developed and instituted, any uneven application of the standard could expose your property to charges of discrimination by the persons who are adversely affected.

---

4. *See Consent Decree, U.S. v. Smith, No. CV 97-0603-N-RHW, wherein the Department of Justice alleged that Defendants imposed and enforced an occupancy standard limiting occupancy of "studio" apartments to one person and one- and two-bedroom apartments to two persons with the intention of making housing unavailable to homeseekers because of their familial status.*

65   Is There a National Occupancy Standard?

No. The closest thing to a National Occupancy Standard is HUD's Keating Memorandum. As stressed before, these are guidelines, not standards, and adherence to them is entirely discretionary. Individual states have also passed legislation governing occupancy standards, but these apply only to the particular state.

Chapter Eight: Familial Status Definitions and Requirements

66   What Does "Familial Status" mean?

The term "familial status" refers to the condition of being part of a household that includes a child or children, actual or anticipated. Discrimination on the basis of "familial status" means discriminating against applicants or residents, on the ground that the household of which they are a part includes or will include a child or children. The prohibition against this type of discrimination was instituted in the Fair Housing Amendments Act of 1988 primarily to address the widespread problem of owners either refusing to rent their property to families with children or restricting families with children in the use and enjoyment of facilities at the property.

67   Who Is Protected Under The Familial Status Provisions of the Fair Housing Amendments Act?

The categories of households that are protected are:

- Households including one or more persons under the age of 18 who live with a parent or other adult who has custody of them or has been designated by the parent to have custody of them;

- Pregnant women;

- Foster families;

- Persons in the process of adopting an individual who is under the age of 18; and

- Households in the process of securing legal custody of an individual who is under the age of 18.

See questions 72 and 207. Certain housing specially designated for "older persons" is excluded from the familial status non-discrimination provisions of the Act, but the exemption is narrow.

68   Examples of Familial Status Discrimination

Illegal discrimination based on familial status may take the form of:

- Refusing to rent, sell, show, or finance a dwelling unit to a household with children, a pregnant woman, or a household that anticipates obtaining custody of a child.

- Requiring families with children to meet additional requirements or pay additional fees not required of others.

- Imposing any conditions or restrictions on the use of a dwelling or housing-related facility, applicable only to families with children.

- Making facilities unavailable to families with children.

- Making, printing or publishing or causing to be made printed or published any notice, statement or advertisement with respect to the sale or rental of a dwelling that indicates preference, limitation or discrimination based on familial status.

- Creating unfair barriers to occupancy by families with children.

- Restricting families with children to certain buildings or to certain units within a building.

The following are examples of conduct that is prohibited by the Fair Housing Amendments Act:

- A landlord tells Ms. Jones that there are no vacant units, when there are such units, because Ms. Jones has children.

- A property is advertised for rent stating "mature couple/mature person" preferred.

- A landlord suggests that Ms. Jones may not be happy living in a property because so few families with children live there.

- A landlord asks Ms. Jones to pay a greater security deposit or a higher monthly rent than is asked of a resident who does not have children (or who has fewer children than Ms. Jones).

- A landlord limits the use of facilities such as swimming pools to adults only (rather than allowing children to use the pools with proper supervision which is a reasonable rule).

- Ms. Jones' housing choices are restricted to a certain section of a property or to certain units (even though other units for which she qualifies are also available) because that is where other families with children live.[1]

- A landlord of a high-rise property refuses to rent to Ms. Jones because the landlord feels the children may not be safe there.

- An owner refuses to rent her property to a family with a child because the property has a swimming pool and she's concerned about liability.

- An owner refuses to rent his property to a family with a child because the property has lead-based paint.

- An owner requires families with children to sign waivers of liability that are not required of others.

See questions 62 and 63.

In general, policies or practices (including overly restrictive occupancy standards) that unfairly limit the opportunities for families with children to rent a dwelling unit or to have full enjoyment of facilities or services available to other residents are violations of the Fair Housing Amendments Act.

See Chapter 7 for a discussion of "Occupancy Standards."

It is clear that intentional discrimination against protected classes is prohibited. However, an action taken in good faith may result in a finding of discrimination if it has an unintended discriminatory effect. A common example of this is when a seemingly neutral maximum occupancy standard has the effect of excluding families with children. In fact many allegations of discrimination on the basis of familial status arise from a refusal to rent because the owner has deemed the applicant's family to be too large for the size of the dwelling unit.

---

1. *See DOJ Woodcrest Settlement Agreement, DJ# 175-37-290. See also U.S. v. Hawthorne Gardens Associates, et al. Civil Action No. 03cv00732 (WGB)*

69 Can I Refuse To Rent My Property to a Household With Children on the Ground that Some Aspect of the Property's Condition Makes it Unsafe for Children?

See question 72 for exemptions for elderly properties.

No. Unless your property is exempted from the provision against discrimination on the basis of familial status (i.e., is an "elderly property"); you cannot exclude households on the basis of familial status. You will need to immediately correct the deficiencies or conditions at your property that make it unsafe for children.

Additionally, it is not permissible to restrict access to the property to families with children on the basis of higher insurance costs.[2]

The decision whether to live in a high-rise building, near a busy street, far from play areas, etc. is for the family to make, not the housing provider. HUD's Counsel has said[3] that under some circumstances property owners may tell prospective residents about perceived hazards at the property without breaching the Fair Housing Act; however, such information must not be misleading or discouraging and must not have the effect of steering families away from the property. In other words, the provider may inform parents of possible dangers but must make it clear that the family will not be excluded nor will the terms, privileges or conditions respecting their occupancy of the dwelling be affected because of those dangers.

In one case* a landlord refused to rent an apartment to a woman who was six months pregnant because it was suspected that the apartment contained lead-based paint. Because of the suspected presence of this paint it was the landlord's policy not to rent to families with children under 6 years old. The applicant complained that she was discriminated against on the basis of familial status.

---

2. *Consent Decree, U.S. v. Kenna Homes Cooperative, CIVIL ACTION NO. 2:04-0783*
3. *Directive Number GME-0010 "Fair Housing Act Enforcement: Safety issues as defenses to familial status discrimination"*

The court ruled that such discrimination had occurred since health and economic considerations (it was estimated that it would cost the landlord between $26,400 and $60,000 to de-lead the property) — were not exceptions to the rule against discrimination on the basis of familial status. In another case of discrimination on the basis of familial status the Administrative Law Judge wrote "...nothing in the Fair Housing Act permits the owner of rental property to determine that his property per se presents unacceptable risks to the health, safety and welfare of children. That decision is for the prospective tenant/parent to make."** In other words there is no "unsafe for children" exemption to the Fair Housing Act's familial status discrimination prohibitions.

---

*HUD v DiBari HUDALJ 01-90-0511-1

**HUD v Schmid HUDALJ 02-98-0276-8

70   Can I Impose Rules Limiting the Use by Children of Certain Facilities at My Property?

Yes, if the limitations relate to the health and safety of children and are reasonable. Examples of restrictions that apply only to children, that have been allowed by HUD, include:

- Prohibiting children under 18 from using a swimming pool unless accompanied by a responsible adult.[4]

- Excluding children from a utility building containing water pumps, shutoff valves and electrical units unless accompanied by a parent.[5]

- Prohibiting children under 14 from using a pool or clubhouse without adult supervision and prohibiting children between 14 and 18 from using the billiard room without similar supervision.[6]

Generally, in order for restrictions or prohibitions to be considered acceptable and non-discriminatory, the perceived danger must be valid, and the rules must be a reasonable means to

---

4. *Legal Opinion GME-0012, Frank Keating, 09/29/92*
5. *HUD v Gugliemi, Fair Housing-Fair Lending (P-H) 25,004 at 25076*
6. *HUD v Murphy, Fair Housing-Fair Lending (P-H) 25002 at 25053*

provide for the health and safety of both the facilities and residents.

An example of a rule that HUD has deemed impermissible is a rule restricting children from using swimming pools at certain hours. There was not a valid health or safety threat for this restriction and it could not meet the "reasonability" requirement.[7]

71 Are There Additional or Special Requirements for Terminating the Lease of a Household With Children?

Generally, no. Households with children are required to observe all the obligations of the lease to the same extent and in the same manner as childless households. Failure to do so will entitle the landlord to terminate the lease in accordance with the relevant provisions. For example, if the behavior of an occupant's child or children is such that it interferes with the quiet enjoyment of other residents, the lease can be terminated as a result of these behaviors because, "[w]hile the Act protects families with children from discrimination, it does not afford them a license to act unreasonably or irresponsibly."[8]

In the event that a charge of discrimination on the basis of familial status is made, it would be wise to have documented the instances of misconduct and complaints about it from other residents, and to have given the resident written warning(s).

Of course, lease provisions must be neutral to the presence of children; instituting requirements that are more likely to result in violations by (and consequences to) families with children could be found to be discriminatory.

72 Familial Status Exemptions for Elderly Properties

The Fair Housing Act provides that certain properties for older persons can exclude children from residency without being

---

7. *Directive Number GME-0012 "Use of Recreational Facilities by Children"*
8. *HUD v Ludwig 05-93-1324-1, per William C. Cregar, Administrative Law Judge*

liable for discrimination on the basis of familial status. However, expert owners and managers advise exercising caution in excluding children from elderly properties because:

- Many properties' legal documents prohibit excluding children (federally-insured mortgage loans generally contain such a provision and properties subject to these provisions may not exclude families with children, regardless of whether they otherwise meet the exemptions in the Fair Housing Act).

- Sometimes, elderly households wish to add grandchildren to their households. A no-children policy would prohibit this.

Owners and managers of properties designed and operated for older persons may exclude families with children in accordance with general exemptions specified in the Fair Housing Act. These include:

- *62 or Over* – Housing intended for, and occupied solely by, persons 62 and over is exempt from the Fair Housing Act's prohibitions against discrimination on the basis of familial status.[9] A property qualifies as "62 or over" housing if *all* occupants of the household, who became residents after September 12, 1988, are 62 years old or older.

- *55 or Over* – Housing intended and operated for households comprised of at least one person 55 years of age or older, per unit,[10] is exempt. In order to qualify, at least 80% of the units must be so occupied. See below for additional discussion.

- *State and Federal Elderly Housing Programs* – Housing operated under a federal or state housing program that the Secretary of HUD has determined is specifically designed and operated to assist elderly persons.[11]

---

9.   *24 CFR, Section 100.303*

10. *24 CFR Section 100.304 (Section 807(b)(2)(c) as amended by the Housing for Older Persons Act of 1995 (42 U.S.C. Section 3607(b)(2)(c).)*

11. *24 CFR, Section 100.302*

Note however, that HUD has a policy of refusing to designate any HUD-assisted or HUD-insured property as exempt from the Fair Housing Act's familial status provisions.[12] Therefore, families with children may not be expressly excluded from any federal housing program. In practice however, all applicants to federal housing programs must meet standard eligibility criteria. In some federal elderly housing programs, because of minimum age requirements for occupancy, this has the effect of excluding families with children.

"Significant Facilities and Services Designated for the Elderly"

As originally written, the Fair Housing Act required properties that sought the 55 or over exemption to "provide significant facilities and services designated for the elderly." The Housing for Older Persons Act of 1995 amended the Fair Housing Act, and removed this requirement.[13]

The Policies and Procedures Requirement

Language requiring policies and procedures consistent with the operation of elderly housing were removed from the HUD Fair Housing regulations and supplanted by identical requirements under the Housing for Older Persons Act (HOPA) of 1995. The HOPA policies and procedures requirement has been reaffirmed in one legal case, and the original factors covering the policies and procedures requirement are still relevant in establishing the property's intention to provide housing for persons aged 55 and older.[14] For this reason these factors should not be ignored, even though they have not been placed into the (amended) regulations implementing the Fair Housing Act. They are:

- The housing facility's written rules and regulations;
- The manner in which the housing is described to prospective residents;
- The nature of advertising;
- Age verification procedures;
- Lease provisions;

---

12. *HUD Handbook 4350.3 CHG 24 2-5(e)*
13. *Federal Register 61-FR-14378, April 1, 1996*
14. *Simovits v The Chanticleer Condominium Association 933 F. Supp. 1394 (N.D. ILL 1996)*

- The actual practices of the management in enforcing the relevant rules and regulations.

Documentation and Age Verification for Properties Claiming the 55 or Over Exemption

Whenever a household is excluded from residency on the ground that it includes a minor child, a complaint of discrimination on the basis of familial status may be made. The housing provider must then prove that the 80% requirement was satisfied when the refusal to rent occurred. Housing providers, therefore, should maintain accurate and current files containing copies of residents' driver's licenses, birth certificates or other identity documents that verify their ages. When residents vacate the premises, the impact on the 80% requirement must also be assessed.

The pitfalls of not maintaining such documentation were demonstrated in one case where a housing provider claimed the 55 and over exemption as a defense to a charge of discrimination on the basis of familial status.[15] The Administrative Law Judge who heard the case ruled that the evidence presented to support the claim was insufficient.

Accurate records of all residents' ages should be maintained because this will also provide evidence that there has been a consistent policy of limiting residence to persons 55 years of age and older. In the case referred to above, the failure to consistently document the ages of residents also weighed heavily against the claim that the property was intended for occupancy by those aged 55 years or older.

In order to establish and maintain housing for older persons status, it is important that the lease or other agreement governing occupancy stipulate that minor children are not permitted to reside at the property. Further, it may be advisable to provide that if residents decide to have a child reside with them, they will move out from the property. HUD has even allowed what was referred to as a "pregnancy" clause in a lease i.e., a clause stating that if a female resident becomes pregnant, the resident will vacate the dwelling by the time the child is born.[16]

---

15. *HUD v Tems HUD ALJ 04-91-0064-1 & HUD ALJ 04-91-0066-1*
16. *Directive Number GME-0006 "Exemptions for Housing for Older Persons"*

Providers who wish to claim exempt status for their properties on the ground that they are providing housing for the elderly are advised to seek advice from professionals who are well acquainted with the requirements of the Fair Housing Act.

Chapter Nine: Fair Housing and People With Disabilities

73 Which Fair Housing Laws Protect People With Disabilities?

See question 74 for definitions, and question 77 for examples of prohibited practices. See question 3 for small property exemptions.

Title VIII of The Civil Rights Act of 1968, as Amended in 1988 ("The Fair Housing Act") — The Fair Housing Act applies to all apartment properties except for certain small properties. An "individual with handicap," or with a "record of" such an impairment, or who is "regarded as" having such an impairment, is protected by the Fair Housing Act from discriminatory housing practices.

See question 13.

Americans With Disabilities Act ("ADA") — Title III of the ADA prohibits discrimination on the basis of disability at business locations; for apartments, Title III generally requires that the rental office and other on-site business locations used by the public be accessible. Title II of the ADA which prohibits discrimination on the basis of disability in all programs, activities and services of public entities, applies to public housing and to other housing programs owned or operated by state or local goverment.

See questions 126 and 128, and Chapter 15 and Chapter 16.

Section 504 of the Rehabilitation Act of 1973 ("Section 504") — Section 504 imposes additional requirements on properties receiving "federal financial assistance"

74 What Is the Fair Housing Act Definition of Handicap or Disability?

"Individual with Handicap"

Under the Fair Housing Act, an "individual with handicap" is defined as:

Any person who has a physical or mental impairment that substantially limits one or more major life activities; has a record of such an impairment; or is regarded as having such an impairment. (42 USC, 3602 §802(h))

A number of further definitions are required in order to interpret the basic definition given above:

"Physical Impairment"

The term "physical impairment" is defined as:

Any physiological disorder or condition, cosmetic disfigurement, or anatomical loss affecting any of the major body systems (the regulations contain a complete list).[1] *This category includes persons testing HIV positive, whether or not they are asymptomatic of AIDS.*

"Mental Impairment"

The term "mental impairment" is defined as:

Any mental or psychological disorder. Examples of mental impairment include: mental retardation, organic brain syndrome, emotional or mental illness, specific learning disabilities, autism, epilepsy and cerebral palsy. The 'mental impairment' category includes alcoholics and recovering drug addicts.

"Major Life Activities"

The term "major life activities" is defined as:

Functions such as caring for one's self, performing manual tasks, walking, seeing, hearing, speaking, breathing, learning and working.

"Record of"

The term "record of" means that the person has a history of having a covered impairment, even if the person is not currently impaired, and even if the history is incorrect.

"Regarded as"

The term "regarded as" having an impairment[2] means having an impairment that does not substantially limit a major life activity but that is perceived by a housing provider or others as doing so. The perception of the provider is a key element. For example:

- A person with a disfiguring birthmark, or severe burns, may be regarded as disabled even though the condition does not limit the ability to perform basic life activities.

- A person may be misclassified as retarded despite the fact that he or she is fully capable of performing basic life activities.

---

1. *24 CFR, Section 100.201*
2. *For relevant cases, see Rodriguez v. Conagra Grocery Products Co 2006 U.S. App. LEXIS 565 (5th Cir. Jan. 10, 2006); Quiles-Quiles v. United State Postal Service 2006 U.S. App. LEXIS 4047 (1st Cir. Feb 21, 2006);*

- A person may be regarded as disabled because he or she is receiving medical treatment for an impairment (despite the fact that the impairment which is being treated is not severe enough to meet the "major life activities" test).

- A person might be capable of all major life activities, but the housing provider might (incorrectly) respond as if the person were impaired.

- A housing provider might (incorrectly) assume the existence of a covered impairment, when the individual may not be impaired at all.

- A housing provider might (incorrectly) deny housing to an individual because of myths, fears, and stereotypes associated with disabilities, even though the individual's physical or mental condition did not meet the Fair Housing Act definition of "disability."

The "record of" and "regarded as" provisions of the definition are included in order to protect persons who are treated as being disabled, regardless of their actual disability condition or lack thereof. When an applicant or resident is 'regarded as' having a disability, courts have differed on whether a reasonable accommodation is necessary.[3]

See question 26 for further information on the appropriate standard to follow when a property is subject to more than one law.

Some states and localities have enacted laws providing additional protections to people with disabilities. In some instances, the definition of "disability" incorporated into these state and local laws may differ from the federal definitions. These laws are intended to result in broader coverage under the law of the state than under federal laws.[4]

---

3. See *Williams v. Philadelphia Housing Authority Police Department, 380 F.3d 751 (3d Cir. 2004), cert. denied, 545 U.S__ (2005), 124 S.Ct. 1725 (2005);* and *Weber v. Strippit, Inc., 186 F.3d 907 (8th Cir. 1999), cert. denied, 528 U.S. 1078 (2000)*

4. See *fpr example Cal. Gov't Code §12926.1(c); Mass. Gen. Laws ch. 151B, §1(17); R.I. Gen Laws §42-87-1(1); N.Y. Exec.Law §292(21).*

75   What Is the ADA Definition of Disability?

Providers of assisted housing should also refer to questions 139, 140, 142, and 143 for various program definitions of disability.

The ADA, protects three categories of individuals with disabilities:

- Individuals who have a physical or mental impairment that substantially limits one or more major life activities;

- Individuals who have a record of a physical or mental impairment that substantially limits one or more of the individual's major life activities; and,

- Individuals who are regarded as having such an impairment, whether they have the impairment or not.

The first category of persons covered by the definition of an individual with a disability is restricted to those with "physical or mental impairment." Physical impairments include:

"Physical Impairment"

- Physiological disorders or conditions;

- Cosmetic disfigurement; or,

- Anatomical loss (Affecting one or more of the following body systems; neurological; musculoskeletal; special sense organs (which would include speech organs that are not respiratory such as vocal cords, soft palate, tongue, etc.); respiratory, including speech organs; cardiovascular; reproductive; digestive; genito-urinary; hemic and lymphatic; skin; endocrine.)

Specific examples of physical impairments include orthopedic, visual, speech, and hearing impairments, cerebral palsy, epilepsy, muscular dystrophy, multiple sclerosis, cancer, heart disease, diabetes, HIV disease (symptomatic or asymptomatic), tuberculosis, drug addiction, and alcoholism.

"Mental Impairment"

Mental impairments include mental or psychological disorders, such as mental retardation, organic brain syndrome, emotional or mental illness, and specific learning disabilities.

"Regarded as"

The ADA also protects certain persons who are regarded by a public entity as having a physical or mental impairment that substantially limits a major life activity, whether or not that person actually has an impairment. Three typical situations are covered by this category:

- An individual who has a physical or mental impairment that does not substantially limit major life activities, but who is treated as if the impairment does substantially limit a major life activity;

- An individual who has a physical or mental impairment that substantially limits major life activities only as a result of the attitudes of others towards the impairment; and

- An individual who has no impairments but who is treated by a public entity as having an impairment that substantially limits a major life activity.

Covered Disabilities

In its regulations implementing Titles II and III of the ADA, the Department of Justice discusses the definition of disability and how it is to be interpreted. While the following statements are not necessarily applicable to the Fair Housing Act or Section 504, they are indicative of the evolving views of the legal community regarding disability rights:

- HIV disease is covered, whether symptomatic (AIDS) or asymptomatic (HIV positive, AIDS Related Complex).

- Contagious disease is included under "physical or mental impairments."[5]

"Substantially Limits"

To constitute a "disability," a condition must substantially limit a major life activity. Major life activities include such activities as caring for one's self, performing manual tasks, walking, seeing, hearing, speaking, breathing, learning, and working. There is no absolute standard for determining when an impairment is a substantial limitation.

"Substantially limits" means:

"... the individual's important life activities are restricted as to the conditions,

manner, or duration under which they can be performed in comparison to most

people. A person with a minor, trivial impairment, such as a simple infected

finger, is not impaired in a major life activity. A person who can walk for 10

miles continuously is not substantially limited in walking merely because, on

---

5. *This arose from the Supreme Court decision in School Board of Nassau County v. Arline. 480 U.S. 273, (1987)*

the eleventh mile, he or she begins to experience pain, because most people would not be able to walk eleven miles without experiencing some discomfort."

"... temporary impairments, such as a broken leg, are not commonly regarded as disabilities, and only in rare circumstances would the degree of the limitation and its expected duration be substantial... The question of whether a temporary impairment is a disability must be resolved on a case-by-case basis, taking into consideration both the duration (or expected duration) of the impairment and the extent to which it actually limits a major life activity of the affected individual."

".... a person with hearing loss is substantially limited in the major life activity of hearing, even though the loss may be improved through the use of a hearing aid. Likewise, persons with impairments, such as epilepsy or diabetes, that substantially limit a major life activity, are covered under the... definition of disability, even if the effects of the impairment are controlled by medication."

Mitigating Measures

Measures which mitigate an individual's disability may be taken into account when determining whether the disability 'substantially limits' a major life activity. For example, if a person cannot walk, they are substantially limited in the major life activity of walking, and while a wheelchair will enable greater mobility, it will not fully mitigate their inability to walk. The ADA Amendments Act of 2008 specifically addresses mitigating measures, stating that the effect of mitigating measures should not be considered when determining whether an individual has a disability.[6]

Not Covered Are...

Simple physical characteristics or disadvantages attributable to environmental, cultural, or economic factors are not considered impairments by the ADA. Examples would be physical characteristics such as blue eyes or black hair or other disadvantages such as an inferior education, a prison record or being poor. However, a person who has these characteristics and also has a physical or mental impairment may be consid-

---

6. *The ADA Amendments Act of 2008 has not been fully enacted as of the publication of this Guidebook.*

ered as having a disability for purposes of the (ADA) based on the impairment.

See question 109 for a discussion on housing admission issues and drug use.

The phrase "physical or mental impairment" does not include homosexuality or bisexuality. Drug addiction, however, is an impairment under the ADA. The decision to deny housing can be made on the basis that an addict is engaged in the current and illegal use of drugs. An individual who no longer takes controlled substances is protected.

The following conditions are specifically excluded from the definition of "disability:" transvestism, transsexualism, pedophilia, exhibitionism, voyeurism, gender identity disorders not resulting from physical impairments, other sexual behavior disorders, compulsive gambling, kleptomania, pyromania, and psychoactive substance use disorders resulting from current illegal use of drugs.

See question 121.
See question 101.

The Department of Justice refused to state definitively that environmental illness, also known as "multiple chemical sensitivity," and allergy to cigarette smoke are disabilities, because only in some individuals will the effect be severe enough to meet the definition of disability. Whether multiple chemical sensitivity constitutes a disability within the meaning of the ADA must be determined on a case by case basis. However, housing providers should be aware that some complaints are being received from persons on the basis of multiple chemical sensitivity; thus, there is the possibility that a judge may rule that these persons are covered by the ADA, and perhaps by the Fair Housing Act and Section 504 as well.

The Supreme Court has heard a number of cases addressing the definition of disability under the ADA.[7]

76   What Is the ADA Amendments Act of 2008?

As of the publication of this Guidebook, the ADA Amendments Act of 2008 had not been enacted as law. It is likely how-

---

7. *See Bragdon v. Abbott 524 U.S. 624 (1998); Sutton v. United Airlines, 527 U.S. 471 (1999); Murphy v. United Parcel Service, 527 U.S. 516 (1999); Albertsons, Inc. v. Kirkingburg, 527 U.S. 555 (1999); and Toyota Motor Manufacturing v. Williams, 534 U.S. 184 (2002).*

ever to ultimately be enacted and if so will reshape some of the legal framework around definitions of disability. The Act sets forth some fundamental ground rules, including (a) the definition of disability should be construed in favor of broad coverage of individuals under the Act; (b) any impairment that substantially limits one major life activity need not limit other major life activities in order to be a disability; (c) an impairment that is episodic or in remission is a disability if it would substantially limit a major life activity when active; and (d) the determination of whether an impairment substantially limits a major life activity shall be made without regard to whether mitigating measures can address the limitations.

77 What Does The Fair Housing Act Require Regarding People With Disabilities?

Prohibited Actions

The following actions are prohibited with respect to rental housing:

- Discrimination in the rental of a dwelling because of a handicap or disability of the renter or of a household member or person associated with the renter.

- Discrimination in the terms or conditions of rental or in the provisions of services or facilities because of a handicap or disability of the renter.

- Inquiries to determine whether a person seeking to rent a dwelling unit is handicapped or disabled.

Allowable Actions

However, the following types of inquiries are permissible so long as such inquiries are made of all applicants:

- An inquiry to determine eligibility based on a handicap or disability, for some federally assisted housing programs.

- An inquiry to determine ability to meet the terms of the lease.

- An inquiry to determine whether an applicant is qualified for a priority available to people with disabilities.

- An inquiry to determine whether any member of the applicant's household engages in the current illegal use of a controlled substance, or has been convicted of illegal manufacture or distribution of a controlled substance.

Allow Reasonable Modifications

Under the Fair Housing Act owners must permit reasonable modifications to dwelling units and common areas, at the expense of a person with disabilities, if necessary to permit the person full use and enjoyment of a dwelling.

Make Reasonable Accommodations

Owners must make reasonable accommodations in rules, policies, practices or services when necessary to afford a person with a disability equal opportunity to enjoy a dwelling, including public and common areas.

Chapter Ten: Accommodations in Policies and Practices

78   Reasonable Accommodation

The Fair Housing Act imposes an obligation on housing providers to make reasonable accommodations in rules, policies, practices and services in order to enable people with disabilities to have equal opportunity to use and enjoy a dwelling unit, including public and common use areas. Title III of the ADA requires private entities that maintain facilities open to the general public to make reasonable accommodations in policies, practices and procedures when such accommodations may be necessary to allow access to any goods, services or facilities.

Professional housing managers recommend that all properties have a written "Reasonable Accommodations Policy."

Reasonable accommodations for vision-impaired persons might include such changes as oral presentation (including audio tape recording) of material normally presented in written form, or the presentation of written materials in large print or Braille.

Reasonable accommodations for hearing-impaired persons might include written presentation of material ordinarily presented orally, provision of such material through an interpreter, or the provision of closed-captioning to televisions located in common areas.

Federally-assisted properties should also refer to question 147 for more on 'assistive devices.'

Under the Fair Housing Act, housing providers are not required to provide individually prescribed items (such as service animals, hearing aids, or reading machines) or personal items (such as telecommunications equipment in the resident's unit, eyeglasses, wheelchair, or a personal reader or interpreter). Note that properties affected by Section 504 are required to provide certain 'assistive devices.'

Allowing a person with disabilities to use an assistive device, special alarm or auxiliary aid would be considered reasonable. For instance, a building that prohibits pets would, as a reasonable accommodation, allow a vision-impaired resident to keep a seeing-eye dog.

*See question 53 for
Fair Housing
considerations in the
leasing process.*

Reasonable accommodation should also be applied to resident selection criteria:

An Example of Reasonable Accommodation

An applicant has a history of behavior that, if displayed by a resident, would violate the lease. The housing provider declines the application for this reason, and the applicant requests a meeting. At the meeting, the applicant presents evidence that she has a mental impairment which causes the behavior, that control of the behavior requires medication and supportive services, and that she has arranged for, and is now receiving, the needed medication and supportive services. The housing provider's resident selection policy provides that these types of mitigating circumstances are not taken into account when there is a history of non-lease-compliant conduct; in this example, it would be a reasonable accommodation to consider the mitigating circumstances. The housing provider would be permitted to verify any information provided as mitigating circumstances, and would make the decision to accept or reject based on the facts and circumstances.

79 How Do You Determine Whether a Request for Accommodation Is "Reasonable"?

*See questions 31, 92,
104, and 105.*

In general, an applicant requiring a reasonable accommodation must first make such a request. Housing providers should not make assumptions about the specific needs of an applicant with disabilities, and should instead rely on the applicant's request to initiate the process.[1] Of course, your screening practices should not serve to discourage people with disabilities from applying to your property, and should encourage applicants and residents to make requests for reasonable accommodations when they feel it would enable them "an equal opportunity to use and enjoy the dwelling."

In order to determine whether a requested accommodation should be given, the following must first be determined:

---

1. *Generally, housing providers may rely upon the applicant or resident to initiate the accommodation process by making a request. However, some courts have imposed a higher standard on housing providers requiring landlords to identify and implement a suitable reasonable accommodation, even when the tenant does not propose one. See Cobble Hill Apartments Co. v. McLaughlin 1999 WL 788517 (Mass. App. Div. June 23, 1999).*

See question 74.

- That the tenant/applicant suffers from a disability as defined in the Fair Housing Act;

- That the housing provider or manager knows of the handicap or should reasonably be expected to know of it; and

- That accommodation of the handicap "may be necessary" to afford the tenant/applicant an equal opportunity to use and enjoy the dwelling.

Case law provides guidance on the factors that one should look at in deciding whether a requested accommodation is or is not reasonable. The following statements from court decisions provide some insight into the standards currently being applied by the courts:

"An accommodation is considered appropriate when it enables the disabled tenant to enjoy the premises to the same degree as that of a similarly-situated non-disabled tenant. In determining what is reasonable accommodation for Complainant, I will consider the following factors: 1) the overall size of the housing provider, including the number of residents, number and type of facilities involved, and the size of the budget; 2) the type of facilities involved, including the composition and structure of the residences; and 3) the nature and cost of accommodation needed." [2]

"We believe that in enacting the anti-discrimination provisions of the FHAA, Congress relied on the standard of reasonable accommodation developed under Section 504 of the Rehabilitation Act of 1973, codified at 29 U.S.C. Section 794. The legislative history of section (sic) 42 U.S.C. Section 3604 (f) plainly indicates that its drafters intended to draw on case law developed under section 504... Thus, Cadman Towers can be required to incur reasonable costs to accommodate Shapiro's handicap, provided such accommodations do not pose an undue hardship or a substantial burden." [3]

---

2. *U.S. v California Mobile Home Park, 29 F3d 1413 (9th Cir. 1994)*
3. *Shapiro v. Cadman Towers 51 F.3d 328 (2d Cir. 1995)*

"The requirement of reasonable accommodation does not entail an obligation to do everything humanly possible to accommodate a disabled person; cost (to the defendant) and benefit (to the plaintiff) merit consideration as well... Similarly the concept of necessity requires at a minimum the showing that the desired accommodation will affirmatively enhance a disabled plaintiff's quality of life by ameliorating the effects of the disability."[4]

In an unusual case, a property owner had refused to rent to a male applicant, in the interest of providing a reasonable accommodation to a female tenant who claimed a disability causing her to have "a great fear of adult males in a residential setting." A consent decree in this case established the accommodation was unreasonable as it required discrimination on the basis of sex against another person.[5]

80 Can I Refuse a Request for an Accommodation on the Grounds that It Will Set a "Damaging Precedent" for the Granting of Future Requests for Accommodation?

Case law has shown that requests for accommodation are sometimes refused by housing providers because they fear that if they grant one request they will be faced with numerous requests of a similar nature in the future, which they will have to grant because they granted the first one. In other words, a potentially "damaging precedent" will be set by agreeing to the first accommodation requested. The attitude of the courts, however, is that each request for accommodation must be assessed in light of the circumstances that exist at the property at the time the request is made. For example, existing circumstances may permit the granting of the first, second and third requests for an assigned parking space. However, when the fourth such request is made the property no longer has the physical space to provide an assigned parking space. The fact that the three previous requests were granted would not oblige the property to grant the fourth.

---

4. *Bronk and Jay v. Ineichen; US Court of Appeals 7th Circuit No. 94-2882*
5. *See Consent Order, U.S. v. Schaberg, CAUSE NO. CV 02-128-M-LBE*

81 Can a Request for Accommodation be Refused on the Grounds that It Will Precipitate Similar, Additional Requests that in the Aggregate Are Not Affordable (and Therefore in the Aggregate Pose a Potential, Unreasonable Burden on the Property)?

See question 94.

Happy Acres Apartments serves a tenant population of seniors and people with disabilities. Resident Gerty has a disabling mental condition and wants to be allowed to have a dog as a 'companion' animal. While the property manager wouldn't object to a single dog, he fears that accommodating Gerty will precipitate numerous similar requests, which will have to be treated consistently. The manager fears that accommodating all of these requests will create an unreasonable burden on the property. Can the property reject a request for a single accommodation, based on its expectation of the aggregate impact of the accommodations?

This question was addressed in a case decided by a HUD Administrative Law Judge[6] who had to consider whether a refusal to grant a reserved parking space to a resident with disabilities was justified on the grounds that similar requests from other residents with disabilities would also have to be accommodated, potentially resulting in non-disabled residents being deprived of parking spaces altogether. The finding was, however, that at the time the request was made there was no shortage of available parking at the relevant property and the cost of assigning the resident a permanent parking space was limited to the cost of affixing a sign to the space. It was therefore ruled that the requested accommodation should have been given. In other cases before HUD, judges have found the fact that granting a single accommodation would create a "domino effect" and lead to an avalanche of similar requests was not a sufficient reason to refuse the accommodation. Each request for accommodation must be assessed in light of the circumstances prevailing at the time of the request and not on speculation about what may transpire in the future if the accommodation is granted. Therefore, if the refusal of the

---

6. *HUD v Dedham Housing Authority; HUD ALJ 01-90-0424-1*

accommodation is based on costs of future similar accommodations this refusal will not be justified. In short, the reasonableness of a specific request must be considered on its own merits in light of current factors.

82   Does the Fair Housing Act Require Me to Provide Support Services to Applicants and Residents?

See question 78.   No. However, housing providers must furnish various types of reasonable accommodations to people with disabilities. Also, if a property holds itself out as providing services, it may be required to provide such services as an accommodation. For example, if a property offers resident services, reasonable accommodations in the provision of those services may be necessary to meet the needs of people with disabilities.

83   Could a Reasonable Accommodation Request for a Unit Transfer Include a Request that the Landlord Pay the Resident's Moving Costs?

See question 78.   This type of request is subject to the same case by case determination as any other request for reasonable accommodation. It is possible that agreeing to the transfer would be reasonable, but that paying the cost of the move would not be reasonable (or, for properties subject to Section 504, would create undue financial and administrative burdens). It is also possible that, in a different situation, it would be reasonable to both agree to and pay for the move.

In order to avoid misunderstanding, housing providers should clarify, at the time a request for reasonable accommodation is made, exactly what is being requested; in this situation, clarify whether the resident is requiring permission to move as opposed to permission to move plus financial assistance.

See Chapter 7.   For properties that are subject to HUD's Occupancy Handbook 4350.3, "owners ... must pay for the transfer unless the request is unreasonable"

Chapter Eleven: Physical Modifications for Accessibility

84   Accessibility Requirements for New Construction

Code requirements addressing accessibility in multifamily housing are complex and subject to change. The answer provided here is intended only as general guidance on the nature of requirements faced in new construction. Developers are strongly advised to seek expert counsel on these issues when designing and constructing properties. In many recent cases courts have required comprehensive retrofitting of non-compliant properties, at the owner's sole expense.

Fair Housing Act   Properties built after March 13, 1991, including dwelling units and non-housing facilities such as roads, walks and common areas, must be designed and constructed to meet specific design and construction standards acceptable under the Fair Housing Act.

See below as well as question 155 for information on requirements that apply to federally-assisted properties; see question 27 for a discussion on the applicable accessibility standard where a property is subject to more than one law.

The following new construction requirements apply to all units in properties that consist of buildings with an elevator and four or more units:

- At least one building entrance must be on an accessible route;

- The public and common use areas must be readily accessible to and usable by people with disabilities;

- All doors must be sufficiently wide to allow entry by wheelchairs;

- There must be an accessible route into and through dwelling units;

- Light switches, electrical outlets, thermostats and other environmental controls must be in accessible locations;

- There must be reinforcements in bathroom walls to allow later installation of grab bars; and,

- The kitchen and bathrooms must be so designed that individuals in wheelchairs can maneuver within those areas.

For buildings that have four or more units but have no elevator the standards listed above apply only to ground floor units.

HUD has published "Fair Housing Accessibility Guidelines" to facilitate compliance with the accessibility requirements of the Act. The primary standard used in the Guidelines is the American National Standards Institute ("ANSI") standard. While the Guidelines are neither "performance standards" nor "minimum requirements," compliance with the Guidelines "shall be a basis for a determination that there is no reasonable cause to believe that a discriminatory housing practice...has occurred or is about to occur in connection with complaints filed with the Department relating to covered multifamily dwellings." [1] The Guidelines are not, however, the exclusive standard for compliance with the Fair Housing Act's accessibility requirements.

In general, the Fair Housing Act requires all newly-constructed premises to contain basic features of "adaptable" design (i.e. easily modifiable to be accessible). "Adaptable" is a less demanding standard than "accessible." For example, an adaptable unit will contain framing to facilitate the future installation of grab bars; an accessible unit will actually contain the grab bars. For elevator properties, all units must be adaptable. For walk-up properties, only units on the ground floor must be adaptable.

See question 127. Areas such as mechanical rooms, which by their nature are not intended to be open to residents or members of the public, need not be adaptable or accessible to the physically disabled members of those groups.

Statute of Limitations The FHA prohibits the design and construction of multifamily dwellings that do not have certain listed accessibility features.[2] The statute provides three enforcement mechanisms.

- First, an administrative complaint may be initiated with HUD and remedies may include actual damages to the aggrieved person, civil penalties and injunctive relief. An aggrieved person-i.e., any person who "claims to have been injured by a discriminatory housing practice,"-must

---

1. *Appendix III to Ch.I, Subchapter A –Preamble to Fair Housing Accessibility Guidelines. 24 CFR Ch.I, Subch.A.,App.II*
2. *42 U.S.C. § 3604(f)(3)(C).*

file this complaint "not later than one year after an alleged discriminatory housing practice has occurred or terminated."[3]

- Second, if a defendant has "engaged in a pattern or practice of resistance" to FHA rights, or if a "group of persons has been denied any [FHA] rights . . . and such denial raises an issue of general public importance" the Attorney General may bring a civil action. The FHA does not provide a statute of limitations for these actions, and courts have held that these actions are not subject to any time limit.[4] Actions seeking damages are subject to the general three-year statute of limitations and those for civil penalties must be commenced within five years.

- Third, the Fair Housing Act explicitly states that an aggrieved person must sue within two years of "the 'occurrence' or the 'termination' of an alleged discriminatory housing practice."[5] However, courts have wrestled with what constitutes an 'occurrence' or 'termination' of discrimination. According to one interpretation, a construction violation represents a single instance of having violated the Fair Housing Act, and the two-year statute would run from the date of construction. Under a different interpretation, properties have an on-going responsibility to provide accessibility and the two-year limitation would commence whenever an individual encounters or is injured by a non-compliant structure.[6] In an important recent case the 9th Circuit Court of Appeals[7] affirmed[8] that "...an aggrieved person must bring a private civil

---

3. *HUD may also file a complaint independently; it is unclear whether HUD is subject to the same limitations period.*

4. *See, e.g., United States v. Inc. Vill. of Island Park, 791 F. Supp. 354, 364-68 (E.D.N.Y. 1992); United States v. City of Parma, 494 F. Supp. 1049, 1094 n.63 (N.D. Ohio 1980).*

5. *42 U.S.C. § 3613(a)(1)(A).*

6. *Kuchmas v. Towson University, Civil Action No. RDB 06-3281, 2008 WL 2065985 (D.Md.), May 15, 2008.*

7. *Other Circuit Courts are not bound by this interpretation. Seek legal counsel on this emerging area of Fair Housing Law.*

8. *Garcia v. Brockway, 503 F.3d 1092 (Sept. 20, 2007)*

See question 88 for further information on reasonable modifications.

action under the FHA for a failure to properly design and construct within two years of the completion of the construction phase, which concludes on the date that the last certificate of occupancy is issued." The Court opined that the unlawful practice in question was the "failure to design and construct" a multifamily dwelling according to FHA standards, which is a single act, rather than an ongoing violation.

Section 504
See questions 125 and 155.

New apartment properties that receive federal financial assistance, and are thus subject to Section 504, must also meet the Section 504 accessibility standards, including the requirement that in new construction and substantial alteration at least 5% of units be accessible to those with mobility impairments and two percent of units be made accessible to those with hearing or vision impairments. There is no threshold for this financial assistance; it is triggered by any amount (even as low as $1).

The Americans With Disabilities Act

Title II of the ADA provides a choice of two standards for new construction and alterations. You can choose either:

See question 84 for a discussion on these standards.

See question 13.

• The Uniform Federal Accessibility Standards ("UFAS"), or

• The Americans with Disabilities Act Accessibility Guidelines for Buildings and Facilities ("ADAAG"). If the ADAAG standard is chosen, you are not entitled to the elevator exemption (which permits certain buildings under three stories or under 3,000 square feet per floor to be constructed without an elevator). In addition, you must also comply with the Fair Housing Act, including the design and construction requirements applicable to covered multifamily dwellings constructed for first occupancy after March 13, 1991.

Title III of the ADA does not provide a choice; it requires that you use the ADAAG standard.

85 Which Standards Should Be Used When Modifying the Property for Accessibility?

Federally-assisted properties should see questions 156, 157 and 158 for a discussion on accessibility requirements that are triggered by various types of alterations.

If a rehabilitation project that is significant enough to trigger accessibility requirements is planned, all components of the modifications generally should conform with ANSI. For buildings whose first occupancy occurred after March 13, 1991, another substantially equivalent standard (acceptable under HUD's Fair Housing Accessibility regulations) can be followed. While the Fair Housing Act does not require accessibility modifications for properties undergoing renovation, §504 does have requirements which are triggered by the nature and extent of the alterations. Providers who are considering substantial rehabilitation should consult with qualified professionals concerning these standards and their applicability.

However, many modifications occur on a case-by-case basis, as part of the reasonable accommodation process. Reasonable accommodations must be appropriate to the needs of specific applicants or residents. It will usually be appropriate for each component of such modifications to comply with ANSI or an acceptable equivalent standard. For example, if a resident's disability can be accommodated by installation of grab bars in a bathroom, the housing provider is under no obligation to make other modifications in the bathroom; however, the grab bars should be installed to ANSI specifications or acceptable equivalent, unless the standard approach would not be effective in allowing the resident to access and use the housing program.

With respect to reasonable accommodations in general, there is a presumption in favor of the applicant's or resident's own assessment of his or her needs. Housing providers who feel that the modifications requested by a resident or applicant are beyond what is needed bear the burden of proving this.

86 Accessibility Requirements for Rehabilitation

Fair Housing Act

There are no accessibility requirements under the Fair Housing Act associated with renovations. In other words, if an existing multifamily building were undergoing renovations, there is no requirement that any of the dwelling units or common areas be retrofitted. However, an applicant or tenant with disabilities must be allowed, at their expense, to make reasonable modifications when necessary to have full enjoyment of the premises.

The Americans With Disabilities Act

Alterations to properties subject to Title II are required to provide accessibility to people with disabilities to the maximum extent feasible and in accordance with UFAS or ADAAG standards. Those subject to Title III should use the ADAAG standard. See question 84.

87 Accessibility Requirements for Existing Housing

The Fair Housing Act

In general, the Fair Housing Act requires:

See questions 78 and 91.

- Reasonable accommodations in policies and procedures, to facilitate accessibility for applicants and residents with disabilities.

See question 88.

- That the housing provider allow applicants and residents with disabilities to make, at their own expense, reasonable modifications to dwelling units and common areas.

Title II of the ADA

Title II of the ADA requires public entities to make their programs, services or activities readily accessible to individuals with disabilities unless this would result in a fundamental alteration in the nature of the program, service or activity or in undue financial and administrative burdens. Alterations that are undertaken to provide accessibility must be in accordance with either UFAS or ADAAG standards.

Title III of the ADA

In general, Title III of the ADA requires that the rental office (and other on-site business locations such as rental offices and community rooms that are used by the public) be accessible.

88 The Fair Housing Act Accessibility Modification Requirements

Under the Fair Housing Act, housing providers must allow accessibility modifications to be made at the expense of the person with disabilities.

The Fair Housing Act regulations allow the housing provider to require restoration of the premises to their former condition following termination of residency, where it is reasonable to do so. Generally, it would be unreasonable to require such restoration where the modifications will not interfere with the next tenant's use and enjoyment of the dwelling. However, experienced housing providers do not agree on whether or not to require restoration following termination of residency. You should consider the following before making a decision whether or not to require restoration of a unit. Your decision can then be based on what is most reasonable for your particular situation.

- Requiring restoration by removal of accessibility modifications will result in a lower supply of accessible units.

- Because the regulations allow the housing provider to condition approval of the modifications on assurances of the quality of workmanship, it should be possible in most instances to have the modifications performed in a way that will be acceptable on a long-term basis.

- Modifications that do not detract from the future marketability of the unit should be permitted to remain.

- Some modifications, such as lowered kitchen cabinets or grab bars in the bathroom around the toilet and shower/bath, could make the unit less marketable.

89 Reasonable Modification

Federally assisted properties should also refer to question 141.

A reasonable modification is an alteration to the physical characteristics of a dwelling unit or to the common areas of a building, requested by an applicant or resident, to allow accessibility by a member of the household.

Depending upon cost and available alternatives, a reasonable modification may include such things as installation of a ramp into a building, the lowering of the unit entry threshold, or the installation of grab bars in a bathroom.

See questions 145, 149, 150 and 159.

In conventional apartments, reasonable modifications are generally undertaken at the expense of the person with disabilities. However, housing providers who are subject to Section 504 (recipients of federal financial assistance) and/or Title II of the ADA (state and local government activities) generally must provide and pay for reasonable modifications unless to do so would result in "undue financial or administrative hardship."

In the absence of compelling evidence to the contrary, housing providers are advised to accept the applicant's or resident's own assessment of what is needed in order to allow accessibility.

Experienced housing providers advise that often there will be multiple methods for providing accessibility, and that the various methods may vary widely in cost. Sometimes, it is possible to provide accessibility through a relatively cost-effective procedural accommodation, instead of a relatively costly structural modification.

90   Accessible Route

Regulations under the Fair Housing Act[9] define an "accessible route" as:

"A continuous unobstructed path connecting accessible elements and spaces in
a building or within a site that can be negotiated by a person with a severe
disability using a wheelchair and that is also safe for and usable by people with
other disabilities."

---

9.   *24 CFR, Section 100.201*

The Americans with Disabilities Act Accessibility Guidelines for Buildings and Facilities ("ADAAG") defines an "accessible route" as:

"A continuous unobstructed path connecting all accessible elements and spaces

of a building or facility. Interior accessible routes may include corridors, floors,

ramps, elevators, lifts, and clear floor spaces at fixtures. Exterior accessible

routes may include parking access aisles, curb ramps, crosswalks at vehicular

ways, walks, ramps and lifts."

ADAAG requires that, in the case of new construction:

*   There must be at least one accessible route within the boundary of the site from public transportation stops, accessible parking spaces, passenger loading zones, and public streets or sidewalks to an accessible entrance.

*   That there must be at least one accessible route connecting accessible buildings, accessible facilities, accessible elements and accessible spaces that are on the same site.

*   That at least one accessible route shall connect accessible building or facility entrances with all accessible spaces and elements and with all accessible dwelling units within the building or facility.

*   That an accessible route must connect at least one accessible entrance of each accessible dwelling unit with the exterior and interior spaces and facilities that serve the accessible dwelling unit.

*   That the surfaces of accessible routes and accessible rooms in newly-constructed or altered buildings and facilities be stable, firm, and slip-resistant. If carpet or carpet tile is used on a ground or floor surface it must be securely attached and have a firm cushion, pad or backing or no cushion or pad. Pile thickness cannot exceed ½ inch.

Interior accessible routes may include corridors, floors, ramps, elevators, lifts, and clear floor space at fixtures. Exterior accessible routes may include parking access aisles, curb ramps, crosswalks at vehicular ways, walks, ramps, and lifts.

The accessible route on a site or within a building or facility must be designed to provide slip-resistant locomotion for both level and inclined travel by people with disabilities. Wheelchair users are also affected by the rolling resistance of the surface of the floor. In addition, cross slopes on walks and ground or floor surfaces can cause difficulty in propelling a wheelchair in a straight line. Wheelchairs are propelled most easily on surfaces that are hard, stable and regular. Materials such as gravel, wood chips, wet clay or sand, often used for outdoor walkways, are neither firm nor stable, nor can they generally be considered slip-resistant. A cobblestone surface is also irregular and significantly impedes wheelchair movement. Thus, walks surfaced in these materials could not constitute an accessible route.

These Regulations require that all new construction must have at least one building entrance on an accessible route, "unless it is impractical to do so because of terrain or unusual characteristics of the site."[10] However, HUD's Accessibility Guidelines provide that all new multifamily properties with elevators should be designed and constructed to provide at least one accessible entrance on an accessible route, regardless of terrain or unusual characteristics of the site. HUD's rationale for not exempting elevator properties from the accessibility requirements due to "site impracticality" is the belief that "the type of site work that is performed in connection with the construction of a high rise elevator building generally results in a finished grade that would make the building accessible". [11] Housing providers should note that, at least for existing housing, there is no requirement that every building be accessible. Thus, overall accessibility can be provided via those units that are located on accessible routes.

Sometimes, due to terrain constraints or building design, no units are located on an accessible route. For example, lack of

---

10. 24 CFR Subtitle B, Ch. I (4-1-99 Edition) Section 100.205. Note also that in U.S. v. Shanrie Co. Inc. et al, (No. 05-CV-306-DRH), the court points out that the impracticality defense can only apply to design issues before construction, not to retrofitting issues after construction.
11. Appendix III to Ch.I, Subchapter A – Preamble to Fair Housing Accessibility Guidelines. 24 CFR Ch.I, Subch. A., App. II

an accessible route could arise where the slope from the parking area to the building is so steep that an accessible route cannot be provided cost-effectively. It might also arise where the building design is such that no units are at ground level (for instance, when entering the building, residents have to walk up or down steps in order to reach their units).

If there are no units on accessible routes, the property will not be able to serve wheelchair users, but will be able to serve other people with disabilities (such as people with hearing or vision impairments and people with various mobility impairments that do not require the constant use of a wheelchair). Accordingly, the common areas should be made accessible to the disabled populations that the property can serve.

Chapter Twelve: Frequently Requested Procedural
Accommodations and Structural
Modifications

91 How Do I Decide Whether To Modify Procedures or Structures, to Accommodate Applicants and Residents With Disabilities?

The term "reasonable accommodation" refers to a procedural change to accomplish accessibility. The term "reasonable modification" denotes a structural change to facilitate accessibility.

Fair housing issues tend to be complex. They also tend not to be susceptible to rigid, standardized solutions. Accordingly, providers will want to develop their own analytical framework for evaluating individual circumstances. Keeping in mind certain basic understandings should help both in establishing policy, and in applying the policy to different situations over time.

Do First Things First

When a property faces the task of achieving accessibility compliance, often the sheer volume of tasks can seem overwhelming. Experienced owners and managers advise prioritizing these tasks.

See questions 28 and 29 for guidance on accessibility reviews and self-evaluations.

• First, perform a physical accessibility review and self-evaluation of the property, its policies and procedures.

• Then, remove barriers and/or adopt methods that enhance accessibility. Make nonstructural changes in programs first. Next, make the common areas accessible. The next priority is structural modifications for existing residents. Modifications for the visually and hearing impaired should follow, as soon as practicable.

Review Basic Requirements for Screening

Applicants with disabilities sometimes request accommodations to admissions and screening procedures, for example a vision-impaired applicant may request that the lease be read aloud.

However, housing providers are not required to waive reasonable, basic requirements for admission of applicants who are members of protected classes. Basic requirements for admission may include the submission of evidence supporting:

• The timely payment of rent and utilities.

- The maintenance of the dwelling in decent, safe and sanitary physical condition.

- That the applicant has not interfered with other residents' enjoyment of the housing.

- That the applicant has not engaged in any criminal activity (or any criminal activity of a nature that would raise the possibility of non-compliance with lease provisions and house rules).

See questions 54 and 105.

Factors such as the likelihood that an applicant will cause excessive wear and tear in a dwelling may also be included, so long as they are reasonable and are applied to all residents equally. A "no excessive wear and tear requirement" cannot, however, be used to exclude the use of wheelchairs or strollers or to discriminate against applicants who intend to use such equipment.

Be Consistent

When reviewing applications for housing, ask each applicant for the same information essential to determining basic eligibility.

Lease Compliance Is the Bottom Line

The test of eligibility of applicants must be their ability to meet the terms of the lease, not a subjective judgment about *how* they will do so. For example, a housing provider may not reject an applicant simply because the applicant does not "appear" capable of maintaining a unit.

92 Professionally Managing Requests for Accommodation or Modification

As a manager, you will be dealing with individuals with disabilities who are eligible for a variety of procedural accommodations and structural modifications. It is the responsibility of the individual to make such requests for accommodations or modifications; it is not your responsibility to offer them. In fact, you should not inquire whether an individual has a disability and may need an accommodation. However, when an individual makes a request, it is your responsibility to deal with it in a timely and appropriate manner.

Expert managers recommend instituting certain practices to ensure fair and proper treatment of all requests for accommodation. Written procedures that describe how to process each request are extremely useful. These should include clear policies on acceptable modifications, methods for verifying disabilities, criteria for accepting and rejecting contractors who make modifications, and on restoration requirements.

Consider implementing a method of documenting accommodations and structural modifications requests (by keeping a logbook for example) that includes information on the date and time when the request was made, the nature of the request, the identity of the person making it and the disposition of the request. Recordkeeping will demonstrate the fairness and professionalism of your management practices in the event of a discrimination charge.

If the request is of a routine nature—such as a request for a reserved, accessible parking space—you should be able to provide an answer within a relatively short time. A more complicated request, where you may need to seek a legal opinion or confer with upper management, may require more time. If the resident has some idea of when to expect a reply, they will be more inclined to think that the request is being taken seriously.

Written policies and procedures are valuable:

- They make it easier for staff to deal equally and fairly with all requests.

- Routine requests, such as for an assigned parking spot, can be quickly processed, following established procedures.

- Complicated requests, particularly those requiring consultation with others, can be handled efficiently, reducing wasted time and mistakes.

- Documentation provides a record of the number and type of requests and their resolutions. This is particularly important when a resident claims that his request was not fairly dealt with or makes repeated or more demanding requests as you will be able to rely on written records to justify your decision on the request.

If at all possible, you should attempt to avoid responding to a request with an outright "no." Most people would be satisfied with an accommodation that takes their needs into consideration and is a reasonable compromise even if it is not what they specifically requested.

93   Reserved Parking Space

For mobility-impaired individuals, the parking arrangements at a property may have a direct impact on their "equal opportunity to use and enjoy their dwelling units." For this reason, requests for reserved parking spaces are probably the most frequently requested procedural accommodations faced by managers.

Such requests are generally for a parking space in close proximity to the resident's dwelling and permanently assigned to the resident. Once you have verified the existence of the disability and have established a link between the nature of the disability and the need for an assigned parking space you should identify an appropriate space and designate it for that particular individual. Once the space is assigned to an individual it should remain with that individual for as long as the disabling condition lasts. Some unacceptable (but common) reasons for attempting to deny an assigned space include:

- Refusal on the ground that it would cause too radical a departure from the existing policies and procedures governing assignment of parking spaces. This is unacceptable even if there is a waiting list for parking and the policy is to assign an available space to the person at the head of the waiting list.

See questions 80 and 81.
- Fear that granting one request will unleash a "floodgate" of similar requests that the property must agree to, with the result that it no longer has any meaningful policy on the matter.

See question 75.
If parking is assigned to accommodate a disability it may be a good idea to ask the resident for re-verification of the disability annually because some disabilities are not permanent.

In response to a request for an assigned parking space you should not ask an individual to use an existing accessible space obtained originally for the use of the leasing office in order to meet either ADA or Section 504 requirements because spaces near the leasing office are regarded as meeting accessibility requirements for the public and not for specific residents.

If you are managing a property that has a high demand for limited, reserved parking you may have to institute a waiting list. This situation is most likely to occur in a high-rise property serving seniors, where many residents could legitimately request reserved spaces. It is recommended that if there are competing requests from residents who all have a disability that justifies a reserved parking space being assigned that priority be determined solely with reference to the date when the request was received. Further, expert managers recommend date stamping all such requests.

Managers are not competent to determine whether, for example, a resident who suffers from rheumatoid arthritis is more mobility impaired than one suffering from multiple sclerosis and therefore more in need of reserved parking. Furthermore the Fair Housing Act neither authorizes nor requires that such a determination be made. Rather than engaging in a guessing game about which disabilities and impairments are more serious, the prudent course is to assign parking on a first-come-first-served basis.

The purpose and litmus test of a reasonable accommodation (including a reserved, accessible parking space) is that it afford the resident "equal opportunity to use and enjoy the dwelling unit." Consequently, a resident's visitors can also reserve a parking space, to the extent that their need for the parking is related to the resident's need for an accommodation. Therefore, it would be reasonable to reserve a space for use by a caregiver or aide who must pick-up and drop-off the resident on a regular basis. On the other hand, it would not be necessary to reserve a space only for use by friends of a resident with disabilities.

Guests, including visiting caregivers, do not always require accommodation. In one case,[1] an appeals court held that parking fees charged to a visiting caregiver need not be waived,

"It is not unusual for any working person to incur parking expenses at their

place of employment. The fact that some of these people may work with

handicapped individuals does not require that their parking fees be waived."

94   Companion Animals

Persons suffering from mental illness or disabilities that severely limit mobility are increasingly making requests that pet policies accommodate their need for a companion animal. They seek this accommodation as a way of addressing the isolation and loneliness that may result from certain disabilities. For this reason, allowing the companion animal is seen by some (including courts of law if the evidence of the benefit provided by the animal is sufficiently strong) to be a reasonable accommodation. In other words, the view is taken that the 'service' provided by the animal is companionship, rather than sight, as in the case of seeing-eye dogs.

See questions 80 and 81 for a discussion on relying on "damaging precedent" in refusing a request for an accommodation.

However, while a request to have a seeing-eye dog is a straightforward reasonable accommodation issue, the issue of "companion" animals is less clear. In a number of cases, property managers have refused requests from residents and housing applicants that they be allowed to keep companion animals. Some managers have expressed concern that they will be unable to enforce "no pets" policies if residents simply need to claim a need for companionship in order to be entitled to this accommodation. If a resident requests an accommodation for a companion animal, here are some points to consider:

- Seek professional third-party verification of the resident's disability. Further, request that the third-party establish a link between the resident's disability, and the need for the service (companionship) provided by the animal. Some firms have developed standard forms for this purpose.

---

1. *US v. California Mobile Home Park; U.S. Court of Appeals for the Ninth Circuit; No. 95-55599*

Although you may desire something concrete from a qualified medical professional such as a psychiatrist, know that courts have supported (in one case) a letter from a social worker stating no more than, *"...the cat is clearly important to Mr. X's well-being and overall health."*[2]

- If the nature of the property or disability is such that a dog cannot conveniently be accommodated suggest a cat instead.

- You may not have to agree to more than one animal.

- A request for a more exotic animal, such as a snake, is more problematic. You may be able to deny a request to keep a snake citing other residents' right to "quiet enjoyment" of the premises.

- Make use of an addendum to the lease covering requirements for the care of the animal, and enforce the terms of the addendum should it become necessary to do so.

- You should not require that a deposit be paid as a condition of allowing the resident to keep a companion or service animal because the animal is a reasonable accommodation to the resident's disability. However, other provisions of your pet rules may be enforceable (i.e. vaccinations, restrictions on the type of animal (no rodents, for instance), and a requirement to clean up after the animal.

95 Service Animals in Projects for the Elderly or People with Disabilities

See question 94. These animals are individually trained to perform tasks such as guiding people who are blind, alerting people who are deaf, pulling wheelchairs, alerting and protecting a person who is having a seizure, or performing other special tasks. The ADA defines a service animal as any guide dog, signal dog, or other animal individually trained to provide assistance to an indi-

---

2. *HUDALJ 09-93-1753-8; Secretary US Dept. of Housing & Urban Development v. River Gardens Apartments , et al.*

vidual with a disability. If they meet this definition, animals are considered service animals under the ADA; they are not required to be licensed or certified by a state or local government.

In housing for the elderly or people with disabilities, the likelihood that service animals will be requested as a reasonable accommodation is high, and providers of housing to these populations should establish a service animal policy to ensure compliance with the Fair Housing Act and Americans with Disabilities Act.

96   Help In Filling Out the Application

Expert managers differ on the matter of assisting applicants with disabilities in completing the rental application form. Some hold that it is not advisable for management to fill out any form for individual applicants, because if a dispute arose over information included on the form, the applicant could argue that what they said was not accurately written on the application. Other experts hold that the applicant still must sign the form, and in so doing is assuming responsibility for its content.

In either case, a refusal to accommodate an applicant with disabilities who needs assistance in filling out the application form may be viewed as discriminatory. If an applicant requests assistance in completing the rental application or paperwork, inquire whether he or she has someone who can assist them with this task.

97   Accommodating Laundry Facilities for People With Disabilities

An individual with disabilities may be unable to access the laundry room and may want to install a washer and dryer in the unit. You may wish to agree to this request if this can be done in a reasonable manner and does not conflict with the provisions of any local codes, necessitate expensive electrical rewiring or create a disturbance to other residents.

See questions 102 and 122. An individual with chemical sensitivities may also request laundry facilities in their unit. The same considerations should apply.

98   Help With Mail

An individual with a disability may be unable to reach the mailbox assigned to their apartment or may be unable to use the key to open it. Whenever possible, you should try to accommodate residents with disabilities by assigning a more accessible mailbox. Other accommodations may include having the resident designate another resident as being authorized to collect mail on the resident's behalf.[3] If either of these methods is chosen it is recommended that you obtain the resident's written authorization for this procedure to be followed. This authorization should be placed in the resident's file. The Post Office also facilitates what are called "hardship extensions" whereby, for example, a person can request and obtain "door delivery" service.[4]

99   Accommodations to Waiting List Policies

Some federally-assisted properties commonly use waiting lists to handle the high demand for their affordable apartments. Properties governed by HUD Handbook 4350.3 should refer to it for guidance on the proper handling of waiting lists and accessible units.[5]

Non-assisted, conventional apartments are less likely to have either accessible units or waiting lists.

---

3. *Domestic Mail Manual (DMM) 042.2.0 permits delivery of mail to an addressee's agent—someone designated by the disabled customer to receive mail on his/her behalf.*
4. *DMM 042.9.2 and 10.2 permit a change in the method of delivery, if the existing method presents an extreme physical hardship to the customer.*
5. *4350.3, 27, 2-30(b)(1)*

100   Visual Fire Alarms

Visual fire alarms afford the hearing impaired a way to be warned of a fire. It is advisable to inform all residents generally about the availability of these devices and to install them in individual dwellings on request. Even where a resident has a known hearing impairment you should not suggest that he or she install one of these devices; you should merely respond promptly to a request for its installation. You should note also that you cannot require hearing impaired persons to absolve the property from liability in the event of a fire or similar event as a condition of living at the property.

101   Help With Trash Removal

An individual with a disability may be unable to walk to a dumpster or be unable to lift a trash bag into a dumpster and may ask that the dumpster be relocated or access to it reconfigured. Consider whether accommodating this request is the best way to meet the resident's needs. If it is not practical or reasonable to move the dumpster, you may propose some alternatives:

- Provide a cart or wagon to the resident for easier transporting of the trash.

- Place a trash can next to the dumpster so that the resident (and if necessary, small children at the property) can properly dispose of trash without having to lift it into the dumpster. Have maintenance empty this trash into the dumpster as often as necessary.

102   Accommodating Chemical or Environmental Sensitivities

See also question 122 for additional discussion on accommodating chemical sensitivities.

HUD has determined that Multiple Chemical Sensitivity Disorder ("MCS") and Environmental Illness ("EI") can, if sufficiently severe, constitute disabilities under the Fair Housing Act.[6] Therefore individuals suffering from these conditions may request reasonable accommodations from their housing providers. Before considering a request for an accommodation, housing providers may seek independent, third party verification of the disability and of the applicability of the request to the disability.

HUD has defined MCS as a condition that causes a person to have severe hypersensitive reactions to a number of different common substances and EI to refer to a condition that causes a person to have any type of severe allergic reaction to one or more substances.[7] Ordinary allergies must be distinguished from MCS and EI as, generally speaking, ordinary allergies are not considered a disability because in most cases they do not substantially limit a major life activity.

The area of chemical or environmental sensitivities is a growing and challenging area for managers. There are many chemicals in use in the daily operation of a multifamily property. Some residents may assert that they are sensitive to one or more of these substances, and that they consequently suffer from physical or mental symptoms, ranging from depression to rashes. When residents assert that they have either of these latter conditions and request accommodations on that basis they should provide some form of written verification to substantiate the existence of the condition.

Typical requests for accommodation and modifications could be:

- To give advance warning that pest control or other maintenance work is scheduled to be undertaken;

- The use of "environmentally correct" pesticides or paint within their unit; or

- More frequent cleaning and/or replacement of filters in air-conditioning or heating ducts.

There have been a number of court cases and HUD determinations related to MCS and EI. While certain aspects of this issue are not yet resolved[8], owners and managers should be pre-

6. *MCS Disorder and Environmental Illness as Handicaps – Directive Number: GME-0009*

7. *Ibid*

8. *Gabbard v. Linn-Benton Hous. Auth., 219 F. Supp. 2d 1130 (D. Or. 2002)*

pared to accommodate simple requests, such as advance notice of pest control or use of alternate products.

See questions 80 and 81 for guidance on "damaging precedent."

Because of the pervasiveness of chemicals in all areas, a person with chemical sensitivities may make repeated requests for accommodation. However, residents with disabilities are not restricted in the number of requests for accommodation they may make and requests cannot be refused on the ground that, in the housing manager's opinion, the person has already made too many. Although the standard for refusing a request for accommodation is uniform across the FHA, the ADA and §504, in the case of properties that are subject to Section 504 a requested reasonable accommodation may, however, be refused on the ground that making it would constitute undue financial and administrative burdens. In the case of other properties that are subject only to the Fair Housing Act or Americans With Disabilities Act reasonable accommodation requests may be refused if, considering all the circumstances of the case, the requested accommodation is not "reasonable."

An Example of An "Unreasonable" Request for Accommodation

The plaintiff, who suffered from multiple chemical sensitivity, requested of her landlords (1) that the carpet in her apartment be removed and not replaced; (2) that the apartment be cleaned with specified products; (3) that the ductwork in the apartment be cleaned; (4) that they refrain from painting the unit before she moved in; (5) that the adjoining tenant use Lysol instead of Pine Sol to clean her floors; and, (6) that the adjoining tenant cover her registers with aluminum foil when she did her cleaning. The landlords and adjoining tenant complied with all of these requests but the plaintiff was still affected by fumes from the adjoining tenant's cleaning activities.

An Example of An "Unreasonable" Request for Accommodation

The plaintiff therefore requested her landlords to evict the adjoining tenant, which they refused to do. The plaintiff vacated the premises and sued the landlords for housing discrimination on the ground that they failed to reasonably accommodate her handicap. The District Court ruled that "such an accommodation [evicting the adjoining tenant] is not required by either federal or state housing discrimination laws, particularly in light of the fact that [the adjoining tenant] was the prior tenant and that her greatest fault appears to be the habit of keeping her premises meticulously clean." On appeal this decision was upheld by the Court of Appeals, which reiterated the ruling in another case* that "The requirement of reasonable accommodation does not entail an obligation to do everything humanly possible to accommodate a disabled person;" consequently, it did not require that the adjoining tenant and her children be deprived of their residence.**

*Bronk V Ineichen, 54 F. 3d 425, 429 (7th Cir. 1995)
**Temple V Gunsalus et al, U.S. Court of Appeals 6th Circuit, 97 F. 3d 1452;

Also refer to question 122 for more discussion on Multiple Chemical Sensitivity.

Note also that, as with other types of disabilities, persons who suffer from MCS or EI are not relieved of the responsibility to observe all the provisions of their leases. Therefore they must take whatever steps are necessary to ensure, for example, that their unit does not become infested with vermin, rodents or insects if the lease has a clause requiring that the dwelling be kept in good and habitable condition. If the resident cannot tolerate the use of any available pest control products he or she will have to devise other methods of dealing with this problem.

103   What is Limited English Proficiency (LEP)?

See question 135.

LEP refers to persons who do not speak English as their primary language and have a limited ability to read, write and speak English. This is an evolving area of fair housing law and practice. Advocates argue that, in order to avoid discrimination based on national origin, landlords have an obligation to provide key information (such as an explanation of the lease) in a language that applicants and residents can understand. Recent legislation has imposed these sorts of obligations on owners and managers of federally-assisted housing but has also required HUD to provide translations of the affected key documents.

Chapter Thirteen: Admissions and Eviction Issues for People With Disabilities

104   General Inquiries Concerning Disabilities

In general, housing providers may not ask an applicant, resident, guest or associate of an applicant/resident whether he or she has a disability, or about the severity of a disability.[1] Experienced housing providers recommend verifying eligibility for occupancy not disability.

Typically, the most a housing provider needs to know is whether an applicant or resident has a disability (for example, in order to decide whether an applicant or resident is entitled to a reasonable accommodation). The housing provider should inquire into the nature of the disability *only to the extent necessary* to determine the reasonableness of a particular accommodation or modification. The provider does not need to know what the specific disability is, the medical diagnosis, the details of the treatment plan, or the likely future course of the disease or disability. Accordingly, administrative processes should be designed to prevent the inadvertent receipt of such unnecessary and unwanted information.

See questions 53 and 54.

Applicants with disabilities should be asked the same questions as other applicants. Ask about their ability to meet residency requirements, such as whether they will be able to pay the rent, comply with the terms of the lease and comply with other pertinent rules and regulations. Housing providers may ask all applicants:

- Whether the applicant can meet the requirements of tenancy.

- Whether the applicant qualifies for a dwelling unit designed for persons with physical disabilities.

- If the property has a priority for admission which is available to people with disabilities, whether any member of the applicant's household qualifies for such a priority.

---

1. *If, however, the existence of a disability is a prime determinant of eligibility, an inquiry is permissible. This situation occurs primarily in federally assisted housing; see Chapter 16, particularly questions 120 and 121.*

- Whether any member of the applicant's household is engaged in the current illegal use of a controlled substance.

- Whether any member of the applicant's household has been convicted of illegal manufacture or distribution of a controlled substance.

105   Applicant Screening and Resident Selection for Persons With Disabilities

Policies and practices must be applied consistently. Because many fair housing complaints arise from a perception of different treatment, a housing provider whose policies are applied consistently will receive far fewer complaints than a provider with more elaborate policies that are applied inconsistently.

The decision to accept or decline an application for residency must be based on the applicant's demonstrated ability and willingness to meet the terms of the lease. Lease terms typically include: non-interference with others, timely payment of rent, proper care of the dwelling, not engaging in criminal activity, and adherence to reasonable rules and regulations. If information obtained during the application process and examination of screening materials, taken as a whole, do not support a conclusion that the terms of the lease will be complied with, the applicant may be rejected.

Applicants who are rejected may have disability conditions of which the housing provider is unaware. In its standard rejection letter, a housing provider may offer rejected applicants the opportunity to request a reasonable accommodation that would enable the applicant to meet the terms of the lease. For example, if an applicant's disruptive behavior is related to his or her failure to medicate, it may be a reasonable accommodation to accept the applicant if he or she can arrange for a live-in or visiting aide who would administer medication as needed.[2]

---

2. *Blalock vs. Amityville Senior Development Corporation, No. 99-CV-5447*

See questions 78 and 79.

Accordingly, housing providers that employ such a technique typically include language such as this in each rejection letter: "If you are a person with disabilities, and the reason your application is being denied is related to your disability, you may contact us not later than (date, time) to discuss whether a reasonable accommodation by us would make your application acceptable."

If the discussion with the applicant identifies a possible accommodation, the housing provider may require verification of the information and must then determine whether the accommodation is sufficient to overcome the reason for rejection.

106   "Independent Living"

Housing providers may *not* make the ability to "live independently" a requirement for admission.

In a major case[3] involving a large public housing authority the court ruled that the inability to live independently is not, in and of itself, a basis for denial of an application for rental housing by a person with disabilities.

The housing provider's decision to accept or deny an application must be based solely on the applicant's ability and willingness to comply with the terms of the lease. An applicant with disabilities may be able to achieve lease compliance, with the assistance of a third party, such as a live-in aide, a relative or a contract service provider.

107   "Direct Threat"

Under the Fair Housing Act, housing providers are not required to rent dwelling units to anyone "whose tenancy would constitute a direct threat to the health and safety" of others or whose tenancy would result in substantial physical

---

3. *Cason v. Rochester Housing Authority 748F. Supp. 1002; 1990 U.S. Dist. Lexis 14229; FHFL 15643. See also Roe v. Sugar River Mills Associates 820 F.Supp. 636)D.N.H. 1993) and Roe v. Housing Authority of Boulder, 909 F.Supp. 814 (D.Colo. 1995).*

damage to the property of others.[4] A determination that an applicant would pose such a threat would necessarily be based upon the documented past history of the person. It would not be permissible to decline an application based on the housing provider's judgment that the applicant might display threatening behavior in the future despite there being no record of such behavior in the past.

The "direct threat" provision affirms HUD's traditional stance that all applicants must meet reasonable basic admissions requirements. A record of behavior that would violate the lease is sufficient grounds to deny an application, even if the behavior is related to a protected disability condition.

See question 78. However, if a reasonable accommodation for a person with disabilities would remove the "direct threat," the housing provider would be required to provide the accommodation, and it would not be lawful to decline the application based on the "direct threat" provision.

The ADA also provides that an individual may be excluded from participation in services, facilities, privileges and accommodations if that individual poses a direct threat to the health or safety of others.

The Department of Justice regulations implementing Titles II and III of the ADA state the following concerning "direct threat:"

- *"A direct threat is a significant risk to the health or safety of others that cannot be eliminated by a modification of policies, practices or procedures, or by the provision of auxiliary aids or services."*

A determination of direct threat may not be based on generalizations or stereotypes about the effects of a particular disability; it:

- *"must be based on an individualized assessment, based on reasonable judgment that relies on current medical evidence or on the best available objective evidence, to determine: the nature, duration and severity of the risk; the probability that the potential*

---

4. *FHA Regulations – 24 CFR Subtitle B Ch. 1 Section 100.202(d)*

injury will actually occur; and whether reasonable modifications of policies, practices or procedures will mitigate the risk."

While these ADA regulations are not necessarily directly applicable to the Fair Housing Act, they are indicative of the evolving views of the legal community regarding disability rights.

In practice, housing providers are not likely to list "direct threat" as grounds for declining an application. Rather, they will simply cite the specific behavior as grounds for denial. The "direct threat" language serves mainly to establish that the provider cannot be required to waive reasonable basic admissions requirements with respect to people with disabilities.

108   Denial or Eviction Based on Drug Addiction or Alcoholism

Neither alcoholism nor drug addiction are lawful grounds for denial of housing. However:

See questions 109, 110, 111, and 112 for additional discussion; federally assisted properties should also see question 144.

- An applicant who is engaged in the current illegal use of a controlled substance may be denied housing on that basis.

- Discrimination is prohibited against an individual who is currently participating in a supervised rehabilitation program and is not engaging in current illegal use of drugs.

See also question 114.

- Subject to what appears below, a resident who violates the lease may be evicted, even if the violation is a manifestation of a disability condition.

- Subject to what appears below, if an applicant has a history of behavior that, if displayed by a resident, would be a lease violation, the applicant may be denied housing, even if the behavior is a manifestation of a disability condition.

In the last two examples, however, if the behavior is a manifestation of a disability condition, the applicant or resident with disabilities must be given an opportunity to demonstrate that a reasonable accommodation by the housing provider (including the consideration of mitigating circumstances) would address the non-lease-compliant behavior.

See question 55.　　　　Persons with addictions, persons who have a "record of" addiction, and persons who are "regarded as" having addictions, are protected under the Fair Housing Act.[5] Housing providers therefore must apply the same screening and selection criteria to addicts or suspected addicts that are applied to all other applicants or residents. Special screening procedures that are used only with respect to suspected drug users would violate the Fair Housing Act.

109　Admissions Requirements and Drug Use

It is permissible to have a basic admissions requirement that no household member be engaged in the current illegal use of drugs.

Experienced housing providers recommend that each applicant household be asked whether any of its members are engaged in the current illegal use of drugs in the written application form, and that this requirement be included in the property's resident selection plan.[6] As with all other resident selection criteria, it is important that this requirement be administered and enforced consistently.

Some properties, particularly those that have experienced significant problems with drug-related criminal activity, may desire to develop a resident selection plan that rejects applicants for specific types of conduct that are suggestive of the current illegal use of drugs and thus are grounds for denial of housing. Housing providers are strongly advised to seek legal guidance in this regard, as this is a rapidly evolving area of fair housing law. Examples might include discovery of controlled substances in a dwelling unit occupied by any member of the household, conviction of any household member for any drug related crime, and recent arrest of any household member for any drug-related crime. Additionally, the Supreme Court has held that public housing agencies may evict tenants for the

---

5. *United States v. Southern Management, 955 F.2d 914 (4th Cir. 1992)*
6. *Experienced housing providers recommend the use of written resident selection plans by all multifamily rental properties, even though such plans typically are required only in federally assisted housing.*

actions of their guests, even if tenant "...did not know, could not foresee, or could not control behavior by other occupants."[7] Housing providers are advised to check carefully any applicable state or local laws, plus applicable case law in this very volatile and controversial area of fair housing practice.

110 Inquiries Regarding "Current Illegal Use of Drugs"

Although it is permissible to inquire concerning "current illegal use" of drugs, it may not be prudent to inquire concerning a period as long ago as five years, which some would consider to extend beyond the meaning of the word "current."

Under the implementing regulations of Title III of the ADA "current illegal use of drugs" is defined as "illegal use of drugs that occurred recently enough to justify a reasonable belief that a person's drug use is current or that continuing use is a real and ongoing problem."

111 Can Evidence of Successful Drug Rehabilitation Be Required?

No, not even if there is direct evidence of the past illegal use of a controlled substance.

A direct inquiry of this nature runs the risk of being regarded as an inquiry into the nature or severity of a disability, and the Fair Housing Act contains broad prohibitions against this type of inquiry.

If an applicant lists a drug rehabilitation center as his or her current or previous address this would not be a justifiable reason for declining the application. In addition it would not be permissible to inquire whether the applicant had successfully completed rehabilitation. It would, however, be permissible to send to the rehabilitation center a questionnaire regarding the applicant's ability and willingness to comply with the terms of the property's lease. This questionnaire should be modeled on the verification materials that the property sends to the land-

---

7. *Department of Housing and Urban Development v. Rucker Et Al. 535 U.S. 125*

lords of applicants who live or lived in standard rental housing.

112   Denial on the Grounds of "Current Illegal Use of Drugs"

See also questions 31 and 124 for additional considerations regarding rejection letters.

The process of denying an application on this basis is straightforward: an applicant who is engaged in current illegal use of drugs would be sent a standard rejection letter, stating that the application was being denied because the housing provider has evidence that the applicant is engaged in the current illegal use of a controlled substance. These are lawful and proper grounds for rejection. If your property is federally-assisted the standard rejection letter must give the applicant an opportunity for an informal meeting to discuss the rejection.[8] Note that a person engaged in the current illegal use of drugs is not protected under the Fair Housing Act.

However, there are several important procedural requirements governing how the housing provider makes the determination of current illegal use.

See question 111.

The information indicating current illegal use[9] must have been obtained via the housing provider's standard application and screening procedures. Providers are specifically permitted to inquire of all applicants whether any member of the applicant household is a current illegal user of a controlled substance. Also, evidence indicating current illegal use may be encountered during the provider's standard applicant screening procedures (for example, landlord references and criminal records), applied consistently to all applicants.

The information should be sufficiently convincing to justify the conclusion that a member of the applicant's household is engaged in the current illegal use of drugs. A recent conviction for illegal drug use should be sufficient. A policy of premising rejections on arrests, rather than convictions, may be possible but also may be challenged. Other forms of evidence may also

---

8. *HUD Occupancy Handbook 4350.3 REV1, 4-9 and Public Housing Handbook 7465.1, 4-4(2)(c).*
9. *See Shafer v. Preston Memorial Hosp. Corp., 107 F.3d 274 (4th Cir. 1997), regarding the definition of 'current'.*

be effective (for instance, statements from qualified professionals knowledgeable of the applicant, and credible statements from other third parties such as landlords).

Some experienced housing providers consider a history of illegal use of controlled substances to be sufficient evidence to deny housing based on current illegal use. In denying such an application, the housing provider must give the applicant an opportunity to submit evidence of rehabilitation (for example, successful completion of a legitimate drug rehabilitation program), or other evidence sufficient to rebut the evidence of current, illegal use. To be acceptable, the applicant's evidence must be verifiable, as with any condition of eligibility, preferably via written verification from a qualified, neutral third party.

Drug addiction, like alcohol addiction, is an affliction that has a long recovery period, and that has a high recovery failure rate. Like alcohol addiction, drug addiction generally requires total abstinence in order to control the addiction. Drug-related activity is also extremely destabilizing when it occurs in apartment properties. Providers should take these facts into account when deciding drug-related issues with respect to applicants for housing.

Federally assisted properties should also see question 144.

Experienced housing providers advise that applicants and residents who are currently using illegal drugs are likely to display other behaviors that violate the lease. Accordingly, drug users are most commonly denied occupancy not on the basis of their drug use *per se* but on the basis of other non-lease-compliant behavior that is less difficult to prove, and which should be the fundamental basis of a housing manager's concerns.

113 Denial on the Grounds of Drug-Related Criminal Activity

Because engaging in drug-related criminal activity would violate the lease, it is lawful to deny an application on the grounds that the applicant has a prior history of having engaged in drug-related criminal activity.

See question 58. This is a legitimate ground for denial, even if the behavior is claimed to be disability-related.

114 Eviction of a Person With a Disability

See question 108. A person with a disability (or disabilities), like all other residents, may be evicted for failure to comply with the terms of the lease, rules and regulations of the property. However, as with initial occupancy, when requested by a resident you are required to make reasonable accommodations to the extent necessary to allow the resident to have an equal opportunity to comply with the terms of the lease. In other words if the lease violations are a consequence of the resident's disability, the housing provider must make requested reasonable accommodations if these would enable the resident to comply with the lease terms.

Chapter Fourteen: Fair Housing Issues for Specific Disabilities

115   Is Disease a Disability?

Regarding HIV and AIDS, see question 124; see questions 74 and 75 for the definition of disability.

Under both the Americans With Disabilities Act (ADA) and the Fair Housing Act a person with a handicap (Fair Housing Act terminology) or disability (ADA terminology) is defined as having a physical or mental impairment which substantially limits one or more major life activities; having a record of such impairment or being regarded as having such an impairment. Although the effect of various diseases may be to limit a major life activity, a disease in itself is not a disability or handicap. The disease becomes a disability or handicap under the Acts when it causes "physical or mental impairment which significantly limits one or more of a person's major life activities."

116   Wheelchair Users

Accessibility of the Office

Wheelchair users want to be able to conduct business at the rental office, regardless of whether the property has any residential units that are wheelchair-accessible. For properties constructed after March, 1991 the Fair Housing Act requires that all common areas of the property and routes to and through them, including the rental office, be accessible to people with disabilities including wheelchair users. Although the Fair Housing Act's new construction requirements will only apply to properties constructed after March, 1991, the rental office is considered a place of public accommodation under Title III of the Americans with Disabilities Act (ADA) and as such must be accessible to persons with disabilities, including wheelchair users, regardless of the date of construction.

See question 84 for FHA accessibility requirements; also see questions 87 and 88.

Accessible Route

Wheelchair users sometimes request modifications to provide an accessible route. The simplest example of a way in which a route may be made accessible is the installation of ramps to eliminate curbs and stoops as barriers to accessibility. Wheelchair users may request improvements to sidewalks, or additional, new sections of sidewalk.

See questions 84 and 90.

Accessible Parking

Spaces must be at least 96 inches wide and must be located on the shortest accessible route to an accessible entrance. Accessible parking spaces must be designated as reserved by signage showing the symbol of accessibility.

Entry Threshold	If the existing entry threshold does not facilitate entry by people with disabilities or wheelchair users, possible solutions include lowering the threshold, or providing a small ramp on both sides of the threshold.
Public Toilet Facilities	If public toilet facilities are provided at a rental office, then these facilities must be accessible. Note that allowing a single member of the public to use your restroom will subject it to accessibility requirements. Note also that if you plan to label a non-accessible bathroom as reserved "for employees only" you may violate laws designed to protect people with disabilities from employment discrimination.
	Accessibility requires that toilet stalls must be on an accessible route and in addition must comply with ADA Accessibility Guidelines (ADAAG) as regards the size and arrangement of toilet stalls, the type of doors used, the amount of clear floor space, the type of flush controls and other features. ADAAG provides that "Unisex" or single-user restrooms are permissible in alterations to existing facilities if it is not technically feasible to construct multiple single-sex facilities.
Wheelchair Damage	Wheelchairs may cause damage to walls and doors. The costs of repainting or repair may not be passed onto a resident or visitor using a wheelchair. Unless the damage is excessive when compared with the normal wear and tear caused by a wheelchair this expense will have to be included in routine maintenance expense.

117   Motorized Wheelchairs and Scooters

While owners and managers may have legitimate concerns regarding safety and property damage from motorized wheelchairs and scooters, the Fair Housing Act requires reasonable accommodations be made for people with disabilities, and in a number of recent cases, courts have concluded that..."permitting motorized wheelchairs and scooters constitutes a reasonable accommodation.[1]

Property owners should establish policies regarding the use of motorized wheelchairs and scooters which attempt to balance the rights of residents with disabilities with the safety of other residents, and with the owner's need to reduce liability at the property. Written policies should consider the following issues:

- Liability Insurance - HUD, reinforced by courts, has held that requiring any form of insurance or indemnification as a condition for the use of a motorized wheelchair is a violation of the Fair Housing Act.

- Additional Fees and Deposits - Concern about damage caused by motorized wheelchairs and scooters may tempt some housing providers to impose increased security deposits or other fees on their users. Experienced owners and managers recommend relying instead on your standard lease provisions. Users of motorized wheelchairs should be held responsible for damage beyond 'normal wear and tear'. Courts have generally ruled against owners who impose additional fees or otherwise subject users of motorized wheelchairs to a different standard of responsibility at the property.

- Restrictions on Use - Housing providers may consider imposing specific restrictions on the hours and locations of use. However such restrictions must be clearly safety related and must be no more restrictive than necessary. For example, an unreasonable restriction would provide little or no safety benefit while imposing a significant burden on users of motorized wheelchairs; conversely, a reasonable restriction would provide a significant safety benefit to other residents while imposing little or no burden on users of motorized wheelchairs.[2] Additionally, housing providers may which to consider speed restrictions as a safety-related policy, which might not unnecessarily burden motorized-wheelchair users.

---

1. See *United States v. Covenant Retirement Communities, Consent Order #1:04-CV-06732-AWI-SMS; United States v. Savannah Pines, Consent Order #401CV3303; and United States v. Twinings Service Corporation, Consent Order.*
2. *United States v.Hillhaven, 960 F.Supp. 269 (D. Utah, 1997),*

- Demonstrations of Competence - Requiring a 'license' or other demonstration of a motorized wheelchair user's competence to operate safely may run afoul of Fair Housing requirements.

- Monitoring for Problems - In the interest of balancing safety at the property with the rights of the disabled, housing providers should monitor the use of motorized wheelchairs, provide written notice when policies are not being followed, and intercede when concerns for the safety of residents at the property dictate.

118   Other Mobility Impairments

An accessible route is essential for wheelchair users. However, properties that lack an accessible route should still be able to serve persons with other mobility impairments not requiring the use of a wheelchair (for example, persons who use walkers or canes).

119   Vision Impairments

Persons with little or no usable vision depend upon environmental cues, including ambient sounds, edges and other physical elements that can be sensed by a cane, and texture changes underfoot, for safe and independent travel. Some people with impaired vision can also use color contrast as a navigational aid.

Cane Detectors   Many people with severe impairments of vision use a cane to aid mobility. To further assist such persons you may consider installing cane detectors. A cane detector is a barrier placed on an accessible route to prevent a person with visual impairment from walking into an obstacle. A visually impaired person approaching an overhanging obstacle (such as a set of stairs) would detect the ground-level barrier with his cane and follow the barrier around the object to the point of clear passage.

Communication

Public accommodations are required[3] to take steps necessary to ensure that no individual with a disability is excluded, denied services, segregated or otherwise treated differently than other individuals because of the absence of auxiliary aids and services, unless the provision of those aids or services would fundamentally alter the nature of the services, facilities or accommodations or would result in an undue burden. The Preamble to those regulations states,

"Implicit in this duty to provide auxiliary aids and services is the underlying obligation of a public accommodation to communicate effectively with its customers... who have disabilities affecting hearing, vision or speech."

See question 173 for further information on communicating with hearing or vision-impaired persons in federally assisted properties.

There is therefore a requirement under Title III to provide effective means of communication. A common procedural accommodation is to provide materials orally instead of in writing. For example, the housing provider could have someone read the lease (and could audiotape this reading, for re-use in the future) and house rules. Some persons with vision impairments may request materials in Braille; however, advocates for people with disabilities report that only some vision-impaired persons are literate in Braille. Remember, however, that the auxiliary aid requirement is a flexible one that allows the public accommodation to choose from a variety of alternatives as long as the result is effective communication. Therefore materials in Braille need not be provided if they can conveniently be read or communicated orally to the individual.

Title II of the ADA (applicable to public entities) requires that when an auxiliary aid or service is required, the public entity must provide an opportunity for individuals with disabilities to request the auxiliary aids and services of their choice and must give primary consideration to the choice expressed by the individual.[4] "Primary consideration" means that the public entity must honor the individual's choice, unless it can demonstrate that another equally effective means of communication is available, or that use of the means chosen would result in a

---

3. *28 Code of Federal Regulations, Section 36.303 (ADA Title III Regulations)*
4. *28 CFR, Section 35.160*

> fundamental alteration in the service, program, or activity or in undue financial and administrative burdens.

120   Hearing Impairments

Materials Normally Delivered Verbally

A common procedural accommodation is to provide materials that are normally provided in a verbal presentation, in written form. For example, instead of a verbal presentation while touring the model unit, a hearing-impaired applicant is provided a written summary of features and benefits.

Sign Language Interpretation

See question 102 and 122.

Unless one of the housing provider's staff members is trained in sign language there will probably be a significant cost attached to providing sign language translation services for hearing impaired applicants or residents, especially considering that other methods of communication are possible—for example written communication.

Telecommunications Device for the Deaf (TDD)

Installation of text telephones is required under certain conditions in new construction and alterations of buildings and facilities covered by ADA. If a total number of four or more public pay telephones (including both interior and exterior phones) is provided at a site, and at least one is in an interior location, then at least one interior public text telephone is required.

Audible Alarms

Audible emergency signals must have an intensity and frequency that can attract the attention of individuals who have partial hearing loss.

Visual Fire Alarms

A visual alarm provides persons with hearing loss the same warning delivered to hearing persons by an audible alarm. Visual alarms are flashing lights used as fire alarm signals. The terms visual alarm signal, visible signal device and visible signaling appliance are used relatively interchangeably within the fire protection community.

See question 100.

Persons with hearing impairments sometimes request the installation of visual fire alarms. This could be as simple as a battery powered smoke detector with a visual alarm, or the request could be to install a visual alarm that is compatible with the building's fire alarm system.

121 Chronic Mental Illness, In General

Myth of Violence

There is a persistent myth that the mentally ill pose a physical danger to their neighbors. However, research demonstrates that persons with chronic mental illness are *less* likely to engage in violent conduct than persons without chronic mental illness. According to the National Alliance for the Mentally Ill, people who have a mental illness are more often the victims rather than the perpetrators of violence.

See question 107 for further discussion on excluding applicants or residents because they pose a direct threat to the health and safety of others.

Remember, however, that you can terminate an existing tenancy or refuse an application for housing if there is evidence that the resident's or applicant's presence at the property poses or will pose a threat to the health and safety of other residents, which cannot be removed or minimized by any reasonable accommodation that the housing provider may furnish.[5]

Failure to Medicate

Many mental illnesses are well controlled by medication. However, a lapse in medication can result in conduct that violates the lease. Should this occur professional managers recommend addressing the lease violation according to standard (written) procedures. If the resident informs you that the lease violation is the result of a disability and requests a reasonable accommodation, consider meeting with the resident and his or her mental health care provider (if there is one) to discuss how the resident's behavior violates the requirements of the lease and to establish what steps the resident must take to become and stay lease compliant. The results of this meeting should be put in writing and a copy given to the resident and care provider. If there are continued documented lease violations then you may consider taking steps towards terminating the tenancy.

---

5. *24 CFR, Section 100.203(d)*

122   Multiple Chemical Sensitivity

Is Multiple Chemical Sensitivity a Disability?

Both HUD and the Department of Justice have taken the position that Multiple Chemical Sensitivity ("MCS") may constitute handicaps or disabilities under the Fair Housing Act or ADA respectively. However, a determination whether an individual who suffers from MCS is handicapped or disabled within the meaning of those enactments depends on whether the disease is sufficiently severe to substantially limit one or more major life activities. However, housing providers are not equipped to make decisions on whether in a particular case the symptoms of MCS are severe enough to qualify as a handicap or disability. Therefore once a resident produces credible evidence that he or she suffers from MCS and requests an accommodation on that basis the same consideration should be given to the request as would be given to requests for accommodation from other residents with disabilities.

Requests for Accommodation frequently made by people with Multiple Chemical Sensitivity include:

Pest Control

Persons with MCS sometimes request that pest control chemicals not be used in their apartments. Expert managers advise that it would be reasonable to agree to this request. However, some alternative method of ensuring that the dwelling does not become infested with pests must be devised. If there is pest infestation in the apartment, the housing provider, the resident, and the pest control professional should work together to find an acceptable pest control method.

Duct Cleaning

In older apartments, residents sometimes request to have the HVAC ducts cleaned on a more frequent basis than the routine HVAC inspections that the property conducts.

Carpet Cleaning

Residents sometimes request that management shampoo the carpets as a disability accommodation.

See question 78 on reasonable accommodation; federally-assisted properties should refer to question 126 on "burdens."

In determining how to respond to the above requests, determine first if the requested accommodation is necessary to afford the resident 'equal opportunity to use and enjoy the dwelling unit." Second, determine if the accommodation is reasonable; for §504 properties, the reasonableness of a request will depend upon whether it would impose an "undue administrative or financial burden."

123   Asthma

Asthma is a health condition involving an excessive immune system reaction that causes inflammation of the bronchial tubes. Inflammation leads to partial or full closure of the tubes, resulting in difficulty in breathing or inability to breathe. Asthma is gaining recognition as a leading health and environmental issue for children. For reasons that researchers have not been able to identify definitively, asthma affects disproportionate numbers of low income and minority children.

Asthma begins with *sensitization*, in which a person becomes highly sensitive to one or more allergens. Subsequently, asthma attacks occur when the sensitized person is exposed to a large concentration of an allergen. Allergens mentioned by researchers as likely major causes of childhood asthma include cockroaches, dust mites, mold, and animal dander. Researchers also believe that stress and environmental tobacco smoke may contribute to, or perhaps can cause, asthma attacks. Persons with asthma are less likely to suffer asthma attacks if their homes are relatively free of allergens.

Is Asthma a Disability?

Yes. Symptoms may vary from individual to individual, but generally requests for accommodation should be considered once there is evidence that the resident suffers from this condition.

Requests for Accommodation frequently made by persons with Asthma:

See questions 102 and 122.

- *Pest Control* - Residents with asthma sometimes request that pest control chemicals not be used in their apartments. As with similar requests from persons suffering from MCS it may often be reasonable to agree to this request.

- *Apartment Location* - Some residents request transfer to a ground floor apartment, or to an apartment nearer to the elevator, to reduce walking distances. If this request is related to the resident's mobility or other impairment to which a qualified professional has attested, it should be granted when an appropriate unit becomes available. You should not, however, displace an existing tenant in order to accommodate this request.

The Maryland district court denied an ADA claim by an individual with asthma, stating: "Since plaintiff's asthma is correctable by medication and since she voluntarily refused the recommended medication, her asthma did not substantially limit her in any major life activity. A plaintiff who does not avail herself of proper treatment is not a 'qualified individual' under the ADA."[6] However the ADA Amendments Act of 2008 asserts otherwise, indicating that a mitigant (such as asthma medication) should not be considered when determining whether a disability substantially limits a major life activity.[7]

124   HIV/AIDS

See question 115 for further information on diseases covered by the ADA.

Human Immunodeficiency Virus (HIV) is specifically mentioned in the Fair Housing Act as an example of a physical impairment. However, people with AIDS, and people who are HIV-positive, are considered people with disabilities under the Fair Housing Act only when their disease substantially limits one or more major life activities. Note however, that under the ADA, HIV need not be symptomatic in order to be regarded as a physical or mental impairment.[8] Note also that people with asymptomatic HIV (or who are erroneously regarded as having HIV/AIDS) may nevertheless be regarded by members of the public as having a physical impairment and are therefore entitled to the protections given to people with disabilities by the Fair Housing Act.

---

6. See *Tangires v. The Johns Hopkins Hospital,* 79 F.Supp.2d 587 (D. Md. 2000), aff'd 230 F.3d 1354 (2000)
7. The ADA Amendments Act of 2008 has not been fully enacted as of the publication of this Guidebook.
8. The Supreme Court found that under the ADA, HIV was a physical impairment that substantially limited a major life activity. See *Bragdon v. Abbott,* 524 U.S. 624 (1998).

Chapter Fifteen: Fair Housing Requirements Affecting Federally Assisted Properties

125   Are There Additional Requirements that Affect Federally Assisted Apartments?

Some federally assisted properties are subject to additional requirements. These include:

Section 504

Also see questions 126, 128, and Chapter 16.

See question 130.

Section 504 of the Rehabilitation Act of 1973 requires recipients of federal financial assistance not to discriminate against "otherwise qualified individuals with handicaps" in their programs which may include services (like counseling), activities (like senior citizen outings) or housing. Additionally, it requires housing providers who are recipients of federal financial assistance to set aside five percent of their units for households with mobility impairments and two percent of their units for households with vision or hearing impairments. See Question 108 and Chapter 16, generally.

1992 Act

See question 16.

The Housing and Community Development Act of 1992[1] *("1992 Act")*. Title VI of this Act allows owners of certain Section 8 properties designed primarily for occupancy by elderly families to elect to give a preference in admission to the elderly and, thereby, limit the number of nonelderly, disabled individuals.

Title VI

Title VI of the Civil Rights Act of 1964 prohibits discrimination on the basis of race, color or national origin in all HUD-assisted programs[2] Title VI covers all HUD housing programs except for its mortgage insurance and loan guarantee programs.

Architectural Barriers Act

The Architectural Barriers Act of 1968 requires certain federal and federally funded buildings and other facilities to be designed, constructed or altered in accordance with standards that ensure accessibility to, and use by, physically handicapped people.

Age Discrimination Act

The Age Discrimination Act of 1975[3] prohibits discrimination on the basis of age in programs receiving federal financial assistance. This Act, however, permits federally assisted programs

---

1. *24 CFR, Part 30 and Part 35*
2. *24 CFR, Part 1.*
3. *24 CFR, 146.13*

and activities and recipients of federal funds to continue to use certain age distinctions if it is a factor necessary to the "normal operation or statutory objective of a program or activity."

Title II of the Americans With Disabilities Act

Title II of the Americans With Disabilities Act applies to activities of state and local governments.

See question 4.

The following is a brief summary of specific federal housing assistance programs and fair housing considerations they face in addition to the Fair Housing Act:

Rural Housing Service

The Rural Housing Service of the Department of Agriculture ("RHS") provides mortgage financing and/or rent subsidies to properties serving rural areas. In general, RHS properties are subject to fair housing requirements under the same laws that govern fair housing for HUD-assisted properties .

See question 133.

Public Housing

Public housing is subject to Section 504 and Title II of the ADA.

Low Income Housing Tax Credit

In 1996, the IRS revised its Form 8823, the Low-Income Housing Credit Agencies Report of Noncompliance, to include the following paragraph, "the failure of Low-Income Housing Credit properties to comply with the requirements of the Fair Housing Act will result in the denial of the low income housing tax credit on a per-unit basis". This means that in addition to other penalties for non-compliance with the Fair Housing Act, Housing Credit properties risk the the loss of credits. Also note that Housing Credit properties do not appear to be subject to 504 regulations. Of course, other federal financing on a Housing Credit property may trigger 504 requirements.

HOME

HOME (The Home Investment Partnerships Program) is a federal program and is therefore subject to Section 504.

Section 8

Section 8 project based assistance is subject to Section 504. Additionally, those who rent to recipients of tenant-based Section 8 subsidy should review question 110.

Community Development Block Grant (CDBG)

Section 109 of the Housing and Community Development Act ("HCD") of 1974, Title 1, prohibits discrimination on the basis of race, color, national origin, disability, age, religion and sex within Community Development Block Grant (CDBG) programs or activities. In addition, CDBG is a federal program and is therefore subject to the requirements of Section 504.

126   What Is "Section 504"?

Summary

Section 504 is a provision of the Rehabilitation Act of 1973, as amended, which prohibits discrimination against an "otherwise qualified individual with handicaps" by "recipients of federal financial assistance." The Section 504 definition of "individual with handicaps" is essentially identical to the Fair Housing Act's definition of "person with disability" The terms "recipients" and "federal financial assistance" are discussed further in question 110. This guidebook will use the term "housing providers" when referring to "recipients."

See also question 139. Chapter 16 contains additional information on the requirements of Section 504.

The Section 504 Regulations

On June 2, 1988, HUD published final regulations[4] implementing the anti-discrimination provisions of the 1973 statute, as they relate to federally assisted housing. The regulation was intended to ensure that otherwise qualified persons with handicaps receive:

- Equal opportunity to participate in programs and services;

- Equal opportunity to gain the same benefits as other persons;

- No denial of rights to dwellings;

- No unnecessary differences in services;

- Provision of assistance in the most integrated setting that is appropriate; and

See question 78 for an in-depth discussion of reasonable accommodation.

- The opportunity to serve on planning and advisory boards.

"Otherwise Qualified"

Section 504 requires the applicant to be "otherwise qualified" (that is, able to meet the requirements for the federal program benefits). This reaffirms HUD's position that all applicants for housing must meet basic screening criteria set out by management in addition to HUD eligibility requirements. An individual who cannot meet all program requirements is not a qualified individual, and his or her application may be declined on that basis, regardless of disability. However, hous-

---

4. *Section 504 Regulations are found at 24 CFR, Part 8. Part 9 was adopted in 1994 and applies primarily to the conduct of HUD's own programs and activities.*

ing providers should note that if a "reasonable accommodation" would allow the applicant to meet the housing program eligibility requirements, the housing provider must make the reasonable accommodation, and the applicant is entitled to the protections of Section 504. Providers are advised to establish clear written guidelines for determining and offering appropriate reasonable accommodations for applicants and residents.

Program Accessibility

See Chapter 1.

Section 504 regulations require subject properties to be "readily accessible to and usable by" people with disabilities. Housing providers must ensure that persons with visual, speaking or hearing impairments can effectively communicate as necessary for their effective participation in the program. In addition, persons with mobility impairments must not be prevented from entering or using premises by virtue of the physical inaccessibility of the property. Reasonable modifications (i.e. structural changes) or reasonable policy accommodations (non structural changes) may be required, at the housing provider's expense, to make the property "barrier free."

Fundamental Alteration

Housing providers are not required to make such physical or policy modifications if to do so would result in a fundamental alteration of the program.

Undue Burdens

Similarly, housing providers are required to make accommodations or modifications up to the point at which doing so would impose undue financial and administrative burdens on the housing provider.

Self-Evaluation

See question 89.

Properties covered by Section 504 were required to perform a self-evaluation of the property and its operations by July 11, 1989, and to modify policies or practices not in compliance with Section 504. Subsequently, properties must make reasonable accommodations in policies and procedures to enable people with disabilities to occupy and make full use of dwellings and facilities.

Transition Plan
See question 127.

If physical modifications are needed to provide accessibility, a transition plan was required to ensure that common areas (including leasing and management offices), programs and facilities become accessible, and to establish a plan for providing accessible dwelling units.

Any necessary structural changes that the plan identified as being necessary to make facilities accessible were to be completed by July 11, 1991.

"Substantial Alterations" and "Other Alterations"

When ongoing maintenance, repair and replacement activities at a property meet the definition of "alterations," accessibility requirements apply (i.e. barriers to accessibility must be removed). These accessibility requirements mandate or strongly encourage housing providers to make a specified number of dwelling units accessible immediately. These accessibility requirements for individual units within a property apply until five percent of the units are accessible to persons with mobility impairments.

See questions 159 and 160.

For substantial alterations only, up to an additional two percent of the units must be accessible to persons with visual or hearing impairments.

Reasonable Modifications

For all affected properties, providers must make reasonable, case-by-case, modifications to units, as needed to accommodate people with disabilities, subject to certain exceptions.

Enforcement

HUD's Office of Fair Housing and Equal Opportunity is responsible for monitoring Section 504 compliance and investigating complaints. Conciliation among parties is encouraged, but HUD may also seek other relief, including termination of federal financial assistance.

Technical Assistance

HUD's Office of Fair Housing and Equal Opportunity staff provide Section 504 technical assistance to recipients of HUD financial assistance and to consumers of HUD services.

127 What Is the Enforcement Process for Section 504 of the Rehabilitation Act?

Complaint and Investigative Procedures for Section 504 of the Rehabilitation Act

Complaints under Section 504 may be filed by persons who believe that they have been discriminated against, or by their authorized representatives. Complaints may be filed either with:

- HUD; or
- In a US District Court

Complaints that are filed with HUD must be filed within 180 days of the alleged act of discrimination. HUD's procedure for handling complaints (which also applies to complaints under Title II of the ADA) is as follows:

1 The housing provider will be notified of the complaint within 10 days of receipt by HUD and will have 30 days from notification to respond to the complaint.

2 The complaint will be investigated and HUD will attempt to resolve the matter informally. Informal resolutions may result in a written "Voluntary Compliance Agreement" signed by the housing provider and HUD.

3 If the matter is not informally resolved, within 180 days of receipt of the complaint, HUD will notify the complainant and housing provider of the results of the investigation. This will be comprised in a "Letter of Findings" that will conclude that there was either compliance or noncompliance with the requirements of the law. This is referred to as a "preliminary finding."

4 Preliminary findings may be reviewed at the request of either the complainant or the housing provider. Such requests must be made within 30 days of receipt of the Letter of Findings.

5 A review of the findings will be concluded within 60 days of the request for review and will either sustain or modify the preliminary findings.

6 If neither party requests a review of the findings HUD will send the housing provider a formal written determination of compliance or noncompliance.

7 If there is a determination of noncompliance the housing provider has 10 days from receipt of the determination to come into voluntary compliance.

If the housing provider does not come into voluntary compliance federal financial assistance may be suspended, terminated or discontinued or the matter may be referred to the Department of Justice with a recommendation that legal proceedings be brought against the housing provider.

128 What Is "Federal Financial Assistance"?

Section 504 covers properties receiving "federal financial assistance," including "market rate" properties that receive some federal assistance. Examples of properties that must comply with Section 504 even though they may appear not to be "subsidized" include:

- Properties receiving even a small amount of federal financial assistance under HUD's Community Development Block Grant (CDBG) or Home Investment Partnerships (HOME) programs.

- Properties with a project-based Section 8 subsidy contract covering some or all of the units.

Section 504 applies to properties subsidized by HUD under the following programs:

- Section 236

- Section 221(d)(3) BMIR

- Section 8, Rental Assistance Payment (RAP) and Rent Supplement (see below)

- Section 202 and Section 811

- Other programs listed in Appendix A to the regulations;

There are some special cases involving Section 8 that deserve additional comment:

- Properties receiving Project Based Section 8 assistance are subject to Section 504. For example:

- New Construction,

- Substantial Rehabilitation,

- State Agency Set-Aside,

- RHS Home Set-Aside,

- Moderate Rehabilitation,

- Loan Management Set-Aside, and

- Property Disposition Set-Aside

See Chapter 16 and Chapter 17, generally. See question 155 for an introduction to §504 accessibility requirements

- If a property has partial Project Based Section 8 subsidy, the Section 504 accessibility requirements cover the entire property's procedures and common areas, and HUD takes the position that all units -- including the unassisted units -- are covered by the Section 504 dwelling unit accessibility requirements.

Properties that receive Resident Based Section 8 subsidies on behalf of residents are not "recipients of federal financial assistance" under the Section 504 regulations. However, housing providers should carefully read their contracts with the housing authority. The entity that provides the voucher (usually the public housing authority) is a "recipient," is therefore subject to Section 504, and must require participating owners to enter into HUD approved contracts which include assurances of nondiscrimination.

FHA Mortgage Insurance does not, by itself, trigger Section 504 requirements.

129 How Do the Fair Housing Act, ADA, and Section 504 Differ?

The following chart illustrates the major differences between these nondiscrimination laws:

Differences in Nondiscrimination Laws

Issue	FHA	ADA	504
Covers federally-assisted properties	Yes	Por-tions*	Yes
Covers all properties	Yes**	Portions	No
Covers employment practices	No	Portions	Yes
Protects families with children	Yes	No	No
In-unit accessibility modifications are paid for by person with disabilities	Yes	n/a	Rarely
In-unit accessibility modifications are paid for by the housing provider	No	n/a	Usually

*The ADA does not apply to apply to apartment units except in those cases where the project is owned or financed by a state or municipality or in transient housing where the rentals are short term. It does, however, apply to places of business that are open to the public such as laundry rooms and offices. Common use areas such as laundry rooms, swimming pools, club house areas (other than areas used in the rental and marketing process) when available only to residents and their guests are not covered by ADA.

**For narrow exceptions: See question 3 regarding small, owner-occupied properties, and See question 5 regarding a non-commercial housing provided by religious organizations.

See question 13 for a discussion of the limited applicability of ADA Title II to apartment properties, and a brief discussion of employment-related issues.

In the preceding chart, the ADA column refers to the ADA requirements shared by all apartment properties: Title I's employment requirements and Title III's requirements for accessibility of the rental office and other public places of business within the property.

The major additional requirements imposed by Section 504 beyond the requirements of the Fair Housing Act and ADA are that the housing provider must make five percent of units accessible to people with mobility impairments and two percent of units accessible to people with hearing or vision impairments, and the housing provider must undertake and pay for accessibility modifications up to the point of undue financial and administrative burdens being created. Title II of the ADA (state and local government activities) imposes a similar requirement.

Of course, under the Fair Housing Act, all housing providers continue to be responsible for ensuring non-discrimination based on race, color, religion, sex, national origin, familial status and disability.

This guidebook addresses rental housing issues only. Accordingly, this guidebook does not cover the Section 504 or ADA provisions regarding employment.

130 What Does "Mixed Populations" Mean?

See Chapter 21.

"Mixed populations" is a phrase used to describe the housing of elderly residents and non-elderly residents with disabilities, in properties originally designed and developed for occupancy primarily by the elderly. As a large number of nonelderly persons with disabilities were admitted over the years, there were 'lifestyle conflicts' with the elderly (i.e., those 62 years of age or older), for whom such housing had originally been built.

See question 125.

On October 28, 1992, Congress passed the Housing and Community Development Act of 1992 ("1992 Act"). Title VI of this Act allows owners of certain Section 8 properties to elect to give a preference in admission to the elderly. However, an owner's right to accord a preference to the elderly is subject to the requirement that a specified number of dwelling units at the property be set-aside for people with disabilities who are under the age of 50. The final regulations were published on December 12, 1994.

131 How Does the Rural Housing Service Implement Fair Housing Act and Section 504 Requirements?

Like HUD, the U.S. Department of Agriculture's Rural Housing Service (RHS), formerly known as the Farmers Home Administration, has incorporated the Fair Housing Act and

Section 504 into its regulatory requirements, as set out primarily in the Multi-Family Management Handbook 1930-C, which is used by all Agency staff, borrowers and managers.

Unlike HUD's 4350.3 Occupancy Handbook, the RHS 1930-C contains no detailed explanation of the purpose of Section 504 or Fair Housing Act. Nonetheless, the requirements are incorporated into the procedures for admission and occupancy of RHS properties, in many instances using actual wording from the Fair Housing Act.

Like HUD, RHS is committed to non-discrimination. RHS has a separate Equal Opportunity Office and a Civil Rights Coordinator in each state for review of compliance and handling complaints. In 1997, HUD and USDA signed a memorandum of understanding (MOU) that outlines how they will coordinate investigation and resolution of fair housing complaints from rural areas.

In a Memorandum dated September 9, 1996, RHS provided more detailed guidance. Copies of the 1930-C Handbook, Administrative Notices (AN's) and the September 9, 1996 Memorandum may be obtained by calling any State or Regional (District) Servicing Office of RHS (at the state and local level, RHS is referred to as Rural Development).

132 Special Requirements for Public Housing

Guidance addressing admission and occupancy requirements for Public Housing are contained in HUD's Public Housing Occupancy Guidebook (June 2003). This handbook provides public housing agencies (PHAs) with HUD policy and advice on occupancy matters related to the Lower Income Public Housing Program. In addition to the Fair Housing Act, PHAs are required to abide by the nondiscrimination provisions of:

- Title VI of the Civil Rights Act of 1964
- Title VIII of the Civil Rights Act of 1968
- Section 504 of the Rehabilitation Act of 1973
- The Age Discrimination Act of 1975

- The Architectural Barriers Act
- Executive Order 11063.
- Title II of the ADA

133 What Are the Consequences of Non-Compliance with Fair Housing on a Housing Credit Property?

Fair Housing laws, of course, apply to Housing Credit properties in the same way as all other multifamily rental properties. In addition, however, violations of Fair Housing Laws on a Housing Credit property can lead to the recapture of all credits. This means, in effect, that fair housing violations on housing credit properties may have more severe consequences than on other properties, and owners and managers of these properties should take compliance very seriously.

Some specific Fair Housing issues raised in the operation of a Housing Credit project include:

Students: Housing Credit regulations do not permit a household comprised entirely of students (with some exceptions) to occupy a unit. This is not a violation of fair housing laws, unless student status (matriculation) is a protected class in your state or local area.

Income Level: Housing Credit apartments are designed to assist low- and moderate-income families. While households cannot earn over a certain amount in order to qualify for a Housing Credit apartment, there is no minimum income. It is not a violation of Fair Housing laws to require a minimum income, and prudent managers establish a minimum that ensures the household can afford the Housing Credit rent while also ensuring a sufficient number of eligible applicants. However, owners and managers should use caution when establishing minimum income requirements that have the effect of excluding Section 8 renters. Experienced managers recommend that any minimum income requirement have an exception for Section 8 renters.

Section 8: While source of income is not a federally protected class according to the Fair Housing laws, Housing Credit regulations prohibit you from refusing to rent based solely on a household's receipt of Section 8 assistance (Section 8 applicants must, however, meet all other program eligibility criteria). In addition, source of income is a protected class in some states and localities.

Placement of Housing Credit:

In properties that have both market rate and income-restricted units, Fair Housing considerations affect the placement of units throughout the property:

- Housing Credit apartments must have substantially the same features and amenities as market-rate apartments. In some states, they must be equivalent in size.

See question 9.

- It is generally thought to be easier to comply with the Housing Credit regulations if Housing Credit and market-rate units are segregated into different buildings. However, this may be viewed as discriminatory, particularly if there are any discernible differences in the quality of service, features, or location of the buildings. In other words, if your Housing Credit residents represent members of one or more protected classes, then any unequal treatment of Housing Credit residents will therefore result in unequal treatment of a protected class. Be aware that your state housing finance agency's approval of placement of Housing Credit units throughout the property will not provide you with any protection from Fair Housing complaints or enforcement action.

- Properties at which all units are Housing Credit apartments but that have multiple set-asides (i.e. some units reserved for households earning less than 50 percent of median area income and some less than 80 percent) must also be careful how these units are distributed throughout the property.

134 What Is Limited English Proficiency (LEP), and What Does It Require of Federally-Assisted Properties?

Persons with Limited English Proficiency (or, "LEP") do not speak English as their primary language, and have a limited ability to read, write and speak English. Title VI of the Civil Rights Act of 1964 prohibits discrimination on the basis of race, color or national origin. As a consequence, and to ensure against discrimination on the basis of national origin, recipients of federal financial assistance must ensure that their programs and services are accessible to persons with LEP. On January 22, 2007, HUD issued comprehensive guidelines on this issue with consequences for the daily management of HUD-assisted multifamily properties. HUD's stated goal for these guidelines is to balance, "...the need to ensure meaningful access by LEP persons...without imposing undue burdens on recipients." LEP is not required for properties which are not HUD-assisted; however, owners of properties which are not affected by the requirements below should appreciate that there is an emerging view that language barriers and discrimination on the basis of national origin are related.

Which Properties Are Affected? All properties defined as federally-assisted[5] must comply with the LEP guidance. For purposes of Title VI of the Civil Rights Act, federal assistance includes those properties with Section 8 project-based assistance, HOME, CDBG, Flexible Subsidy, §236, §202 and §811, ELIPHA and LIHPRHA, as well as all public housing. It does not include properties with FHA-insured mortgages or tax credits which do not otherwise have federal financial assistance.[6] Also excluded are owners of properties that accept housing choice vouchers, unless they are also recipients of an otherwise applicable form of federal financial assistance.

LEP is more than a regulatory issue: it is a fair housing issue. All properties-including those not explicitly required to adhere to the HUD guidelines-should review their procedures. A failure to provide access to LEP persons may constitute a form of discrimination on the basis of national origin in violation of fair housing laws.

---

5. *A complete listing of affected housing programs can be found in the November 24, 2004 Federal Register.*
6. *At publication of this Guidebook, the IRS has not yet concluded that low-income housing tax credit properties are 'federally-assisted' for purposes of LEP. Owners and managers of LIHTC properties should be alert to any rulings from the IRS on this issue.*

135 How Should Federally-Assisted Properties Determine the Need for and Extent of Their LEP Program?

In the context of multifamily housing, LEP refers to persons who have limited ability with the English language, and who are (or potentially are) applicants to or residents of your property. Within the framework of HUD's guidance, you must provide 'meaningful access' to your housing, which includes marketing and outreach, and all critical communications with applicants and residents.

See Chapter 1.
NOTE: HUD requires properties to consider whether LEP populations are 'least likely to apply' when developing their affirmative fair housing marketing plans.

Affected properties are required to perform a 'four-factor analysis' to determine when it is necessary to provide either interpreters or translations of certain documents.

The Four-Factor Analysis
To determine the extent of your obligation to provide meaningful access to LEP persons, you must consider the following four factors:

Factor 1:
The number or proportion of LEP persons eligible to be served or likely to be encountered-a demographic analysis may be necessary to determine whether there is a large number or significant proportion of LEP persons from any language group (or groups). Managers should not rely only on their own experiences: various language groups may be eligible for your program, but may have historically been underserved as a result of language barriers. In addition to your own experiences serving the community, sources of data for your analysis might include the U.S. Census, local schools, community organizations and state and local government. Once you have compiled this information, consider whether a 'significant number or proportion' of LEP persons from one or more language groups may have diminished access to your programs because of language barriers.

TIP: Distinguish between LEP persons (for whom you may have to provide interpreters or translations of documents), and those who may speak another language while being proficient in English (for whom you do not have to make any such provisions).

The HUD guidance does not provide a threshold number or proportion of LEP persons that would trigger certain requirements. However, the guidance suggests:

- When there are more than 1,000 eligible persons, vital documents should be translated into the language of that population; or,

- When there is more than five-percent of the total eligible population and more than fifty persons, vital documents should be translated into the language of that population; or,

- When there is more than five-percent of the total eligible population and less than fifty persons, managers should arrange for oral interpretations of documents; or,

- When there is less than five-percent of the total eligible population and less than fifty persons, written translations of documents is not required.

These thresholds are guidelines only and should be considered alongside the frequency of interactions with an LEP group, and in the context of your property's financial and administrative resources. See below for more about these considerations.

Factor 2:   The frequency of contact with LEP persons-in addition to considering the number and proportion of LEP persons who are (or potentially are) applicants to or residents of your property, you must consider the frequency of these contacts. For example, if the number and proportion of non-English speaking Swedes in your market is small but is reflected heavily among your residents and applicants, you should accommodate this group. It is the nature of housing to continuously serve residents, on a daily basis. Greater frequency of contact requires a greater standard of accommodation.

Factor 3:   The nature and importance of the communication-housing is an essential service, and communications about housing with potential applicants, applicants and residents is viewed by

HUD as having high importance, and a consequently greater standard of accommodation is required. Consider whether the failure to provide language-accessibility could have a serious implication. Vital communications include: applications-from which the applicant's eligibility for housing is determined; leases-in which the residents' rights and responsibilities are communicated; notifications and legal proceedings; and all other interactions on which the availability or cost to the resident of housing depends.

Factor 4: The resources available to the property and the costs to provide the access-housing providers must only provide meaningful access to LEP persons if doing so does not impose undue administrative and financial burdens on their operations. Smaller properties with limited budgets are not expected to provide the same level of language services as larger properties with larger budgets. However, properties are expected to creatively solve resource and cost issues through the use of technology, shared resources, and reasonable business practices. Properties in large portfolios that share common documents must consider the overall need for language accessibility, against the overall shared resources of the portfolio. Properties must bridge the language barrier through a variety of means, particularly when providing access to LEP persons through qualified interpreters and translations of documents becomes cost-prohibitive.

The 'cost' test is not absolute. There is no threshold for cost or level of effort stipulated in the guidelines. Instead, housing providers must consider cost and resource issues relative to the other factors.

Costs of translations, interpreter services and staff training, are eligible project expenses.

Balancing the Need to Provide 'Meaningful Access' with Cost and Administrative Burdens

The grid below illustrates the dynamic relationship between your responsibility for providing language-accessibility and the burden (cost and resources) of those undertakings.

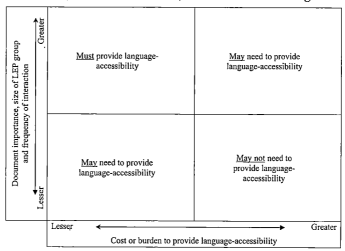

136 What Are the Considerations Regarding Document Translation and Interpretation Services for LEP Populations at Federally-Assisted Properties?

Document Translation

Competently translated documents are an effective means of providing critical information to an LEP population. Translations can be expensive, but may be necessary for critical documents, for key LEP populations. The quality of translation-which generally impacts its cost-should be viewed in the context of the importance of the document. More important documents require higher-quality translations.

HUD intends to translate the model lease into Spanish, Chinese, Russian, Vietnamese, Portuguese, Amharic, Korean and French. Depending on the four-factor analysis, housing providers may be responsible for translating other documents into these languages, or other languages. All translated documents should be clearly marked, 'For Informational Purposes Only'. Only the original English language document is legally binding.

Interpretation Services

Qualified interpreters can be an important link between LEP populations and your property. Consider informing smaller, eligible LEP populations (in the appropriate language or languages), that your property will pay for qualified interpreters as needed. This can take the form of a standard announcement stapled to the front of all important documents or notices, and posted conspicuously in the rental office.

Housing providers should not rely on informal interpreters, including family or friends (particularly minors). While LEP applicants and residents may feel comfortable with individuals they know and trust, the quality of interpretation services they provide may be inadequate or may create a conflict of interest for the interpreter. If an LEP person insists on using a personal interpreter consider obtaining a statement that they declined the offer of a qualified interpreter at the property's expense.

Properties with a compelling and ongoing need to provide language assistance should strongly consider hiring bilingual staff. HUD has stated, however, that it does not necessarily consider bilingual staff to meet the standard for professional interpretation services.

137 What are the Considerations for Federally-Assisted Properties When Developing a Language Assistance Plan (LAP) for Limited English Proficiency LEP Populations?

A Language Assistance Plan (LAP) is not required, but expert housing providers advise it as a standard business practice for properties that have clearly eligible LEP populations. A well-constructed LAP should summarize the elements of the four-factor analysis, and provide policies and procedures to follow when providing services to LEP persons. Consider, as an outline:

- A summary of the data used to establish the identity and extent of any LEP populations, including the estimated number of persons and their estimated proportion within your market.

- A summary of the nature of your interactions (marketing, application processing, landlord/tenant dealings).

- A statement of policy regarding how your property will bridge any language barriers to ensure fair access for any eligible populations. This should include how to handle LEP callers, or in-person interactions.

- (If applicable) policies for bilingual staff, including situations in which they may not provide interpretations because of the need for professional interpreters or conflict of interest.

- A list of translated documents to be made available 'for informational purposes.'

- Procedures for accessing and using interpreters, as needed.

- Provisions for training to ensure all staff-particularly those who interact with LEP persons-understand and can administer the policies and procedures.

Chapter Sixteen: Disability-Related Requirements in Federally-Assisted Housing

Partial Compliance

138 Who Is Protected by Section 504 of the Rehabilitation Act?

Section 504 of the Rehabilitation Act of 1973 protects against discrimination of "qualified individuals with handicaps" who participate in programs and activities conducted by HUD or that receive financial assistance from HUD. A qualified individual is one who is "eligible to participate in a program or activity" (in other words, who meets the housing program's eligibility requirements). This would include individuals who, if they were to receive a "reasonable accommodation" from the housing provider, could meet the housing program requirements.

139 What Is the Section 504 Definition of "Individual With Handicaps"?

In both the Fair Housing Act and Section 504, an "individual with handicap" is defined as:

"Any person who has a physical or mental impairment that substantially limits one or more major life activities; has a record of such an impairment; or is regarded as having such an impairment."

Refer to questions 73 and 75 for the definitions of disability according to the Fair Housing Act and Americans With Disabilities Act.

The similarity of the definitions in both laws is not accidental: the Preamble to the Fair Housing Regulations explains that:

"Congress intended that the definition of 'handicap' in the Fair Housing Amendments Act be interpreted in a manner that is consistent with regulations interpreting the meaning of the similar provision found in Section 504 of the Rehabilitation Act of 1973." [1]

---

1. *54 FR 3232 – Implementation of the Fair Housing Amendments Act of 1988*

140   What Is the HUD Handbook Definition of Disability?

See questions 73, 139, 142, and 143.

Some federally assisted properties are subject to HUD Occupancy Handbook 4350.3. This handbook defines disability for the purposes of admission to certain federal housing programs (Exhibit 2-1 of the Handbook), as well as for eligibility for protection under the Fair Housing Act and Section 504 of the Rehabilitation Act (Exhibit 2-2). Refer to these documents to ensure that you are applying the correct definitions for a given situation.

141   Does Section 504 Require Me To Modify My Procedures or My Property?

See questions 28, 29, and 152 for further information on the requirements of a self-evaluation and accessibility review.

Section 504 requires that "the [housing] program, when viewed in its entirety, is readily accessible to and useable by individuals with handicaps." Section 504 requires properties to perform a "self evaluation" (to ascertain the existence of barriers to accessibility) and prepare a "transition plan" (setting out a timetable and methodology for removing such barriers). A self-evaluation generally reviews policies, practices and procedures that the property may have in place and identifies any barriers to accessibility that are found to result from these policies, practices and procedures. In order to prepare the transition plan it may be necessary to perform an accessibility review to evaluate the nature and extent of any physical barriers to accessibility, as well as any procedures, practices or policies that may restrict the use of the housing program by people with disabilities.

See question 78 on reasonable accommodation, and question 89 on reasonable modification.

Section 504 also requires housing providers to modify their procedures, practices and policies to ensure that they do not discriminate against a qualified individual with handicaps and to undertake reasonable modifications to dwelling units and common areas, when requested by applicants and residents with disabilities, as needed to provide accessibility. Section 504 requires that the housing provider pay for these changes.

See questions 145 and 149 for further information on what constitutes a fundamental alteration and undue financial and administrative burdens.

These changes do not have to be made, however, if making them would result in a fundamental alteration in the nature of the program under which the housing is provided or in undue financial and administrative burdens; however, changes have to be made up to the point that undue burdens are created.

142 What Are the Housing Assistance Program Definitions of Handicap and Disability?

See Chapter 6 for guidance on resident selection criteria.

In order to be admitted to federally-assisted housing, an applicant household must meet housing program eligibility requirements and also satisfy the housing provider's uniform, nondiscriminatory resident selection criteria. The remainder of this question will be devoted to questions of program eligibility (i.e. eligibility requirements that arise from the federal legislation, regulations, contracts and handbooks governing the particular housing programs under which a given property operates).

See question 143.

Once admitted, households meeting program definitions of "disability" or "handicap" may be entitled to certain deductions that may reduce the amount of rent the household will pay.

Eligibility Requirements Common to All Programs

The following are the program eligibility requirements that are common to all regulated housing properties:

- Household income must not exceed the income limit for the program (with rare exceptions).

See also question 143.

- Household size must be appropriate for at least one of the unit types available at the property. Recent legislative and handbook changes provide that single persons are eligible for all HUD-regulated housing programs.

Additional Requirements for Family Properties

In general, for properties designed and operated for families, HUD housing programs impose no additional eligibility requirements. As discussed above, however, applicant households must also satisfy the housing provider's resident selection criteria.

Properties Exclusively for the Elderly

For the few HUD-assisted properties designed and operated solely for the elderly (i.e., with no provision for also serving non-elderly people with disabilities), there is one additional program eligibility requirement: the head of household or spouse must be age 62 or over .

Properties for the Elderly and Non-elderly People with Disabilities

Historically, the majority of HUD-regulated housing properties serving the elderly also included a number of units (typically 10 percent of the total number of units) designed for people with disabilities regardless of age (usually these apartments were designed to be accessible to wheelchair users). For these properties, households are required to meet one of the following additional program eligibility requirements:

- The head of household or spouse must be age 62 or over; or

- The household must meet the applicable program definition of "disabled" or "handicapped."

Housing Program Definition of "Disability"

The program definition of "disability" or "handicap" varies by housing program, with some programs offering a number of criteria under which a household might be eligible. Usually, it may be sufficient if any member of the household meets the criteria, but in some programs, either the head of household or spouse is required to have the disability or handicap condition.

Following is a summary of the most common regulated housing programs that have their own definition of "handicap" and/or "disability" for purposes of program eligibility. If a housing program in which you participate is not listed, you should check the applicable regulations to determine whether it, too, has its own definitions.

Some general principles should be kept in mind during the discussion of program definitions of "disability" and "handicap:"

- Typically, households with a member who has mobility impairments will be eligible under most of the programs. This is because the typical "handicap" accessible apartment was designed specifically to be accessible to wheelchair users.

- Whether households with other types of disabilities are eligible depends on HUD's determination of the purpose for which the housing program was enacted by Congress.

- Where, for instance, a given program requires non-elderly households to have a mobility impairment in order to be eligible, the existence of other disabilities in addition to the mobility impairment does not affect the eligibility. For example, a household with both a mobility impairment and a chronic mental illness would still be eligible.

- A household that meets the Section 504 definition of "individual with handicap" but which does not satisfy the other applicable housing program definition(s) would not be eligible for housing set aside for people with disabilities. This is because Section 504 protects "*otherwise* eligible individuals with handicap;" if the household does not meet the program eligibility requirements, then the protection provided by Section 504 does not apply.[2]

The Section 8 Programs

The Housing and Community Development Act of 1992 ("the 1992 Act") changed the terms used in these programs. Prior to the 1992 Act, the terms "handicapped person" and "disabled person" were used. With the enactment of the 1992 Act, only one term is used: "person with disabilities," defined as a person who:

1 *"Has a disability as defined in Section 223 of the Social Security Act, which reads: "an inability to engage in any substantial gainful activity because of any physical or mental impairment that is expected to result in death or has lasted or can be expected to last continuously for at least 12 months; or, for a blind person at least 55 years old, inability because of blindness to engage in any substantial gainful activities comparable to those in which the person was previously engaged with some regularity and over a substantial period of time;" or*

---

2. *For relevant cases, see: Beckert v. Our Lady of Angels Apartments, Inc., 192 F3d 601 (6th Cir. 1999); Knudsen v Eben Ezer Lutheran Hous. Ctr., 815 F.2d 1343 (10th Cir. 1987); Brecker v. Queens B'Nai B'Rith Hous. Dev. Fund Co., 798 F.2d 52 (2nd Cir. 1986).*

2   *"Is determined, pursuant to regulations issued by the Secretary of HUD, to have a physical, mental, or emotional impairment which is expected to be of a long-continued and indefinite duration; substantially impedes the person's ability to live independently; and is such that this ability to live independently could be improved by more suitable housing conditions; or*

3   *Has a developmental disability as defined in Section 102 of the Developmental Disabilities Assistance and Bill of Rights Act, which reads: "a severe, chronic disability of a person 5 years of age or older which*

   (A) is attributable to a mental or physical impairment or a combination of mental and physical impairments;

   (B) is manifested before the person attains age 22;

   (C) is likely to continue indefinitely;

   (D) results in substantial functional limitations in three or more areas of the following areas of major life activity:

      (i)   self-care,

      (ii)   receptive and expressive language,

      (iii) learning,

      (iv)   mobility,

      (v)   self-direction,

      (vi)   capacity for independent living; and

      (vii) economic self-sufficiency.

   (E) reflects the person's need for a combination and sequence of special, interdisciplinary, or generic care, treatment, or other services which are of lifelong or extended duration and are individually planned and coordinated; except that such term, when applied to infants and young children, means individuals from birth to age 5, inclusive, who have substantial developmental delay or specific congenital or acquired conditions with a high probability of resulting in developmental disabilities if services are not provided."

This definition, which merely combines the definitions of the previously used terms with little or no substantive changes, is applicable to all housing assisted under the Section 8 program. Prior to the 1992 Act, the terms in effect were defined as follows: "Handicapped person" (see definition (2) above) and the only change by the 1992 Act is the inclusion of "emotional impairment," and "disabled person." (See definitions (1) and (3) above). There were no changes to these definitions as a result of the 1992 Act.

See Chapter 21 regarding Mixed Populations.

It should be noted that until the enactment of the 1992 Act, the Section 8 program had defined "elderly family" to include households whose members all were under age 62 but whose head, spouse or sole member was handicapped or disabled. The 1992 Act provided a new definition of "elderly families" for properties that give a preference in admission to elderly families. This definition excludes from preferential admission non-elderly handicapped or disabled households and includes only those households where the head spouse or sole member is 62. (Eligible households, i.e. those with an elderly head or spouse can also include other members who are handicapped or disabled, however.) Properties that do not grant a preference to elderly families will continue to use the pre-1992 Act definition of elderly household.

See Chapter 20 for further information on assisted properties that are entitled to provide a preference for the elderly.

Section 202 Of The Housing Act Of 1959 And Section 811 Of The National Affordable Housing Act

The Cranston-Gonzalez National Affordable Housing Act of 1990 ("the 1990 Act") made significant changes in the Section 202 program with respect to the manner in which housing under the program will be offered in the future. The 1990 Act provided that, in the future, separate housing would be provided for the elderly and for people with disabilities: supportive housing for the elderly would be provided under Section 202 and supportive housing for people with disabilities would be provided under Section 811. Under the Section 811 program disabilities are separated into three major categories: physical disability, developmental disability and chronic mental illness. An owner may, with HUD approval, limit occupancy of Section 811 housing to persons with similar disabilities.

As a result of the 1990 Act, the following definitions apply to properties approved as Section 202 or Section 811 properties on or after October 1, 1991, or such properties for which a loan had been approved but had not yet closed and were converted to the new category (referred to as "post 1990 Act property").

Post-1990 Act Section 202 program

For the post-1990 Act Section 202 program, the following definitions apply:

- "Elderly person" means a household composed of one or more persons, at least one of whom is age 62 or older.

- "Frail elderly" means an elderly person who is unable to perform at least three of five activities of daily living adopted by the Secretary for purposes of this program. The five activities of daily living are: (1) eating; (2) bathing; (3) grooming; (4) dressing; (5) home management activities (for example housework, grocery shopping, laundry).[3]

Section 811 Program

For the Section 811 program the following definitions apply:

- "Person with disabilities" means a household composed of one or more persons, at least one of whom has a disability.

- "Disability" means a physical, mental, or emotional impairment, which (a) is expected to be of a long-continued and indefinite duration; (b) substantially impedes the person's ability to live independently; and (c) is such that this ability to live independently could be improved by more suitable housing conditions.

- A person shall also be considered disabled if such person has a "developmental disability" (see definition 3 for the Section 8 program above).

Post-1990 Act properties are identified by the letters HD or EE in the HUD project number. The letters HH or EH identify a pre-1990 Act property.

Pre-1990 Act, Section 202

For pre-1990 Act Section 202 properties the following definitions apply:

- "Handicapped person" means any adult having a physical, mental, or emotional impairment which (1) is expected to be of a long-continued and indefinite duration; (2) substantially impedes the person's ability to live independently; and (3) is such that this ability to live

---

3. See 24 CFR, Chapter VIII, Section 889.105 and Handbook 5471.3, Rev. 1, pp. 113.

independently could be improved by more suitable housing conditions.

- A person is also considered handicapped if he or she (1) has a 'developmental disability' (see definition 3 for the Section 8 program above), or (2) has a chronic mental illness (defined as a severe and persistent mental or emotional impairment that seriously limits his or her ability to live independently (e.g., by limiting functional capacities relative to primary aspects of daily living such as personal relations, living arrangements, work, recreation, etc.), and whose impairment could be improved by more suitable housing conditions.

Section 221 For purposes of Section 221 properties, persons are considered handicapped if they are handicapped within the definition which applies to pre 1990 Act Section 202 properties (see above).

Section 236 Under the Section 236 program, the definitions of "handicap" and "disability" are the same as those for the Section 8 program prior to the 1992 Act:

- "Handicapped person" means any adult having a physical or mental impairment which is expected to be of a long-continued and indefinite duration; substantially impedes the person's ability to live independently; and is such that this ability to live independently could be improved by more suitable housing conditions.

- "Disabled person" means a person who has a disability as defined in Section 223 of the Social Security Act (see Section 8, definition 1 above), or who has a developmental disability (see Section 8, definition 3 above).

143 Fair Housing Act vs. Program Definition

To the extent that being disabled/handicapped is a requirement of eligibility for admission to certain types of housing, the specific program definition of disability or handicap, which may be more restrictive than the Fair Housing Act or Section 504 definition, will prevail.

See question 104 for a discussion of inquiries.

The housing program definitions may come into play in two situations: firstly, when satisfying one of the applicable definitions is a prerequisite to establishing the household's eligibility; and secondly to establish eligibility for certain allowances against income. In both situations, it is acceptable to request verification of the existence of a disability. In the second situation, it is acceptable to request information regarding expected medical or assistance expenses. Housing providers should be aware however that while program definitions of disability will determine whether a particular individual qualifies for a particular housing program or whether an allowance against income should be applied, all individuals continue to be protected under the Fair Housing Act, Americans with Disabilities Act and §504 of the Rehabilitation Act.

To illustrate the first situation: a person applying for admission to a pre-October 1991 Section 202 property for the physically disabled must meet the housing program definition for having a "physical impairment" (in addition to all other applicable requirements for admission). In this instance, if the person has an impairment which meets the fair housing definition of "handicap" but which does not meet the applicable housing program definition, the housing provider must decline this person's application, because the person does not meet basic admission requirements for the particular housing program.

See question 104 for a discussion of inquiry technique, and question 105 for a general discussion of applicant screening and eligibility procedures. See question 165 regarding inquiries regarding disabilities.

To illustrate the second situation: if a four-person family, that includes a child with a disability, applies for an apartment in a Section 8 property for families, program eligibility is satisfied by virtue of the family status, and it is neither necessary nor appropriate to inquire about the disability for purposes of determining housing program eligibility. However, the household may be entitled to an allowance against income for certain expenses related to the child's disability condition. Therefore, at the point where the housing provider is determining final eligibility income, a limited inquiry into the disability condition is permissible in order to establish qualification for the allowance.

To decline the four-person household's application because of the child's disability condition would violate both Section 504 and the Fair Housing Act.

144   Are Drug or Alcohol Related Illnesses Considered Handicaps Under Section 504?

See questions 107 through 113.

Yes, both drug addiction and alcoholism are included in the definition of "individual with handicap" contained in the Fair Housing Act and Section 504. However, an individual who is engaged in the "current, illegal use of a controlled substance" (i.e. illegal drugs) is not protected and may be denied housing. The most detailed discussion of the meaning of "current illegal use" is found in DOJ's ADA regulations (see below). Individuals whose tenancy would pose a direct threat to the health or safety of others may also be denied housing.

This is not an artificial distinction. Congress intended to protect addicts who are drug free and in recovery, but not persons who are engaged in the current, illegal use of a controlled substance (whether addicted or not).

The Department of Justice, in its regulations implementing Titles II and III of the ADA, made the following points regarding "current, illegal use":

- Current illegal use is defined for ADA purposes as "illegal use of drugs that occurred recently enough to justify a reasonable belief that a person's drug use is current or that continuing use is a real and ongoing problem."[4]

- "The key question is whether the individual's use of the substance is illegal, not whether the substance has recognized legal uses."

- Alcohol is not a controlled substance, so use of alcohol is not lawful grounds for denial of services or benefits under the "current illegal use" exception. Alcoholics are protected under the Fair Housing Act, the ADA and Section 504.

- "A distinction is also made between the use of a substance and the status of being addicted to that substance. Addiction is a disability, and addicts are individuals with disabilities protected by the [ADA]. The protection, however,

---

4. *Section 36.104*

does not extend to actions based on the illegal use of the substance. In other words, an addict cannot use the fact of his or her addiction as a defense to an action based on illegal use of drugs."

Some Housing providers may wish to require evidence of recovery. In its final report, the HUD Occupancy Task Force stated: "When an individual claims recovery, the regulations for all programs should authorize the housing provider to require the person to present evidence of recovery from a qualified, neutral third party in order to be admitted (in the case of an applicant) or allowed to continue to reside in the unit (in the case of a resident). See also 24 CFR 966.4(a)(5)(i): 'A PHA may require a family member who has engaged in the illegal use of drugs to present evidence of successful completion of a treatment program as a condition to being allowed to reside in the unit" (Occupancy Task Force Report, Chapter 3, page 3-10).[5]

Examples of Drug Addiction as a Disability

The claiming of a handicap on the basis of drug addiction was seen in one case where the managers of an apartment complex denied an application for housing. *The application was made by the Board of a drug rehabilitation program which intended to house drug program participants at the property. The intended occupants were all in the second or "reentry" phase of the rehabilitation program, meaning that they had been drug-free for a year but would continue to be supervised and monitored by employees of the rehabilitation program. This supervision included twice-monthly drug tests with any participant testing positive for drugs being discharged from the program and evicted from the apartment. In reviewing the attitude of the housing managers to this application the court stated that "...we can see that there is no question that [the housing managers] denied housing to the Board on the basis of the substance abuser status of the prospective tenants; ...The clients are clearly impaired and their ability to obtain housing... was limited by the attitudes of [the leasing managers]. Thus we conclude that the clients qualify as having a handicap under the general definition at 42 USC "3602(h)(1)-(3)."*

5.*U.S. V Southern Management Corporation, 955 F.2d 914; US Court of Appeals for the 4th Circuit.*

Examples of Drug Addiction as a Disability

> *The court went on to consider whether the exclusion of "current, illegal use of or addiction to a controlled substance" from the definition of handicap applied to the applicants. The housing managers contended that the term "addiction" included persons addicted to but no longer using controlled substances, that "once an addict always an addict" and addicts may not seek the Act's protection. In the view of the Court the question was whether "...a person who was previously using and is addicted to illegal drugs may, after a period of abstinence and rehabilitative efforts be said to no longer have an "addiction", as that term is used in the statutory exclusion." The court concluded that "...we believe that Congress intended to recognize that addiction is a disease from which, through rehabilitation efforts, a person may recover, and that an individual who makes the effort to recover should not be subject to housing discrimination based on society's "accumulated fears and prejudices" associated with drug addiction." The court therefore concluded that the refusal to rent was unlawful and awarded the Board substantial damages.*

145   What Is a "Fundamental Alteration"?

A fundamental alteration is an action which would cause a basic change in the nature of the housing program offered at the property; for example an action requiring:

- The elimination or substantial modification of essential lease or housing program requirements;

- The property to provide supportive services; or

- The property to offer housing of a fundamentally different nature than the type of housing currently offered.

See question 78.   Actions that may be requested as "reasonable accommodations" may actually constitute fundamental alterations and thus would not have to be done. For example, a request to allow people with disabilities to rent a dwelling by the day or by the week would be a fundamental alteration in an assisted housing program, where monthly or annual leases are the norm. On the other hand, making arrangements for residents to pay their rent by mail rather than in person might not result in a fundamental alteration.

A housing provider is not required to offer housing of a fundamentally different nature from the type of housing currently provided. Moreover, there must be a direct connection between the requested accommodation and the individual's disability.

See questions 78 and 84.

An example of a request for accommodation that is really a request for supportive services might involve a request for housekeeping or personal care services to enable an applicant with a disability to meet basic admissions requirements. Unless the property is designed as an assisted living facility where such services are provided routinely to all residents, agreeing to such an accommodation would likely constitute a fundamental alteration to the nature of the housing program.

146 Can Housing Providers Be Required to Provide Non-Housing Services as a Reasonable Accommodation?

See question 82.

As a general principle, housing providers are not required to provide supportive services for residents (e.g. counseling, medical or social services) that fall outside the scope of the property's housing program. The test of eligibility for admission is whether, with appropriate modifications or accommodations, the applicant or resident can comply with the requirements of the program offered, not whether he or she could benefit or obtain better results from some other program that the property does not offer.

Applicants who need supportive services may still qualify for housing if they can obtain and arrange for these services on their own.

147 Does the Provision of "Auxiliary Aids" Constitute a Fundamental Alteration?

Auxiliary aids are services or devices that enable persons with impaired sensory, manual or speaking skills to have an equal opportunity to participate in, and enjoy the benefits of, programs or activities receiving federal financial assistance, by, for example facilitating effective communication. These do not include individually prescribed items or personal items.

Examples of auxiliary aids for persons with vision impairments include readers, Brailled materials, taped texts, large print materials and audio recordings.

For persons with hearing impairments, auxiliary aids include telecommunication devices for the deaf (TDDs), interpreters, note-takers, transcription services, closed caption decoders, open and closed captioning, videotext displays and written materials. Managers are generally not required to provide TDDs for a resident's personal use. You are required to either have a TDD on the property or an equivalent service. If, however, you have a gated community with a telephone available to call residents to have the gate opened, you might have to provide a TDD for both the resident and at the gate.[6]

Auxiliary aids do not include individually prescribed items such as hearing aids, service animals or eyeglasses; or personal items such as telecommunications equipment in the resident's unit, personal readers, or personal interpreters.

Section 504 Regulations require housing providers to provide "appropriate auxiliary aids" where necessary to allow individuals with handicaps to have an equal opportunity to participate in and enjoy the benefits of the particular housing program. This includes providing TDDs or an equally effective alternative system for communicating with hearing-impaired persons. It does not, however, include taking any action that would result in a fundamental alteration in the nature of the program or in undue financial and administrative burdens.

RHS properties are also required to provide auxiliary aids (electronic, mechanical or personal assistance), excluding individually prescribed devices, to handicapped or disabled residents.

---

6. *Even though this is an 'individually prescribed item' the existence of a gate would make provision of a TDD necessary to afford the resident equal opportunity to use the property.*

148 What About "Undue Administrative and Financial Burden"?

"Undue administrative and financial burdens" are justifications for failing to provide accessibility under Section 504 of the Rehabilitation Act and Title II of the ADA. They do not excuse a failure to provide reasonable accommodations as required by the Fair Housing Act. However, only accommodations that are "reasonable" have to be provided. Whether an accommodation is "reasonable" "is a question of fact, determined by a close examination of the particular circumstances." [7] It has also been said, "The reasonable accommodation inquiry is highly fact-specific, requiring case-by-case determination." [8]

A reasonable accommodation would not be required if it would impose an undue administrative and financial burden or would result in a fundamental alteration in the nature of the program or service offered (e.g., an owner who has previously not accepted Section 8 certificates may not be required to reasonably accommodate a person with disabilities by accepting Section 8 certificates).

Note that the standard is 'undue administrative *and* financial burden.' Owners should document both when rejecting a request for reasonable accommodation. Courts will consider the aggregate cost of both when hearing cases.

149 What Are "Undue Financial and Administrative Burdens" in Providing Accessibility?

See questions 156, 157, and 158.

The following discussion refers to the situation of an existing property that is not undergoing "substantial alteration" or undertaking "other alterations." For new construction and substantial alterations to existing buildings, accessibility must be provided. For existing properties undergoing "other alter-

---

7. *Jankowski Lee & Associates et al V Cisneros & Rusinvo US Court of Appeal 7th Circuit, No. 95-3051*

8. *U.S. v. California Mobile Home Park Management Co. 29 F.3d 1413 (9th Circuit 1994)*

ations," accessibility must be provided "to the maximum extent feasible;" that is, other alterations to a dwelling unit or common area to provide accessibility need not be made if doing so would impose undue financial and administrative burdens.

Definition of Undue Financial and Administrative Burdens

Undue financial and administrative burdens are "modifications" or "accommodations" (i.e. procedural changes for accessibility); that would cause a property to incur an expense or undertake an activity that would put an unreasonable strain on the capacity of the property to operate in a manner consistent with the legal and contractual obligations of the owners. There must be both financial and administrative impact in order to create "undue financial and administrative burdens."

Under §504, housing providers are, however, required to make modifications and accommodations up to the point before undue burdens are created.

Undue Burdens and Physical Modifications

The Section 504 regulations contain a specific exception for accessibility modifications that "have little likelihood of being accomplished without removing or altering a load bearing structural member;" such modifications do not have to be performed.

A modification which entails a lesser redesign of a building or dwelling unit however, may not create undue burdens, depending upon the financial circumstances of the property and the needs of the resident or applicant.

If as a result of a proposed modification, basic maintenance to the property must be postponed, a defensible argument could be made that undue burdens would be created if the modification were undertaken. A determination of undue burdens will be based upon the specific circumstances of every property, taking into account such things as the constraints of the site and existing structure, plans for major renovations to the property, the needs of the resident, and the financial condition of the property. If major structural modifications (for instance, to create or enlarge bathrooms or bedrooms for wheelchair accessibility) would be required separate from a planned "substantial alteration" of the property, they could be considered undue burdens, depending significantly on the financial resources of the property and the specific needs of the resident or applicant. Owners cannot however claim an 'undue burden' for failure to provide accessible units which are required under the Fair Housing or Rehabilitation Acts.

Substitution of Alternative Methods

There is no requirement to make structural modifications if other methods of achieving accessibility are effective. For instance, the availability of suitable modified units in the buildings, or in other buildings in the area under control of the owner, or other properties in the area with which the owner has a referral agreement, may constitute an acceptable alternative to undertaking structural modifications. Owners however should consider the reasons that a household has requested to occupy a modified unit, rather than move to an alternative unit.

Similarly, there is no requirement to make a structural modification if accessibility can be accomplished via a less onerous procedural accommodation. Modifications (except in connection with a substantial alteration) may create undue burdens if they would cause the property to:

- Operate at a deficit or contribute to worsening of an existing deficit condition;

- Take funds away from necessary maintenance and repairs; or

- Result in a curtailment of basic services to the property.

Administrative Burdens

Similarly, "undue administrative burdens" might result from an accommodation that requires a housing provider to provide support services to a person with disabilities, if the provision of such services would impair the ability of the provider to deliver basic administrative services to other residents. For example, if a provider were asked to provide trash collection services for a person with disabilities, and the provision of such services would result in a cutback in existing management services, it would pose an undue administrative burden.

See question 78.

Undue administrative burdens might also result from accommodations that required a replacement of property staff with new staff having different qualifications and capabilities.

Partial
Compliance

If a housing provider determines that full compliance with a request would create undue burdens, it may be possible to comply partially without creating undue burdens. In this instance, the housing provider would be required to comply up to the point that undue burdens were created. For instance, a wheelchair user may request that the bathroom be enlarged and provided with grab bars; if the enlargement would constitute undue burdens and providing the grab bars would not, the housing provider would follow the steps outlined in the following question to determine if the disability could be accommodated in some other manner which would not create undue burdens. If alternatives are not feasible, the housing owner would provide the grab bars but not the enlargement.

The final report of the Public & Assisted Housing Occupancy Task Force contained a useful discussion on reaching agreement on reasonable accommodation methods.

150 Procedures for Making Undue Burden Determinations

The following discussion refers to the situation of an existing property that is not undergoing a "substantial alteration" or "other alteration." For new construction, and for existing properties undergoing "alterations," accessibility must be provided (and there is no "undue burdens" exception).

Experienced housing providers suggest that a determination that providing an accommodation or modification would result in undue burdens be made by a senior person, perhaps the supervisor or the off-site property manager responsible for the property, and that the determination be made in writing.

The goal is to place the applicant household in a unit that meets the household's needs. Thus, it is appropriate to consider all methods for accomplishing the goal, beyond the specific method that initially is being considered. Experienced housing providers advise that, in many instances, a creative solution can be found that does not create undue burdens, for example:

- Can the disability be accommodated within a reasonable period of time, say 30 days, at a nearby, similar property under the owner's control or with which the owner has a referral agreement?

- Can the disability be accommodated within a reasonable period of time at an existing accessible unit within the property?

- Are there any practicable non-structural methods for accommodating the disability? For instance, if a wheelchair user cannot access the laundry facility, the normal accommodation would be to make the laundry facility accessible. The owner might, however, incur less cost by offering to subsidize a laundry service that would pick up, clean and deliver the resident's laundry.

- Are there less burdensome structural methods for accommodating the disability? For instance, a wheelchair user may not be able to access the bathroom in its current configuration. Rather than tearing out, enlarging and reconstructing the existing bathroom, it may be possible for the resident to operate the wheelchair in the existing bathroom if (a) the vanity and lavatory are replaced with a wall-mounted lavatory and (b) the bathroom entry door is widened and made to swing out into the hall instead of into the bathroom itself.

- Has the housing provider discussed alternative methods for accommodating the disability with the person requesting the modification, and with local disability-oriented organizations?

Assuming that the housing provider has followed the above procedures, and has determined that undertaking the least burdensome method for accommodating the disability is not within the property's present financial and administrative resources:

See question 31.

- Document that you have acted in good faith, in an overall context of disability-awareness. If the determination of undue burdens results in an official complaint, this will be a key factor in the investigator's decision.

- Document your good faith efforts to consider seriously the household's request, and to accommodate the disability in a less burdensome manner.

- Demonstrate that the least burdensome method for accommodating the disability involves both financial and administrative burdens. The Section 504 regulations require that both types of burdens be present before a determination of undue burdens can be made.

- The Transition Plan includes timetables and funds sources for making structural modifications to the property over time, as needed to provide accessible routes plus a reasonable number of accessible units. If, in comparison to the timetables and funds sources contained in the Transition Plan, the requested modification occurs dramatically sooner, or at dramatically higher cost, or the anticipated financial or administrative resources do not exist, this would support a conclusion of undue burdens.

- Document the property's present financial condition. The HUD surplus cash calculation is a useful indicator; a property with zero surplus cash has exactly enough cash resources to cover its short-term financial obligations. If the property has negative surplus cash, or has insufficient positive surplus cash to cover the cost of the modification, this would support a conclusion of undue burdens.

- Is there any reason to expect that the property's financial condition will soon improve sufficiently to support the cost of the proposed modification? If so, it may be possible to accommodate the disability when the financial condition improves.

- Document your attempts to locate funding from third party sources. State and local governments and local disability-oriented organizations may have information about alternative funding sources.

151   What Are the Differences Between the ADA's "Readily Achievable" Standard, and 504's "Undue Burden" Standard?

The ADA and Section 504 use different standards for determining when a property should undertake modifications. For properties subject to Section 504, properties must make changes unless doing so poses an "undue financial and administrative burden". Properties or portions of properties that are subject to Title III of the ADA must make changes that are "readily achievable without too much difficulty or expense". These are tangibly different cost standards which could result in different decisions depending on which standard is used. If a property is affected by both standards, a safe approach is to follow the more restrictive approach (higher standard).

Chapter Seventeen: Accessibility and Federally-Assisted Properties

152 What Is a Section 504 Accessibility Review?

In general, the steps discussed in questions 23, 24 and 25 will meet Section 504's requirements for a "self evaluation" and "transition plan." However, the following additional points should be considered:

- For existing properties, the Section 504 regulations required nonstructural changes to be made not later than September 11, 1988.

See question 128 for the definition of "federal financial assistance."

- For existing properties, the transition plan was required to be completed by January 1, 1989. If your property has not completed a transition plan, this should be done as soon as possible. For properties not now subject to Section 504 but which receive Federal Financial Assistance in the future, a transition plan is required to be completed within six months following receipt of assistance.

- The 504 regulations require that you "consult with interested parties (local disability organizations and groups, persons with disabilities who are living in the property, etc.)" regarding the Accessibility Review, Self Evaluation and Transition Plan. Experienced housing providers advise that this participative process is valuable in developing a high quality approach to accessibility. In most areas, local disability organizations (such as Independent Living Centers) are available to participate in this process.

See question 147 for more on "Auxiliary Aides."

- The issue of communicating with residents or applicants with visual or hearing impairments should be addressed. Properties that are subject to the provisions of Section 504 of the Rehabilitation Act are required to provide auxiliary aids such as telecommunication devices for hearing impaired persons (TDD's) to ensure effective communication with these residents and applicants. A TDD is an acceptable form of accommodation. Other properties should also consider the use of such devices.

153 What Are the Accessibility Requirements Under Section 504?

See question 126 for a description of subject properties.

Regulations under Section 504 of the Rehabilitation Act[1] define "accessible" to mean that a facility can be approached, entered and used by individuals with physical disabilities.

See question 155 for the accessibility requirements for new properties. See questions 141, 156, 157, 158, and 159.

Section 504 requires that all new multifamily housing projects (i.e. projects constructed after July 1988) that are subject to the Act must be designed and constructed to be readily accessible to and usable by individuals with disabilities. In the case of existing multifamily housing the regulations require that the housing program must be readily accessible to and usable by individuals with handicaps and that if certain types of alterations to such properties are undertaken that accessibility up to a specified level must be given.

154 Does RHS Impose Special Accessibility Review Requirements?

In general, the United States Department of Agriculture's Rural Housing Service (RHS) requirements for the self-evaluation and transition plan are identical to HUD requirements. USDA regulations implementing Section 504 were issued on June 11, 1982. These regulations address the self- evaluation and transition plan.

- Handbook 1930-C[2] addresses Handicap signage (accessible parking spaces must have a sign showing the international symbol of accessibility), the use of Handicap logos and the need for an unobstructed accessible route through common areas and to the primary building entrance.

- Some state RHS offices required submission of transition plans for review by RHS.

- RHS has taken the position that, to the extent possible, barriers to common use areas that prevent any mobility-impaired person from having full access will be removed.

---

1. *24 CFR Part 8 Section 8.22*
2. *Exhibit B VI C 2b(2)*

155 Accessibility Requirements for New Construction of Federally Assisted Housing

See questions 128 and 160.

New apartment properties that receive federal financial assistance, and are thus subject to Section 504, must also meet the Section 504 accessibility standards. Section 504 requires that new developments have a minimum of 5 percent of the total dwelling units or at least one unit, whichever is greater, accessible for persons with mobility impairments. An additional 2 percent of the units must be accessible for persons who have hearing or vision impairments. For properties without an elevator, all ground floor units must meet the Fair Housing Act accessibility requirements; in properties with an elevator, all units must meet the Fair Housing Act accessibility requirements. HUD may prescribe a higher percentage of units to be accessible based upon the need for such units in the area.

Once the above test is met, no additional units need be made accessible unless:

- An eligible applicant with disabilities requiring an accessible unit reaches the top of the property's waiting list;

- There is no accessible unit in the subject property; and

- There is no accessible unit in a nearby (suitable) property with which the owner has a referral agreement.

For new construction, there is no exception for "undue financial and administrative burdens:" the property must be accessible to people with disabilities.

Also see question 84 regarding accessibility requirements for new construction under the Fair Housing Act.

Section 504 accessibility standards are based on the Uniform Federal Accessibility Standards ("UFAS"), and Fair Housing Act accessibility standards are based on the ANSI standard. Providers who are considering new construction should consult with knowledgeable professionals regarding these standards and requirements.

156   What Is an "Alteration"?

In certain instances where alterations to an existing property are undertaken Section 504 requires that these alterations provide accessibility to people with disabilities.

Maintenance, repair or replacement activities may fall under the Section 504 definition of alteration, which is defined as, "Any change in a facility or its permanent fixtures or equipment. It includes, but is not limited to, remodeling, renovation, rehabilitation, reconstruction, changes, or rearrangements in structural parts and extraordinary repairs. It does not include normal maintenance or repairs, re-roofing, interior decoration, or changes to mechanical systems."

See question 149.   Alterations may be categorized as either "substantial alterations" or "other alterations," and there are different accessibility requirements for each. If an alteration falls into the "other alteration" category, accessibility must be provided to the maximum extent feasible that would not impose undue burdens.

157   What Is a "Substantial Alteration"?

See question 155.   The accessibility requirements for new construction (including the requirement that 5 percent of the units must be accessible for the mobility impaired and 2 percent of the units must be accessible for persons with hearing or vision impairments), apply to an existing facility undergoing substantial alterations.

Section 504 defines "substantial alterations" as:[3]

• Alterations to properties with 15 or more units, and

• *Where the cost of alteration is 75 percent or more of the replacement cost of the completed property.*

---

3.   *24 CFR Part 8.2*

"Replacement cost" is defined as:[4]

"...the current cost of construction and equipment for a newly constructed housing facility of the size and type being altered. Construction and equipment costs do not include the cost of land, demolition, site improvements, non-dwelling facilities and administrative costs for project development activities."

158   What Are "Other Alterations"?

Under Section 504, "other alterations" are modifications that go beyond normal maintenance into the "alterations" category, but that are of lesser cost than "substantial alterations."

"Other alterations" must, to the maximum extent feasible, make a property or dwelling, including common areas, readily accessible to and usable by a person with disabilities. Accessibility must be provided only up to the point of infeasibility or undue burdens.

If alterations to single elements or spaces of a dwelling unit amount to an alteration of the dwelling unit the entire dwelling must be made accessible. Once five percent of all the dwelling units at the property have been made accessible no additional elements within dwelling units or entire dwelling units are required to be made accessible.

Housing providers are cautioned that the "other alterations" definition may be construed to impose especially burdensome requirements. For instance, if a property's bathrooms are being renovated and if such renovations constitute "other alterations," each bathroom would have to be made accessible until at least 5 percent of the units are fully accessible. In this instance, the housing provider might incur lower costs by immediately making 5 percent of the units accessible, in order to avoid the additional costs in making 100 percent of the bathrooms accessible. As with new construction and substantial alteration, once the 5 percent threshold is met, the above requirements no longer apply.

---

4. *24 CFR Part 8.3*

The distinction between normal maintenance and "other alteration" is not as clear as housing providers might like. For instance, it is unclear whether restoration of a fire-damaged unit would constitute an "other alteration." In this case, it might be prudent to restore fire-damaged units to accessible or adaptable condition where unit design (and reconstruction cost) permits, and where the unit is on an accessible route, if the 5 percent requirement had not been met.

The purpose of the "other alteration" provision is to encourage providers to make 5 percent of dwelling units accessible immediately, in order to avoid the perhaps troublesome "other alteration" requirements. Providers who proceed quickly with accessibility modifications to dwelling units thus gain the benefit of exemption from a potentially problematic requirement.

Housing providers considering "alterations" should consult with professionals knowledgeable about accessibility requirements.

159 Requirements for Existing Housing

Section 504 also imposes accessibility requirements for existing properties that are not undergoing either "substantial alteration" or "other alterations."

Also see the discussion of Accessibility Review in questions 28, 29, and 30 for an introduction to accessibility in this global sense.

The requirement is that "the program, when viewed in its entirety, is readily accessible to and usable by individuals with handicaps." This requirement pertains to *program* accessibility rather than *physical* accessibility. The following discussion outlines the general areas of accessibility requirements, and refers to other portions of this guidebook for more detailed discussion of each area.

The program accessibility requirement does not necessarily mean that a housing provider must make each facility accessible to and usable by individuals with handicaps. A housing provider may meet its obligations through such means as referral to other properties, provision of services in an accessible building, or reassignment of services to an accessible building.

See questions 78 and 89 for discussions of reasonable accommodations [in procedures] and reasonable modifications [to structures]; see question 145 for a discussion on "fundamental alterations" and questions 149 and 150 on "undue burdens."

If requested by an applicant or resident with disabilities at the top of the waiting list, the provider must make a dwelling unit accessible, at the property's expense, unless to do so would result in a fundamental alteration in the nature of the program or in undue financial and administrative burdens.

Section 504 does not require a structural modification when a less troublesome procedural modification or method would be effective. For instance, the availability of suitable modified units in the buildings, or in other buildings in the area under control of the owner, or other properties in the area with which the owner has a referral agreement, would be such an alternative method.

If an accessibility modification is unreasonable, would result in a fundamental alteration, or would result in undue burdens, the modification does not have to be made. However, the Fair Housing Act provisions continue to be applicable.

See question 88 for the accessibility requirements under the Fair Housing Act.

The Section 504 regulations require that, in choosing among the methods for compliance, priority must be given to methods that offer housing to qualified persons in the most integrated setting appropriate (i.e. methods that do not have the effect of segregating residents with disabilities from residents without disabilities).

160 The 5-Percent/2-Percent Thresholds

Suppose an existing property has satisfied the five-percent/two-percent accessibility thresholds. Must an additional unit be made accessible if requested by an applicant with disabilities?

If at least 5 percent of a property's units are fully accessible (in the case of new construction, this would include having an additional 2 percent of the units accessible to persons with hearing and vision impairments), there is no obligation to make additional elements, or entire units, accessible unless an individual with disability requires an accessible unit (or some accessibility feature in a unit).

Thus, this new request for modifications must be granted (subject to the restrictions on undue burdens and fundamental alterations).

Housing providers are advised to treat accessible units as precious resources. If one of these units is rented to a household that does not need the accessibility features, it is advisable to require the household to execute a lease addendum agreeing to transfer to a non-accessible unit, when the accessible unit is required to accommodate a household that does need the accessibility features.

161 What Is RHS' Position On The 5-Percent/2-Percent Thresholds?

The USDA Section 504 regulations require that 5 percent of units built after June 11, 1982 be constructed as accessible units. The regulations also require that all new facilities be constructed in accordance with the Uniform Federal Accessibility Standards (UFAS).

Unlike the HUD Section 504 regulations, the USDA regulations are silent concerning units for the visually or hearing impaired. The RHS merely encourages developers to construct units that are designed for the hearing or visually impaired.

162 Applicability of the UFAS Standards for Physical Modifications

Section 504 Regulations provide that design, construction or alteration of buildings that conform to UFAS (or a substantially equivalent standard) will comply with accessibility requirements.

HUD's Occupancy Handbook[5] provides that after 5 percent of the property's units are accessible to persons with mobility impairments the owner must adapt additional units only if:

- The specific accessibility feature requested is reasonable;

---

5. *4350.3 REV1 Section 2-35(E)2 and (E)3*

- An accessible unit cannot be provided within a reasonable period of time; and

- Fulfilling the request will not result in undue financial and administrative burdens or in a fundamental alteration in the nature of the project or program.

See question 157. If a "substantial alteration" is planned, all components of the modifications generally should conform with UFAS, or to another substantially equivalent standard acceptable under the Section 504 regulations. Providers who are considering substantial alterations should consult with qualified professionals concerning these standards.

For other properties (and for properties undertaking substantial alterations once the major renovation is completed), case-by-case modifications must be appropriate to the needs of specific applicants or residents. It will usually be appropriate for each component of such modifications to comply with UFAS or acceptable, equivalent specifications. For example, if a resident's disability can be accommodated by installation of grab bars in a bathroom, the housing provider is under no obligation to make other modifications in the bathroom; however, the grab bars should be installed to UFAS or an acceptable equivalent standard, unless the standard approach would not be effective in removing the resident's barriers to occupancy.

In general, there is a presumption in favor of the applicant's or resident's own assessment of the best methods for meeting his or her needs. Housing providers who feel that the modifications requested by a resident or applicant are beyond what is needed therefore bear the burden of proving this.

163   Sources of Funds for Reasonable Modifications

In Chapter 2 of HUD's Occupancy Handbook 4350.3, HUD indicated that it will allow the following funding approaches to cover modification costs:

- Residual Receipts funds may be used.

- Use of Replacement Reserve funds is discouraged; any Reserve funds withdrawn must be replaced, generally within one year. Often, this will require a rent increase; see further discussion below.

See also questions 149 and 150.

- Where a rent increase is necessary in order to fund a modification, this creates a presumption of undue burdens. Thus, the Handbook seems to indicate that modifications will often constitute undue burdens unless the property currently has excess cash sufficient to pay for them.

- For properties using the Annual Adjustment Factor rent increase method, rents may not be increased to cover the cost of modifications.

Experienced housing providers recommend that, whenever a significant capital improvement plan is contemplated, needed accessibility modifications be taken into consideration and be made a part of the plan.

Housing providers should note that other resources may be available to pay for accessibility modifications. Examples might include Community Development Block Grant funds. Housing providers should network with local disability advocacy organizations, and with their state and local governments in order to obtain information on available sources of funding for undertaking alterations and modifications to provide accessibility.

Experienced housing providers also recommend that determinations of undue burdens be made carefully, because this is a volatile area of Fair Housing practice where significant differences of opinion can be expected between housing providers, advocates, regulatory agencies and the courts.

Properties affected by HUD's occupancy requirements should refer to Handbook 4350.3 REV1, Section 2-43, 'Limits on Obligations to Provide Reasonable Accommodations'.

Chapter Eighteen: Occupancy, People With Disabilities, and Federally-Assisted Housing

164 How Can I Implement Federally Regulated Housing Programs in a Disability-Aware Manner?

For federal housing programs, disability status may sometimes determine program eligibility; hence it may be necessary to ascertain whether either the applicant or a member of the household has a disability. Generally, the rule of thumb is that the housing provider should verify the applicant's eligibility not disability. However, in order to determine eligibility, housing providers may sometimes have to ask questions related to the applicant's disability that would not be permissible in non-regulated properties (except when necessary to respond to a request for reasonable accommodation). In addition, inquiries about applicants' disabilities may be necessary because the amount of residents' medical expenses typically is a consideration in determining the amount of rent residents will pay.

See question 31.   These factors mean that providers of federally regulated housing must venture into areas that have high risk for fair housing complaints to arise. In addition to considerations applicable to all apartments, providers of federally regulated housing should also consider the following:

- If practical, develop your application procedures so that you will not be aware of disability conditions until the last possible moment. For most applicants at federally regulated properties, disability status and medical expenses can be determined and verified relatively late in the application process. If feasible, you will want to delay obtaining information on these matters until after you have decided to (tentatively) accept or decline the application.

See question 168.   - If your property normally has a waiting list (for example, because its rents are well below market), develop written procedures for filling vacancies in your accessible units. Some federal assistance programs have special waiting list priorities for applicants with disabilities.

- When you can't avoid a medical question, ask only what you absolutely need to know. Typically, when you inquire about medical expenses, you need to know only how much the applicant is likely to spend in the next 12 months; you do not need to know the diagnosis, details of the treatment plan, or the likely future course of the disease.

- When you can't avoid a disability question, ask only what you absolutely need to know. When you are verifying disability, you need only to find a qualified third party who will state in writing that the applicant meets one of the official or program definitions of a person with disabilities. Again, you do not need to know the medical details.

- When accepting applications, offer your accessible units. If your property has accessible or adaptable units, ask the applicant if anyone in the household needs the accessibility features only after you have made the tentative decision to accept the application. This can be done (in writing, requiring a written response) as a part of your normal process of deciding to which unit type the household will be assigned.

- When accepting applications, ask about modifications that may be required. For households who select standard (non-accessible) units, ask (in writing, requiring a written response) whether anyone in the household will need reasonable modifications to the unit in order to accommodate a disability condition.

- When responding to applicant requests for reasonable accommodations, remember that housing providers cannot be required to waive basic requirements for admission. For federally regulated programs, these basic requirements may include:

  - Compliance with housing program eligibility requirements.

See question 195.
  - Age (for properties which have appropriately elected to proceed under the 1992 Act and have established a preference for admission of the elderly).

165 Inquiries Concerning Disabilities, for Federally Regulated Properties

In general, an applicant, resident, guest or associate of an applicant/resident may not be asked whether he or she has a disability, or about the severity of a disability. For federally regulated housing, however, there are two scenarios where the owner can ask about the existence of a disability:

- The existence of a disability may often be a prime determinant of eligibility for admission; in these situations, an inquiry as to disability status is permissible. Additionally, an owner can ask for verification of a disability if a resident asks for a reasonable accommodation.

- Applicants and residents may not be asked to waive their right to confidentiality or be asked to reveal medical details about a disability. For instance, for an applicant to be eligible for an allowance for medical expenses, (available only to households whose head or spouse is "handicapped" or "disabled" as defined in the housing program), the provider must establish:

See questions 142 and 143.

- That the head or spouse meets at least one of the applicable housing program definitions, and that there is a qualified, neutral third party who can provide written verification that this is true.

- The amount of the household's expected qualified medical expenses over the next twelve month period, and that there are qualified, neutral third parties who can provide written verification of the expected medical expenses.

In this example, the provider does not need to know the medical diagnosis, the details of the treatment plan, or the likely future course of the disability. The inquiry and verification processes should be designed to prevent the inadvertent receipt of such unnecessary and unwanted information.

One good approach is to revise all application materials so that applicants are advised of situations where it may be to their advantage to disclose their disability status, for example:

- If disability will be a prime determinant of eligibility for admission (for instance, an applicant for a unit at a Section 811 property for the chronically mentally ill will need to establish that this particular disability exists); and

- If disability will entitle the household to an allowance (such as the allowance for medical expenses and the allowance for handicapped assistance and care costs).

HUD's Occupancy Handbook 4350.3 (REV1)[1] requires that owners tell applicants for certain assisted housing programs that they are permitted to verify the existence of a disability only if eligibility for admission is dependent on the existence of handicaps or disabilities or if the applicant is claiming allowances that are given to persons with handicaps or disabilities. Note that the applicant may elect to forego the benefit of any allowances available on the basis of disability, in which case a housing provider should not pursue any inquiry on the matter.

Rural Housing Service (RHS) provisions are similar to HUD's. In its September 1996 Memorandum entitled "Federally Assisted Programs and Accessibility Issues" RHS addressed disability-related requirements:

"Once a tenant/applicant requests their handicap status be considered,

inquiries can be made but only to the extent necessary to verify disability.

Management should not attempt to make any determination concerning a

tenant/applicant's handicapping condition. The tenant/applicant may provide

acceptable verification from a number of sources. For example, documentation

that the tenant/applicant is eligible for Social Security Income Disability is

preferable to requiring verification from their physician. The verification

method that is least intrusive should be accepted."

The Memo also advised against including the question, "Are you handicapped?" on application forms. Instead the Memo suggested that questions be designed to read from the perspective of eligibility. So, for example, the aforementioned

---

1. *See 4350.3, Section 2-31.E.2. and Exhibit 15-B.*

question should read: "If you are applying for residence at an elderly project and you are under 62 are you aware that you must be handicapped or disabled to be eligible?" and "Are you requesting the elderly household deduction and medical expenses?" It is up to the household to answer these questions and provide documentation proving eligibility.

The application materials should include explanatory information that discusses how these allowances affect the amount of rent paid, so that the household can judge whether the potential benefit of lower rent outweighs any privacy concerns about disclosing disability status. Providers who use this approach will be able to avoid inquiry into disability status, until the applicant brings up the subject.

In addition, a federally regulated housing provider may ask all applicants for assisted housing:

- Whether the applicant qualifies for a dwelling unit designed for persons with physical disabilities.

- Whether the applicant qualifies for a medical expense deduction or another allowance which is a part of the housing program(s) offered at the property.

- Whether any member of the applicant's household is engaged in the current illegal use of a controlled substance.

- Whether any member of the applicant's household has been convicted of illegal manufacture or distribution of a controlled substance.

- If the property has a priority for admission that is available to people with disabilities, whether any member of the applicant's household qualifies for such a priority.

A number of housing providers have established a phased screening process to ensure that information is obtained only to the extent needed to determine eligibility. In these instances, in the application process providers obtain only the information that would affect a decision to accept or reject an applicant. Unless the condition of a disability is a factor in determining program eligibility, a provider has no need at the initial stage of the application process to make inquiries about the existence of a disability. If, however, the fact of a disability is a prime determinant of eligibility, a provider must from the start verify the existence of a disability condition as defined in the applicable housing program.

See also questions 81 and 145.

When the tentative decision is made to accept the applicant to the property's waiting list, the provider then inquires as to the applicant's need for a unit with accessibility modifications.

See questions 112 and 197 for discussions of procedures regarding applicants who are denied housing.

Later, when a unit becomes available and the applicant approaches the top of the waiting list, the provider will seek to obtain the more detailed information relevant to the determination of eligibility for an accessible unit and rent payment, including provision for any allowances.

166 For Federally Regulated Properties, What Additional Considerations Affect My Decisions When Applicants and Residents Request Changes to My Property and Procedures?

Would Granting These Requests Create Undue Financial and Administrative Burdens?

With respect to people with disabilities, reasonable modifications to dwelling units, or reasonable accommodations in rules and regulations, need not be made if they pose undue financial and administrative burdens to the property. Modifications must be made, however, up to the point at which further modifications would result in undue burdens. To sustain an argument that an undue burden would be created if a request is granted, providers must show real and credible evidence, such as the impairment of the ability of the property to provide essential services or to meet basic financial obligations.

Would Granting These Requests Result in a Fundamental Alteration of the Housing Program Under Which the Property Operates?

A fundamental change in the nature of the housing program, for example in the type or extent of services provided, is not required to accommodate the needs of a person with disabilities. An example of a request that would result in a fundamental alteration of a program if it were to be granted is a request from an applicant who suffers from a neurological disorder for 24 hour nursing care. The owner does not provide this type of medical service in the housing that he offers. Although he must allow the applicant to obtain the nursing care on his own, it would constitute a fundamental alteration in the nature of the program if the owner were required to provide this medical service at the owner's expense. Again, however, requests for accommodations to provide accessibility must be granted up to the point that further accommodations would result in a fundamental alteration in the nature of the housing program under which the property operates.

Limit Inquiries to What You Need To Know

Follow an objective process for reviewing eligibility for residency. Where the applicant has protected status and this status is related to eligibility under a federally regulated housing program (e.g., a mentally disabled person applying for a Section 811 property for the chronically mentally ill), use the least intrusive means available to verify the existence of a disability. Ask only those questions which tell you whether a person is eligible for admission. In this example, ask simply, does a disability, as defined in the program regulation, exist? Ask disability-related questions in a sensitive manner. Ask only at the point you need to know, not before.

167 "Independent Living" and Federally Regulated Properties

See question 106.

Housing providers may *not* make the ability to live independently a requirement for admission or continuing occupancy. Both HUD and RHS explicitly prohibit use of an "independent living" requirement.

168 Are There Any Occupancy Requirements for Accessible Units in Federally Assisted Housing?

See question 174.

Yes, the Section 504 regulations are specific on this issue. There are two requirements: one dealing with marketing and the other with priority for housing.

First, housing providers who have accessible units must adopt marketing approaches that ensure that eligible people with disabilities are aware of this availability. The marketing efforts should be focused on the populations that would benefit from the particular accessibility features offered at the property.

Housing providers should note that this marketing requirement is applicable regardless of the length of the waiting list.

See question 203. Second, accessible units are allocated using a special priority approach. When accessible units become available, the housing provider must offer the units in the following order (for properties that have appropriately elected to proceed under the 1992 Act):

- First, to current residents (of the property or of nearby properties under common ownership or control) having disabilities which would benefit from the available unit's accessibility features, but whose current units do not have such features. These households with disabilities should be ranked in the order indicated by the priorities and preferences included in the housing provider's resident selection plan.

- Second, to eligible households on the waiting list having disabilities which would benefit from the available unit's accessibility features. These households with disabilities should be ranked in the order indicated by the priorities and preferences included in the housing provider's resident selection plan.

- Third, to other eligible and qualified households on the waiting list (i.e. those without disabilities), in which case the provider is permitted (and advised) to require the household to agree, in writing, to transfer to an available non-accessible unit at the provider's request. HUD also strongly recommends that the lease permit the owner to transfer non-disabled family members to a non-accessible unit in the event the household member with disabilities moves out of an accessible unit, while other household members remain.

When an accessible unit becomes available, households that need the unit's accessibility features move to the top of the waiting list, ahead of households with earlier application dates.

This requirement implies that housing providers must determine, at or soon after the time of application, whether applicant households would benefit from accessibility features. Because this determination involves inquiry into the existence of disabilities, it is a sensitive process that providers will want to handle with care and tact, using standard written forms as opposed to less formal methods of communication.

169 Is Eligibility for Section 202 Properties Affected By the Type of "Handicap"?

Yes. In the case of Section 202 properties constructed prior to October 1991, HUD required owners to specify the target population which each property would serve, from among four distinct sub populations—elderly, physically handicapped, developmentally disabled, and chronically mentally ill. Note, however, that it is permissible to serve more than one of those categories, for example many properties serve the elderly and physically handicapped. HUD approval must be obtained if the property intends to serve another or different target population.

Consider a Section 202 assisted elderly housing property that was originally designed only for the elderly and the mobility impaired. In this example, the property would admit only those applicants who were "elderly" and/or "mobility impaired" as defined in the program regulations. Note that non-elderly persons with mobility impairments are eligible only for accessible units. Of course, applicants who meet the appropriate program definition would remain eligible regardless of any additional disabilities: an elderly person who is also vision impaired would be eligible, as would a mobility impaired person who is also chronically mentally ill.

170 Can Physician's Statements Be Required as a Condition of Eligibility, in Federally Regulated Housing?

See question 171 for a discussion of acceptable means of verification.

No. If the existence of a disability must be verified, a physician's statement is only one of a number of acceptable verification methods. HUD's Public Housing Occupancy Handbook 7465.1 in fact prohibits a Public Housing Authority from requiring verification from a physician when adequate verification is available from other sources.

HUD Handbook 4350.3 does not permit housing providers to require either a physical examination or any form of medical test as a condition of eligibility.[2]

171 What Are Acceptable Methods For Verifying Disability Status, in Federally Regulated Housing?

Experienced owners and managers recommend the use of verification methods that take into account the following guidelines:

- Providers should not inquire into the nature or extent of the disability. For instance, in determining eligibility, the provider need only establish that the applicant meets one of the applicable housing program definitions. It is not necessary or lawful to inquire into the precise nature or medical details of the disability.

- Given a choice of verification methods, choose the method that is least likely to reveal unwanted medical details. Receipt of SSI disability benefits is, by itself, proof of disability status. Note, however, that HUD's Occupancy Handbook 4350.3 provides guidelines for methods of verifying the existence of a disability and its suggested third-party verification form includes questions (requiring a "Yes" or "No" answer) whether the person has a physical disability, developmental disability or mental illness.[3]

Limit the verification to what is needed. For example, to determine the allowance for medical expenses, the housing provider needs only to establish the amount expected to be spent over the next twelve months, and to identify a neutral, qualified third party with whom the amount can be verified. There is no need to establish the medical details of the treatment plan.

---

2. *See 4350.3 REV1, Section 4-8.*
3. *See 4350.3, Section 2-31.E.2. and Exhibit 15-B.*

A requirement that third party verifications come only from a physician is not reasonable if other available sources (for example, a therapist or a counselor) are qualified to give the verification.

An approach used by one provider is to send a letter to a qualified healthcare professional listing the applicable housing program definitions of a person with disabilities, and asking the professional to indicate whether the applicant meets at least one of those definitions.

Similarly, HUD's suggested disability verification form (referred to above) recommends that the form contain the definition of "disability" or "handicap" applicable to the particular program under which the property operates and should ask the third party to identify any of the relevant definitions that apply to the individual by indicating "Yes" or "No."

172   In Federally Regulated Housing, May Managers Deny Applicants Who Display Threatening Behavior?

See question 107 for a discussion of this issue. Experienced providers advise that it may be more effective to concentrate on the issue of lease compliance, rather than the "direct threat" provision.

The Fair Housing Act and Section 504 include specific provisions that providers may properly decline applicants whose tenancy would pose a "direct threat to the health and safety of others" or would result in substantial physical damage to the property of others. RHS regulations also provide that applications for housing may be refused if the proposed tenancy would threaten the health and safety of other individuals or would result in substantial physical damage to the property of others, *unless the threat can be removed by applying a reasonable accommodation.* (Our emphasis).

Federally regulated housing leases impose a specific obligation on residents to observe standards of conduct that do not interfere with the right of others to the full and safe enjoyment of their dwelling and common facilities. The screening process to determine an applicant's qualification for residency must be based on the applicant's demonstrated ability and willingness to meet this and all other terms of the lease (for example: timely payment of rent, proper care of the dwelling, and adherence to reasonable rules and regulations).

If the application and screening materials, taken as a whole, do not support a conclusion that the terms of the lease will be complied with, the applicant may be rejected.

Experienced housing providers suggest that, when rejecting any applicant the standard rejection letter should inquire whether there is a reasonable accommodation that would make the applicant acceptable. It is critical to do this consistently, for all applicants, rather than selectively. In fact HUD's Occupancy Handbook 4350.3 provides that upon receiving written notice of the rejection of an application for housing all applicants may, within fourteen days, request a meeting to discuss the rejection.[4] Be aware that neither the Fair Housing Act nor Section 504 requires this formal rejection notification and appeals process, and so this requirement applies only to properties governed by the 4350.3.

Applicants who are rejected because they have histories of non-compliance with lease provisions may have disability conditions of which the housing provider is unaware. The rejection letter should offer all applicants the opportunity to request a reasonable accommodation that would enable the applicant to meet the terms of the lease. For example, if it is disclosed that an applicant's disruptive or threatening behavior is related to his or her failure to medicate, it may be a reasonable accommodation to accept the applicant if he or she can arrange for a live-in or visiting aide who would administer medication as needed. In order to meet this requirement, a housing provider might include language such as this in each rejection letter: "If you are a person with disabilities, and the reason your application is being denied is related to your disability, you may contact us not later than (date, time) to discuss whether a reasonable accommodation by us would allow your application to be acceptable."

If this discussion identifies a possible accommodation, the housing provider may require verification of the information and must then determine whether the accommodation is sufficient to overcome the reason for rejection of the application.

---

4. *4350.3 REV1, 4-9.C.2.(b)*

See question 78.   HUD's Occupancy Handbook 4350.3 provides that owners may include the consideration of "extenuating circumstances" in their screening criteria. If a property's screening practices allow for the consideration of extenuating circumstances, then the extent to which an applicant's disability has affected his or her application should be considered.[5] In addition, regardless of any such provision in a property's screening criteria, the Fair Housing Act requires all properties to make reasonable accommodations for people with disabilities.

173 Do Federally Regulated Housing Providers Have Any Special Requirements for Communicating With Individuals With Hearing or Vision Impairments?

Yes. Section 504 requires housing providers to communicate effectively with applicants, residents and members of the public. Housing providers must provide communications in alternative formats (for example, taped readings of the lease and related documents for vision-impaired persons; and printed copies of materials normally delivered orally, for hearing-impaired persons).

The choice of communication method should give primary consideration to the requests of individuals with handicaps. Local Independent Living Centers, or similar organizations, can provide information to assist in making these choices.

See question 147.   If the housing provider communicates with applicants or residents by telephone, then the provider must use a TDD [Telecommunications Device for the Deaf] for communicating with persons with hearing impairments, or an "equally effective" communication system or provide auxiliary aids, if necessary for communicating with persons with hearing impairments

RHS regulations also require housing providers to take appropriate steps to ensure effective communication with applicants and tenants with handicaps and disabilities including providing auxiliary aids (electronic, mechanical or personal assistance) where necessary.

---

5. *See 4350.3 REV1, 4-28.B.*

174 Do HUD and RHS Allow Accessible Apartments to Be Rented to Households Who Do Not Need the Accessibility Features?

In certain cases, yes.

HUD-Regulated Properties

In HUD-regulated housing, Handbook 4350.3 provides that accessible units must be assigned in accordance with the order set out in question 146.[6] However, if there are no current tenants or qualified applicants on the property's waiting list who have disabilities requiring the accessibility features of the particular unit the owner may offer the unit to another household and may incorporate into the lease an agreement that the tenant will move to a non-accessible unit of the proper size within the same property when one becomes available. The lease provision should state who would pay for the cost of the move.

RHS-Regulated Properties

Handbook 1930-C[7] provides that units may be rented to households not needing the accessibility features, when:

- No applicants needing the features have applied for housing, and management has made a diligent effort to identify such individuals;[8] and,

- The non-disabled resident agrees to transfer to another apartment when one becomes available and someone has applied who needs the accessibility features. The leasing section of the RHS Handbook includes a lease clause for this situation.[9] If a non-disabled applicant refuses to sign this lease clause , the housing provider would not be required to rent to that household. If an applicant who signs the lease clause later refuses to move, this would constitute grounds to terminate the tenancy or not renew a lease.

---

6. *See 4350.3, REV1, 2-32.C.*
7. *Exhibit B, VI, D, 2, g*
8. *Handbook HB-2-3560, Appendix 1, 3560.158(d)(3)(ii)*
9. *Handbook HB-2-3560, Appendix 1, 3560.156(c)(16)*

175   What Is a "Live-In Care Attendant"?

Both RHS and HUD[10] use the same definition. A Live-in Care Attendant is a person who resides with an individual with disabilities or an individual who is elderly, and who:

- Is determined to be essential to the care and well-being of the person;

- Is not obligated for the support of the person; and

- Would not be living in the unit except to provide the necessary supportive services.

A family member may serve as a Live-in Care Attendant, so long as the above criteria are met.

176   Does RHS Require That Residents Be Able to Sign Their Own Legal Documents?

The Rural Housing Service allows guardian signatures in all RHS programs as a reasonable accommodation for applicants with disabilities.[11]

177   Does RHS Impose Special "Reasonable Accommodation" Requirements?

The RHS Handbook addresses the issue of reasonable accommodation:

- The Project Management Plan must discuss reasonable accommodations in communication, and how the borrower will make reasonable accommodation decisions.[12]

- The borrower must establish and enforce rules to ensure there are reasonable accommodations to persons who are handicapped or disabled.[13]

---

10. HUD 4350.3 REV1, 3-6.E.3.(a).
11. See USDA Memo dated September 9, 1996
12. Handbook HB-2-3560, Appendix 1, 3560.156(c)(16)
13. Handbook HB-2-3560, Appendix 1, 3560.156(c)(16)

- The management section of the Handbook[14] restates fair housing law in regard to reasonable accommodations, stressing parking and service/companion animal issues — two of the most common that managers must face.

178 Does RHS Impose Special "Reasonable Modification" Requirements?

On September 9, 1996, RHS issued a memo addressing accessibility issues. The Memo restates Section 504 policies and adds Agency guidance in dealing with modifications. In part, the Memo reads:

"The borrower is responsible for bearing the expense of providing these modifications or other special accommodations, needed by individuals with handicaps unless the borrower can show that it would cause an 'undue financial burden.' If this position is taken, the borrower must prove such a burden exists in order to receive a waiver from the Secretary. Reserve funds and subsequent loans, operating funds, and alternative funding sources such as State and local Agencies, must be considered. Most modifications are not expected to create undue financial/administrative burdens. All waiver reports will be reviewed for approval by the Secretary of Agriculture."

Section 504 requires that at least 5 percent of units in buildings constructed after June 1982 meet the Uniform Federal Accessibility Standards. The September 9, 1999 RHS Memorandum clarifies that on RHS-regulated properties these accessible units must be comparable in variety (of unit types) to other units at the property.

In addition, the Project Management Plan must discuss any planned accessibility modifications.[15]q

---

14. *Handbook HB-2-3560, Appendix 1, 3560.156(c)(16)*
15. *See HB-3560, Section 3660.102(b)(1)(xii)*

Chapter Nineteen: Fair Housing Marketing and Admissions Issues for Federally-Assisted Properties

179   Affirmative Fair Housing Marketing Requirements

Affirmative Fair Housing Marketing Plans (AFHMPs) are required for many rental properties and programs that receive FHA mortgage insurance, HUD subsidies, RHS loans, and/or RHS subsidies. The purpose of the plan is to attract renters of all groups regardless of sex, disability and familial status. Some examples of multifamily programs that require the submission of a written AFHMP are:

- Multifamily mortgage insurance under sections 207, 220, 221(d)(3) and 221(d)(4) of the National Housing Act.

- Project-based Section 8 Rental Assistance.

- Housing for the Elderly or Handicapped under Section 202 of the Housing Act.

- Projects financed under Section 515 of the Housing Act of 1949 by the Farmers Home Administration Section 8 Set-Aside.

- Supportive housing for people with disabilities under Section 811 of the National Housing Act.

Many other affordable housing programs do not require a formal plan, but are required to conceive, implement and maintain records of their affirmative marketing efforts with special emphasis on attracting the "least likely to apply" segment of the population.

The AFHMP process is particularly concerned with attracting those segments of the population that are considered "least likely to apply" for housing at the particular property unless special outreach efforts are implemented. For example, if the property is built in an area with a low percentage of African-Americans, they would be judged "least likely to apply," and the AFHMP rules would require additional "outreach" to African-American applicants. This outreach might include advertising in media that reach that audience predominately, and/or provision of marketing materials to organizations that serve that community. Some populations may require marketing materials in a language other than English.

AFHMPs will frequently need to include a description of outreach efforts geared towards people with disabilities in the community because they are considered among those 'least likely to apply' without special outreach activities.

An AFHMP must include a description of the methods to be used to market the property generally and the special outreach steps that will be taken to attract the group(s) identified as being least likely to apply. Details about the commercial media to be used in advertising must also be included in the plan. AFHMP's must also include a description of the indicators that will be used to measure the success of the marketing program and an indication of the capacity to provide staff with training on fair housing laws.

The AFHMP must be submitted to HUD for approval on HUD Form 935.2. The same form is used for HUD and for RHS, although RHS uses slightly different instructions.

HUD Requirements

HUD's approval of the Plan is based on whether HUD determines that the Plan has the potential to effectively attract renters from all groups within the property's market area, whether it has the potential to attract people with disabilities and their families to the property, whether the provider has identified the appropriate group(s) for special outreach and whether the fair housing training proposed for the management staff is adequate.

On HUD-regulated properties the Plan must be available for public inspection in the property office. The Plan remains in force throughout the life of a multifamily project mortgage and/or the period for which a HUD subsidy is provided.

HUD requires that the AFHMP be updated every five years or when the local Community Development jurisdiction's Consolidated Plan is updated.[1]

Rural Housing Service Requirements

In the case of RHS properties the approved AFHMP must be posted at the property's project site, rental office or any other location where tenant applications are received.[2]

---

1. *See HUD 4350.3 REV1, Section 4-12F*
2. *Handbook HB-2-3560, Appendix 1, 3650.104(b)(3)*

Unlike HUD, RHS requires that Affirmative Marketing be updated as needed[3] even if there are an adequate number of applicants on the property's waiting list.

Unlike HUD, RHS does NOT allow waiting lists to be closed. Applications must always be made available.[4]

180   Additional RHS Requirements for Fair Housing Posters

RHS requires two additional items to be displayed in the property's rental office:

- The "And Justice for All" poster (a USDA Equal Opportunity Non-Discrimination poster);[5] and,

- A copy of the Applicant/Tenant 1944-L Grievance and Appeal Procedure.[6]

If the rental office is not on site these items must be displayed in a prominent place on the site.

See question 52.   All properties, regardless of federal financial assistance are required to display the Fair Housing poster.

181   What Household Types Are Eligible for RHS "Family" Properties?

Occupancy[7] requirements for the four different types of RHS properties are as follows:

- Family housing may be occupied by any combination of elderly, disabled or handicapped and/or non-elderly, non-disabled or non-handicapped tenants including tenants with minor children,

---

3. *Handbook HB-2-3560 Appendix 1*
4. *7CFR 3560.104*
5. *Available at http://www.usda.gov/da/cr/just.htm*
6. *7CFR 3560.160*
7. *Handbook HB-2-3560, Appendix 1, 3560.155*

- Elderly housing must be occupied by tenants who are elderly, disabled and/or handicapped but children cannot be excluded if they are members of the elderly household,

- Mixed housing (i.e. housing that consists of specific units in a project designated as family housing and other units designated as elderly housing units) occupancy is governed by the family and elderly housing provisions, and

- Congregate housing and group homes must be occupied by elderly, handicapped or disabled persons or families requiring the supportive services provided by the property.

The RHS definition of familial status clarifies who has protection from familial status discrimination under the Fair Housing Act.[8]

182 Does RHS Allow Single Person Households to Be Admitted to RHS "Family" Housing?

Yes, in fact "Household" is defined as "One or more persons who maintain or will maintain residency in one rental or cooperative unit."[9] However, RHS typically does not allow single person households to be admitted to units larger than one bedroom.

Although RHS has always permitted reasonable accommodations for single applicants with disabilities, or pregnant women, who may request two bedrooms, an Administrative Notice (AN #3285) was issued on August 30, 1996 reminding housing providers not to permanently fill large units with single people. Managers are permitted some flexibility if warranted by market conditions such as high vacancy or physical conditions such as projects with all two bedroom units.

---

8. *See Handbook HB-2-3560 Appendix 1 3560.11*
9. *See Handbook HB-2-3560 Appendix 1 3560.11 Definitions*

183 Criminal Background Checks on Federally Regulated Properties

See also questions 9 and 58.

Increasingly, managers are using criminal background checks as an additional screening measure. In fact, HUD guidelines contained in PIH Notice 96-16 require Public Housing Authorities to review the police and court records of public housing applicants as well as members of their household aged 16 and older. It is proposed to extend this requirement to all Section 8 assisted housing programs as well as other HUD assisted housing programs such as Section 221(d)(3) BMIR programs, Section 202 and 811 programs and Section 236 programs. In the case of properties that can exercise their own discretion on whether or not to use such screening, the use of criminal background checks will be considered discriminatory *only* if the basis of checking or not checking is related to membership in a protected class. For example, such checks are only performed on applicants who are members of a particular race.

Managers must get written consent from an applicant before undertaking a criminal background check. Even where such checks are required (for example in public housing) the tenant or applicant must give his or her signed consent for this information to be released. In the case of public housing the PHA may obtain criminal conviction records directly from the National Crime Information Center, police departments and other law enforcement agencies under the Housing Opportunity Program Extension Act. Owners of project-based section 8 properties may request the PHA in whose jurisdiction the property is located to obtain criminal records and perform determinations for the owner regarding screening applicants. The owner is not entitled to receive the record or be informed of its contents. Instead, the PHA uses the record to screen or evaluate the applicant based on the owner's standards of admission and occupancy.

When refusing admission to an applicant because of information uncovered by a criminal background check, the applicant should be told-in writing-the reason for the refusal.

184 Non-Citizens in Federally-Assisted Properties

Certain federally-assisted properties are required to establish the citizenship/immigration status of applicants for purposes of determining eligibility for their housing programs.

Applicants are eligible to live in, and benefit from federal rental assistance in, housing built under the following programs, regardless of their citizenship or immigration status: Section 221(d)(3) BMIR, Section 202 PAC, Section 202 PRAC, Section 811 PRAC, and other Section 202 units without Rent Supplement or Section 8.

For all other HUD multifamily programs (including Section 236, 202 with Section 8, other project-based Section 8, RAP, and Rent Supplement), federal rental assistance may be provided only to U.S. citizens and eligible noncitizens.

To be eligible for assistance, eligible noncitizens must:

Sign a declaration that they have eligible immigrant status;

Sign a verification consent form authorizing the property manager to verify the family members' eligible immigrant status; and

Have one of the documents approved by the Department of Homeland Security (DHS), as shown in HUD Handbook 4350.3, Figure 3-4, documenting their eligible status.[10]

Mixed Families

In cases when some members of a family are citizens or eligible noncitizens, while others are ineligible noncitizens, the family is termed a "mixed family." Mixed families may be eligible for "prorated assistance" at properties with citizenship/immigration restrictions. However, until the citizenship status of all family members has been determined, the family is eligible for 'conditional assistance.'

Conditional Admission Pending Completion of Verification

Families that have submitted the requested information regarding their immigration status in a timely manner may not have their assistance delayed if the process of verifying that information is still ongoing. In other words, "if a unit is avail-

---

10. See Handbook 3-12(B)(4).

able, the family has come to the top of the waiting list," the family is otherwise eligible and meets the property's screening policies, and "at least one member of the family has submitted the required documentation in a timely manner and has been determined to be eligible, the owner must offer the family a unit and provide conditional assistance to those family members whose documents were received on time. Owners continue to provide full assistance to such families until information establishing the immigration status of any remaining non-citizen family members has been received and verified."

Residence Without Assistance

Under certain circumstances, households composed entirely of ineligible noncitizen may be able to live in a HUD-assisted property even though they are not eligible to receive rental assistance such as Section 8 (because the rental assistance program has citizenship/immigration restrictions). In these situations, ineligible noncitizens do not receive "assistance," but rather pay the full rent (i.e., the Section 236 "market" rent, or the Section 8 "contract" rent).

Chapter Twenty: Familial Status Issues in Federally-Assisted Housing

185   Verifications and Familial Status

In assisted housing, the size and composition of an applicant's household may often determine:

- Eligibility for residence at the particular property;

- The amount of rent that should be charged; and/or

- The size of the rental unit that will be offered to the applicant.

As a general rule housing providers must verify any factor that is a prime determinant of eligibility for federal housing assistance at the property. This may include verifying the familial status of applicants for such housing by ascertaining, for example whether the applicant:

- Has children;

- Is pregnant; or,

- Is in the process of obtaining custody of a minor child.

See question 143 for further information on the eligibility of single persons for the Section 8 program.

Single people are eligible for admission to assisted housing, so that the fact that an applicant is childless, unmarried or intends to live alone would not be a disqualifying factor. However, it may limit the applicant's choice of the size unit to be assigned.

The methods for verifying familial status must be reasonable. Acceptable verification methods are minimally intrusive, and are geared towards obtaining the basic information necessary for ensuring compliance with the program requirements under which the particular property operates.

Housing providers are advised to interpret the above guidelines as prohibiting the requirement of any type of medical examination or medical test (including sonogram testing) in order to verify any familial status assertions. The RHS Handbook 1930-C does, however, provide that a housing provider can request written verification of an unborn child by a doctor or other qualified third party.

See question 186 for a discussion of "minimum occupancy standards."
As stated at the outset, the size and composition of an applicant's family will often determine the size of the unit that will be offered to the applicant, because assisted properties typically apply minimum occupancy standards for each type of unit at the property.

See question 69.
HUD's Occupancy Handbook 4350.3 advises housing providers against making recommendations or decisions about whether or not to rent based on the housing provider's opinion of what is in a family's best interest.

HUD's Occupancy Handbooks (Public Housing 7465.1 and Assisted Housing 4350.3) also require that in establishing occupancy standards owners comply with State and local laws as well as the Handbooks. Owners therefore need to familiarize themselves with these codes.

186 What Is a "Minimum Occupancy Standard"

A minimum occupancy standard is a requirement that each unit type be occupied by a minimum number of persons. The purpose of a minimum occupancy standard is to make the best use of scarce affordable housing resources by avoiding under-utilization of affordable rental units.

Owners of HUD-assisted housing are required to adopt minimum occupancy standards. These standards must be both acceptable to HUD and defensible under the Fair Housing Act (i.e. should not have the effect of discriminating against any members of a protected class). HUD's guidelines for occupancy standards are contained in Handbook 4350.3 for Subsidized Multifamily Housing Programs and in Handbook 7465.1 REV 2 for Lower Income Public Housing Programs. RHS properties must also adopt occupancy standards that will prevent overcrowding (maximum occupancy standards) and under-utilization (minimum occupancy standards). Guidelines for these properties are contained in Handbook Number 1930-C.

Minimum occupancy standard violations ("under-utilized" apartments) typically occur when members of a family leave the household, resulting in too few household members for the apartment size. HUD's Occupancy Guidelines for Subsidized

Multifamily Housing Programs (Handbook 4350.3) provides that if a unit becomes under-utilized because of changes in household composition, the owner should require the family to move to an appropriate size unit within the property when one becomes available.

RHS guidance also provides that when a unit becomes over-crowded or under-utilized and there is a waiting list for a unit of that size the tenant must move to another unit of adequate size when one becomes available. If the tenant refuses to move or there is no such available unit, the tenant must vacate the property within a reasonable time period. All RHS lease agreements must contain these provisions.

187 May Housing Providers Base Minimum Occupancy Standards on the Age, Gender or Relationship of Household Members?

No. Minimum occupancy standards should refer to the number of persons required to occupy a unit of a particular size and not the gender of the occupants or their age or relationship to each other.[1] HUD permits housing providers to consider age, gender and family relationship in certain circumstances. However, the *initial* designation of the number of persons required for each unit size should be based strictly on the number of persons in the household.

Following this initial designation, the housing provider might offer a larger unit, based on legitimate need including accommodation of a disability, and/or considerations of gender, age or relationship of household members. For example it may be reasonable for young siblings of the opposite sex to share a bedroom. To require adolescent siblings of the opposite sex to do so may not be. Therefore, despite a minimum occupancy standard that provides for a minimum of five persons in a three bedroom unit, in the case of a household that consists of two parents and two adolescent children of the opposite sex,

---

1. *United States v. Cherrywood Associates, LP, et al., CIV-00-0724-S-BLW (D. Idaho)*

offering them a three bedroom unit on request may be appropriate. It is most unlikely that a policy of this type would be found to unfairly exclude or discriminate against families with children.

HUD's Handbooks require that occupancy standards:

- Must consider the number of persons residing (or anticipated to reside) in the unit.

- May consider, when it is reasonable to do so, both the number of persons in the household and the relationship and sex of those persons.

- Should consider the size of the unit as well as the size and number of bedrooms.

Regarding relationship and gender, HUD allows owners to use the following guidelines in developing occupancy standards:

- Children of the same sex may share a bedroom.

- No more than two persons would be required to occupy a bedroom.

- Unrelated adults would not be required to share a bedroom.

- Persons of the opposite sex (other than spouses) would not be required to share a bedroom.

- A child may share a bedroom with a parent if the parent so wishes. However, children, with the possible exception of infants, would not be required to share a bedroom with persons of different generations, including their parents.

Persons of different generations (for example, grandparent and grandchild) would not be required to share a bedroom.

These approaches suggested above (initial assignment based strictly on number of persons, then giving the household an opportunity to request a larger or smaller unit size) will allow families to choose smaller or larger units, depending on the family's needs. For example a family may request a smaller unit on the basis that they wish their two children of the opposite sex to share a bedroom, even though the property's occupancy policy does not require this.

RHS Guidelines can be found at Handbook HB-2-3560 Appendix 1 Section 3560.155, Assignment of Rental Units and Occupancy Policies.

188 Typical Minimum and Maximum Occupancy Standards for Federally-Assisted Housing

In assisted housing, most households can be appropriately accommodated at two persons per bedroom. However, some households will need larger units as a result of disability, privacy considerations, or other legitimate needs. Generally, providers can choose to adopt a flexible standard, where applicant households choose from, at most, two unit types; or a more structured standard, where applicant households are assigned to one unit type but allowed to request one additional bedroom if there are acceptable reasons for this request.

An Example of a Flexible Occupancy Standard

Number of Bedrooms	Number of Persons	
	Minimum	Maximum
One	1	2
Two	2	4
Three	3	6
Four	5	8
The applicant may select any unit size for which the household size qualifies.		

An Example of a Structured Occupancy Standard

Number of Bedrooms	Number of Persons	
	Minimum	Maximum
Zero	1	1
One	1	2
Two	3	4
Three	5	6
Four	7	8
The applicant household may request a unit that is one bedroom larger than shown above, on the basis of disability, or other acceptable reasons.		

Some housing providers choose to disregard infants for purposes of their occupancy standards. For example, two adults and an infant would qualify as two persons and may therefore, on request, be accommodated in a one-bedroom unit.

189 How Should Assisted Housing Providers Determine Overcrowding and Under-utilization, for Purposes of Making Needed Unit Transfers?

Written occupancy standards for assisted housing should address the issues of overcrowding (i.e., too many occupants in a unit) and under-utilization (i.e., too few occupants to justify the governmental subsidy for the unit size).

Overcrowding

Typical occupancy standards provide that households with more than the maximum number of occupants are considered overcrowded and are subject to unit transfer. HUD requires that occupancy standards must comply with all reasonable State or local restrictions regarding the maximum number of occupants permitted to occupy a dwelling. Failure to abide by these standards will constitute a breach of both HUD's directives and local and State laws. RHS has amended their policy[2] on assignment of rental units. Over- or under-housed households must be offered an available unit before it may be offered to a household on the waiting list. A household is over-housed if there are more occupants than bedrooms; a household is under-housed as defined by the property's occupancy standards.

Under-utilization Typical occupancy standards provide that households with less than the required minimum number of occupants are considered to be under-utilizing the governmental subsidy and are subject to unit transfer. This will usually occur where, during the course of the tenancy, there is a reduction in the number of family members occupying the unit. However, transfer is generally not required if at the inception of the tenancy the unit size, though inappropriate, was approved by management. This typically happens when, to reduce vacancies at the property, a family is allowed to rent a unit that is larger than appropriate for the family size. In those circumstances it is advisable that the lease provide that the family will move to a smaller unit when another family needs the larger one and a suitable smaller unit is available.

It is generally recommended that the property's standard lease provide that, in the event of overcrowding or under-utilization, the household will agree to be transferred to a unit of the appropriate size if and when one becomes available. In the case of under-utilization, HUD's Occupancy Handbook 4350.3 provides that if a family refuses to move, after a request to do so has been made, they may be permitted to remain in the unit but must pay the HUD-approved market rent for it. If they fail to pay this rent they may be evicted. HUD's model lease for multifamily subsidized housing also provides that families in under-utilized units will be required to move within thirty days of the availability of an appropriate size unit or pay the market rent for the occupied unit.

---

2. *HB-2-3560 Appendix 1*

190 May Federally Assisted Elderly Properties Exclude Children?

Also see question 72 for exceptions which allow certain properties to exclude children.

Generally the answer is no, even though under the Fair Housing Act certain elderly properties are exempted from the provisions prohibiting discrimination on the ground of familial status. HUD has determined that the various mortgage insurance programs under the National Housing Act (including Sections 220, 221, 223, 231, and 236) contain a statutory requirement that households with children may not be excluded. Thus, properties developed under these mortgage insurance programs may not exclude otherwise eligible households with children (for example, a grandchild living with grandparent), even if the property was designed and operated for the elderly. Excluding households with children from residing at those elderly properties will therefore constitute illegal discrimination on the basis of familial status.

For federally assisted properties for the elderly not developed under these mortgage insurance programs (for instance, Section 202 properties, or Section 8 with a non-FHA-insured mortgage loan), the Fair Housing Act also prohibits discrimination against families with children.

191 What Is the RHS Definition of "Elderly"?

"Elderly" is defined[3] as a person who is at least 62 years old. The term elderly also means individuals with handicaps or disabilities regardless of age as separately defined in the Handbook. RHS therefore uses the term "elderly" to denote a person of age 62 or older, a person with a handicap, or a person with a disability. "Elderly family" means a household where the tenant, cotenant, member *or* co-member is at least 62 years old, disabled or handicapped.

Like HUD, in RHS practice the term "elderly" does not refer to a nonelderly household that includes an "elderly" relative or a handicapped child. The tenant, cotenant, member or co-mem-

---

3. *Handbook HB 2-3560, Appendix 1, 3560.11*

ber (in the case of cooperative housing) must be either elderly or disabled or handicapped.

The RHS definition of tenant/cotenant is a person who has signed a lease and is, or will be, an occupant of a unit.

192 Are Any RHS Elderly Programs Exempted from the Familial Status Requirements of the Fair Housing Act?

The practical answer is no. On July 9, 1991, the Department of Housing and Urban Development determined that certain RHS housing qualified for an exemption from the prohibitions against discrimination because of familial status. The exemption applies to housing RHS designated as housing for the elderly or handicapped under the Section 515 program. The determination stated that the exemption would exist as long as the units are rented to elderly persons in accordance with the terms of the program.

However, if an owner were to prevent an elderly household from occupying a unit because the household included children, the owner would not be complying with the terms of the program. Therefore, although the exemption is technically available, in actual practice owners may not exclude elderly households with children from RHS properties.

193 Are Families With Children Eligible for Admission to RHS Elderly Housing?

Yes, provided that the household otherwise qualifies. The RHS provisions governing elderly housing state that non-elderly household members are permitted when the tenant or co-tenant is an elderly person.[4] In addition, leases on RHS properties are forbidden from including any provisions that prohibit occupancy by families with children under 18, and this applies also to housing designated as elderly.

---

4. *Handbook HB 2-3560, Appendix 1, 3560.152(c)(1)(ii)*

Chapter Twenty-One: "Mixed Population" Issues in Federally-Assisted Elderly Properties

194 Which Properties May Provide a Preference for the Elderly?

See question 207 for further information on these programs.

There are various types of properties that are entitled to limit admission to the elderly, for example:

- Section 202 Supportive Housing for the Elderly properties; and,

- Section 221 and 236 properties, if they were originally designed for occupancy by elderly families.

See question 130 for a definition of "mixed populations."

In addition, the Housing and Community Development Act allows certain properties to provide a preference for the elderly while still admitting other categories of residents in certain circumstances.

Properties that are entitled to provide this preference for the elderly are properties that were originally designed primarily for occupancy by the elderly and were assisted in their construction or substantial rehabilitation under one of the following Section 8 programs:

- The Section 8 New Construction Program;

- The Section 8 Substantial Rehabilitation Program;

- The State Housing Agencies Program (if it involves new construction and substantial rehabilitation);

- The New Construction Set-Aside for Section 515 Rural Rental Housing Program; and

- The Section 8 Housing Assistance Program for the Disposition of HUD-Owned Projects (if it involves substantial rehabilitation).

It does not matter if a property is FHA-insured or not. If a property falls within one of the above programs and it was originally designed primarily for occupancy by households whose head, spouse or sole member is elderly, the manner in which the property was financed is irrelevant: the property is entitled to provide a preference for the elderly.

195   Providing a Preference for the Elderly

Before an owner elects to provide a preference to the elderly, it must first determine whether the property was originally designed primarily for occupancy by the elderly. The 1992 Act is silent on how an owner should make this determination.

Regulations made under the Act,[1] on the other hand, do provide detailed guidance on this issue. These regulations do not cover housing developed under Section 202, Section 221, or Section 236.

Documentation Requirement

The regulations include a "documentation requirement." This requirement states that elections be supported by at least one "primary source" or at least two "secondary sources."

Primary Sources

Primary sources include, but are not necessarily limited to, identification of the project (or portion of the project) as serving elderly families in one of the following documents:

- The application in response to the notice of funding availability;

- The terms of the notice of funding availability under which the application was solicited;

- The regulatory agreement;

- The loan commitment;

- The bid invitation;

- The owner's management plan; or

- Any other underwriting or financial document collected at or before the loan closing.

Secondary Sources

Secondary sources include, but are not necessarily limited to:

- Lease records from the earliest two years of occupancy, for which records are available, showing that occupancy had been restricted primarily to households whose head, spouse or sole member was 62 or older;

- Evidence that services for the elderly have been provided, such as services funded by the Older Americans Act,

---

1. *These Regulations may be found at 24 CFR Ch. VIII 880.612a.*

transportation to senior citizen centers, or programs coordinated with the Area Agency on Aging;

- Property unit mix with a higher percentage of efficiencies and one bedroom units (HUD's Occupancy Handbook 4350.3 for Subsidized Multifamily Housing provides that virtually no project with a large percentage of two, three or four bedroom units would have been approved as elderly housing); or

- Any other relevant type of historical data.

When to Consider Secondary Sources

If there is a conflict between primary sources as to the original design of the property, the owner may not make an election by relying on primary sources alone. In these cases, the owner would need to rely on secondary sources to support the election. In other words, two or more secondary sources may be used in the event that primary sources conflict or do not provide clear evidence of the property's original design.

If there are no primary or secondary sources to support a claim that the property was originally designed to house the elderly, then a preference for the elderly cannot be given and all eligible applicants must be housed in the appropriate order.

Making the Election

See question 197 for set-aside requirements.

Once an owner has determined that the property was originally designed primarily for occupancy by the elderly, the owner does not have to take any formal action. The owner need only revise the property's admissions policies to reflect the election and to conform to the statutory and regulatory provisions. In certain circumstances the owner will also need to inform non-elderly applicants who are currently on the property's waiting list that an election in favor of the elderly has been made and that it may affect their application for housing. This notification is required if all the units set-aside for non-elderly disabled families are already occupied or if there are no units required to be set-aside for non-elderly disabled families. In either of those events there may be a reduced likelihood that the property will be able to accommodate non-elderly applicants. Nevertheless, such applicants should not be removed from the waiting list.

196 Is HUD Approval of the Preference for the Elderly Necessary?

See question 195.

No. However, an owner, if challenged on its election, must be able to produce evidence that supports the property's eligibility to give a preference in admission to the elderly. In addition, HUD may, at any time, review and determine whether the property was eligible to elect such a preference.

It would be wise for an owner to keep all documentation which was relied upon in making the election. That way, if challenged, it will be a simple matter to produce the requisite proof.

197 Calculating The Set-Aside

The law requires that even if a property has elected to exercise a preference for elderly families the owner must nevertheless reserve a specific number of units in the property for occupancy by applicants with disabilities who are neither elderly nor near-elderly (i.e., aged 50 and over but less than 62).

See the next page for an example.

To calculate the number of units which must be set aside for this purpose, the owner must first determine the percentage of units occupied by households whose head, spouse or sole member was a person with disabilities under the age of 50, as of January 1, 1992, and as of October 28, 1992. The owner should take the number of units corresponding to the higher percentage and compare it to 10 percent of the property's units. Whichever of those two numbers is less is the number of units that must be reserved or set aside for non-elderly disabled occupants. In no case will the maximum number of units that must be set aside exceed ten percent of the total number of units at the property.[2]

---

2. *24 CFR 880.612a (c) (1)*

Example: Calculating the Set-Aside

You have a 100-unit property. On January 1, 1992, 5 percent of the units were occupied by residents with disabilities under the age of 50; on October 28, 1992, 12% of the units were occupied by such residents. Since the October 28 percentage is greater, you take that number, which amounts to 12 units and compare it to 10 percent of the property's units (10 units). The lesser of those two numbers is the number of units required to be set aside; in this case, 10 units or 10%.

In contrast, if on January 1, 1992, 6% of the units were occupied by residents with disabilities under the age of 50, and 8% of the units so occupied on October 28, 1992. Taking the larger of the two numbers, 8% which amounts to 8 units, and comparing it to 10 percent of the units, (10 units), the number of units required to be set aside would be 8% or 8 units. Of course, if no units were occupied by non-elderly disabled persons at January 1, 1992 or October 28, 1992 then no set-aside will have to be made.

Keep a copy of the resident profile information, and a written record of the set-aside calculation in the property's permanent files.

198 Can I Exceed the Set-Aside?

The number of units required to be reserved at any time is the number calculated based on the formula outlined in question 197.

Yes. The regulations state that the calculated set-aside is only a minimum. Accordingly, an owner may, at any time, reserve a higher number of units for the non-elderly disabled. Moreover, the regulations state that an owner who chooses to exceed its set-aside is not obligated to continue to provide that greater number of units.

However, an owner who chooses to exceed its set-aside and then return to the set-aside should not do so in a manner that could be interpreted as discriminatory. For example: choosing to exceed the set-aside for physically disabled non-elderly applicants but returning to the set-aside when a person with mental disabilities applies or reaches the top of the property's waiting list.

199 How Do I Comply With the Set-Aside Requirements When Filling Vacant Units?

In selecting applicants to fill vacant units, the owner must first determine the property's current position in relation to set-aside compliance. If the required number of non-elderly disabled units has been set aside the owner would fill vacancies with elderly families. If the required number of non-elderly disabled units has not been set-aside the owner must fill vacant units, up to the number of units required to be set aside, with households whose head, spouse, or sole member of the household is under age 50 and is a person with disabilities.

It is advisable to perform the set-aside compliance calculation each time an admission decision is made, and to retain a written record of the calculation in the property's permanent files.

200 What Is the Secondary Preference for Near-Elderly?

In certain circumstances, properties that provide a preference to the elderly may elect to provide a secondary preference to "near elderly" people with disabilities (i.e., 50 and over but less than 62) rather than "younger" or non-elderly people with disabilities. This preference can be exercised in two situations:

- If all the units required to be set-aside for non-elderly disabled families have been so reserved, and there are no elderly applicants on the waiting list then near-elderly disabled applicants can be housed in units reserved for the elderly; or

- If the number of units set-aside for non-elderly disabled residents exceeds the number of applicants eligible for those units then near-elderly disabled applicants can be housed in those units.

201 What If There Are an Insufficient Number of Applicants?

What if the owner elects to exercise the secondary preference, but there are an insufficient number of near-elderly disabled applicants to fill existing vacancies?

See question 195.   If there are an insufficient number of applicants in any of the three preferential categories (i.e., elderly, non-elderly disabled and near-elderly disabled) to fill vacant units, the units are to be made generally available to any otherwise eligible applicant on the waiting list, without regard to the preferences or reservation of units provided by Title VI of the Housing and Community Development Act of 1992 and its regulations. Likewise, if the secondary preference is not exercised and there are no elderly or non-elderly disabled applicants on the waiting list, vacant units can be made available to any eligible applicant on the waiting list. This is why applicants who do not fall within any of the preferential categories should be kept on the waiting list. They may still become eligible for housing if there are vacancies at the property and no preferential category applicants on the waiting list.

See question 179.   However, the regulations provide that before an owner determines that there are an insufficient number of applicants who qualify for housing on the basis of any of the preferences, the owner must first conduct marketing and other outreach activities in accordance with applicable HUD regulations to attract such applicants. These regulations require an owner to undertake marketing of the property in accordance with the property's HUD-approved Affirmative Fair Housing Marketing Plan and all Fair Housing and Equal Opportunity requirements.

202   What If Non-Elderly Residents With Disabilities Exceed the Set-Aside?

If the number of units occupied by non-elderly disabled residents exceeds the number of units required to be set-aside for them, the owner may *not* evict those residents in order to reduce the number of units occupied by the non-elderly disabled to the level of the required set-aside. However, as non-elderly people with disabilities move out of the property, the owner may fill the resulting vacancies with elderly families until the number of units occupied by the non-elderly disabled is equivalent to the property's set-aside.

It is also forbidden for owners to evict residents solely because the units occupied by them are required in order to satisfy any preference or set-aside.

203   Resident Selection for Accessible Units

There is nothing explicit in either the regulations or the statute governing how owners should fill accessible units. However, the preamble to the regulations makes it clear that an accessible unit need not be given to the next applicant on the waiting list in need of such a unit if that applicant would not otherwise be eligible pursuant to the new preference provisions.

An Example of Unit-Assignment

A property has reached its set-aside. The only applicant in need of an available accessible unit is under age 50. The property may, nevertheless, make the unit available to an elderly person (or a near-elderly disabled person if there are no elderly on the waiting list) not in need of the unit's accessibility features.

See also questions 168 and 160.

With respect to projects or parts of projects for the elderly, to be eligible for a unit made accessible under Section 504 of the Rehabilitation Act of 1973 the applicant must meet the definition of elderly family and a member of the household must have a disability requiring the accessibility features of the unit.[3] On the other hand, the preamble also states that when the next eligible applicant for a unit (elderly or non-elderly) is in need of an accessible unit and the only available unit is not accessible, then the owner is to accommodate the applicant either by:

- Making that unit accessible; or

- By transferring a resident who is living in an accessible unit and who does not need the unit's features.

---

3. *HUD Occupancy Handbook 4350.3, REV1, Section 2-6*

204   What If I Make No Election?

If an owner does not elect to give a preference to the elderly, the property must continue to admit residents pursuant to the rules in effect prior to the 1992 Act. In other words, applicants with disabilities who are under age 62 must be admitted as if they were elderly, without any numerical limitation.

205   Do I Have To Decide Now?

No. Although it is not specifically stated, the regulations seem to sanction the making of the election to give a preference to the elderly at any time the owner chooses. Consequently, an election could be made in the future.

Regardless of when the owner makes the election, in determining the number of units to be set aside for the non-elderly disabled occupancy levels by that group as at January 1, and October 28, 1992 must be calculated as set out above.

206   Other Mixed Populations Provisions

Two changes are noteworthy: the definition of "elderly families," and the status of older properties designed for elderly occupancy.

This definition applies to all Section 8 programs, not just to those listed in question 194.

Prior to the 1992 Act, the term "elderly families" was defined under the United States Housing Act of 1937 to include people with disabilities under the age of 62. It was this inclusion that required the admission of non-elderly people with disabilities into Section 8 elderly properties prior to the 1992 Act. The 1992 Act changed the definition of "elderly families" to mean specifically those whose head, spouse or sole member is age 62 or older.

Title VI of the 1992 Act also made it clear that properties designed exclusively for elderly occupancy under the 236 program, the 221(d)(3) BMIR program and the 202 program may continue to restrict occupancy to elderly families in accordance with the rules, standards, and agreements governing occupancy in such housing in effect at the time of the development of the housing. Owners should carefully study these rules, standards and agreements, to determine whether their property was designed exclusively for elderly occupancy.

207 Are Federally Assisted Apartment Properties for the Elderly Allowed to Exclude or Restrict the Number of Non-Elderly People With Disabilities?

Yes, certain programs permit the number of non-elderly disabled admissions to be restricted, and other programs permit the total exclusion of the non-elderly disabled. Following is a summary of the most common programs and what they permit:

Section 202 and Section 811

Section 202 Supportive Housing Program for the Elderly provides capital advances to finance the construction and rehabilitation of structures that will serve as supportive housing for very low-income elderly persons (i.e. aged 62 years and older) and provides rent subsidies for the properties to help make them affordable. Prior to the 1990 National Affordable Housing Act applicants for admission to Section 202 housing had to be either elderly or disabled and low-income. This Act established a separate program for people with disabilities—"Supportive Housing Program for Persons with Disabilities" - under Section 811.

See question 142 for additional information.

Occupancy in Section 202 housing is open to any household comprised of one or more persons (one of whom is 62 years of age or more at the time of initial occupancy), if other occupancy requirements are met (for example, income eligibility). On the question of adult children of Section 202 residents coming to live with an elderly parent, HUD has ruled that this is permissible only where the adult children are essential for the care or well being of the elderly tenant(s).[4] In other words adult children qualify for occupancy only as long as the tenant requires their supportive services.

Under Section 811, owners are expressly authorized, with HUD approval, to limit occupancy of housing for persons with disabilities to people with similar disabilities.

---

4. *HUD Directive Number 97-74 "Occupancy In Section 202/8 Projects*

Sections 221 and 236

Admission to Section 221 and 236 properties may be restricted to the group of persons for whom the property was originally designed, for example all Section 236 programs were originally designed to serve either families or the elderly and/or disabled. Section 221 properties were originally intended to serve the elderly or disabled.

Under Section 658 of the Housing and Community Development Act an owner of any federally assisted project that was designed for occupancy by elderly families may continue to restrict occupancy in such projects to elderly families. Section 221 and 236 properties fall within that provision and can limit admission exclusively to elderly families (i.e., families whose heads or their spouses or whose sole members are at least 62 years of age) if that was the group for whom the project was specifically designed. The non-elderly disabled would have no rights of admission to such elderly properties. If, however, the properties have accessible units then non-elderly disabled persons requiring accessibility features must be accepted for accessible units. In order to identify the particular group that the project was intended to serve, HUD's Occupancy Handbook 4350.3 provides that documents such as regulatory agreements, loan commitment papers and financial documents should be examined. If the property documentation is unclear as to the category of persons intended to be served and the owner claims that it was originally designed for the elderly, then approval must be obtained from the Director of Housing Management. It is recommended that owners obtain the advice of counsel before designating their property as one designed for exclusive occupancy by a particular class.

208   Does RHS Allow People With Disabilities, Under the Age of 62, to Live in Elderly Housing?

Yes. Under RHS Handbook 1930-C the term "Elderly" includes individuals with handicaps or disabilities regardless of age and "Elderly family" includes a household where the tenant, cotenant, member or co-member is disabled or handicapped. It is also expressly provided that elderly housing must be occupied by tenants who are either elderly, disabled and/or handi-capped.

209 Does RHS Allow Non-Elderly or Non-Disabled Persons to Live in Elderly Housing?

Yes, non-elderly and non-disabled persons may live in elderly housing but they do so as part of the elderly or disabled tenant's household and they may not themselves be the qualifying tenant. Elderly housing must be occupied by tenants who are elderly, disabled and/or handicapped but not at the exclusion of children if they are members of the "elderly" household.[5] In addition, surviving members of an elderly, disabled and/or handicapped tenant's household may continue occupancy of the elderly unit even if they are not elderly, disabled or handicapped.[6]

---

5. *Handbook HB 2-3560, Appendix 1, 3560.152(c)(1)(ii)*
6. *Handbook HB 2-3560, Appendix 1, 3560.158(d)*

SUBCHAPTER A—FAIR HOUSING

PART 100—DISCRIMINATORY CONDUCT UNDER THE FAIR HOUSING ACT

AUTHORITY: 42 U.S.C. 3535(d), 3600–3620.

SOURCE: 54 FR 3283, Jan. 23, 1989, unless otherwise noted.

Subpart A—General

§ 100.1   Authority.

This regulation is issued under the authority of the Secretary of Housing and Urban Development to administer and enforce title VIII of the Civil Rights Act of 1968, as amended by the Fair Housing Amendments Act of 1988 (the Fair Housing Act).

§ 100.5   Scope.

(a) It is the policy of the United States to provide, within constitutional limitations, for fair housing throughout the United States. No person shall be subjected to discrimination because of race, color, religion,

§ 100.10

sex, handicap, familial status, or national origin in the sale, rental, or advertising of dwellings, in the provision of brokerage services, or in the availability of residential real estate-related transactions.

(b) This part provides the Department's interpretation of the coverage of the Fair Housing Act regarding discrimination related to the sale or rental of dwellings, the provision of services in connection therewith, and the availability of residential real estate-related transactions.

(c) Nothing in this part relieves persons participating in a Federal or Federally-assisted program or activity from other requirements applicable to buildings and dwellings.

§ 100.10 Exemptions.

(a) This part does not:

(1) Prohibit a religious organization, association, or society, or any non-profit institution or organization operated, supervised or controlled by or in conjunction with a religious organization, association, or society, from limiting the sale, rental or occupancy of dwellings which it owns or operates for other than a commercial purpose to persons of the same religion, or from giving preference to such persons, unless membership in such religion is restricted because of race, color, or national origin;

(2) Prohibit a private club, not in fact open to the public, which, incident to its primary purpose or purposes, provides lodgings which it owns or operates for other than a commercial purpose, from limiting the rental or occupancy of such lodgings to its members or from giving preference to its members;

(3) Limit the applicability of any reasonable local, State or Federal restrictions regarding the maximum number of occupants permitted to occupy a dwelling; or

(4) Prohibit conduct against a person because such person has been convicted by any court of competent jurisdiction of the illegal manufacture or distribution of a controlled substance as defined in section 102 of the Controlled Substances Act (21 U.S.C. 802).

(b) Nothing in this part regarding discrimination based on familial status

applies with respect to housing for older persons as defined in subpart E of this part.

(c) Nothing in this part, other than the prohibitions against discriminatory advertising, applies to:

(1) The sale or rental of any single family house by an owner, provided the following conditions are met:

(i) The owner does not own or have any interest in more than three single family houses at any one time.

(ii) The house is sold or rented without the use of a real estate broker, agent or salesperson or the facilities of any person in the business of selling or renting dwellings. If the owner selling the house does not reside in it at the time of the sale or was not the most recent resident of the house prior to such sale, the exemption in this paragraph (c)(1) of this section applies to only one such sale in any 24-month period.

(2) Rooms or units in dwellings containing living quarters occupied or intended to be occupied by no more than four families living independently of each other, if the owner actually maintains and occupies one of such living quarters as his or her residence.

§ 100.20 Definitions.

The terms Department, Fair Housing Act, and Secretary are defined in 24 CFR part 5.

Aggrieved person includes any person who—

(a) Claims to have been injured by a discriminatory housing practice; or

(b) Believes that such person will be injured by a discriminatory housing practice that is about to occur.

Broker or *Agent* includes any person authorized to perform an action on behalf of another person regarding any matter related to the sale or rental of dwellings, including offers, solicitations or contracts and the administration of matters regarding such offers, solicitations or contracts or any residential real estate-related transactions.

Discriminatory housing practice means an act that is unlawful under section 804, 805, 806, or 818 of the Fair Housing Act.

Office of Asst. Secy., Equal Opportunity, HUD   **§ 100.50**

Dwelling means any building, structure or portion thereof which is occupied as, or designed or intended for occupancy as, a residence by one or more families, and any vacant land which is offered for sale or lease for the construction or location thereon of any such building, structure or portion thereof.

Familial status means one or more individuals (who have not attained the age of 18 years) being domiciled with—

(a) A parent or another person having legal custody of such individual or individuals; or

(b) The designee of such parent or other person having such custody, with the written permission of such parent or other person.

The protections afforded against discrimination on the basis of familial status shall apply to any person who is pregnant or is in the process of securing legal custody of any individual who has not attained the age of 18 years.

Handicap is defined in § 100.201.

Person includes one or more individuals, corporations, partnerships, associations, labor organizations, legal representatives, mutual companies, joint-stock companies, trusts, unincorporated organizations, trustees, trustees in cases under title 11 U.S.C., receivers, and fiduciaries.

Person in the business of selling or renting dwellings means any person who:

(a) Within the preceding twelve months, has participated as principal in three or more transactions involving the sale or rental of any dwelling or any interest therein;

(b) Within the preceding twelve months, has participated as agent, other than in the sale of his or her own personal residence, in providing sales or rental facilities or sales or rental services in two or more transactions involving the sale or rental of any dwelling or any interest therein; or

(c) Is the owner of any dwelling designed or intended for occupancy by, or occupied by, five or more families.

State means any of the several states, the District of Columbia, the Commonwealth of Puerto Rico, or any of the territories and possessions of the United States.

[54 FR 3283, Jan. 23, 1989, as amended at 61 FR 5205, Feb. 9, 1996]

Subpart B—Discriminatory Housing Practices

§ 100.50 Real estate practices prohibited.

(a) This subpart provides the Department's interpretation of conduct that is unlawful housing discrimination under section 804 and section 806 of the Fair Housing Act. In general the prohibited actions are set forth under sections of this subpart which are most applicable to the discriminatory conduct described. However, an action illustrated in one section can constitute a violation under sections in the subpart. For example, the conduct described in § 100.60(b)(3) and (4) would constitute a violation of § 100.65(a) as well as § 100.60(a).

(b) It shall be unlawful to:

(1) Refuse to sell or rent a dwelling after a *bona fide* offer has been made, or to refuse to negotiate for the sale or rental of a dwelling because of race, color, religion, sex, familial status, or national origin, or to discriminate in the sale or rental of a dwelling because of handicap.

(2) Discriminate in the terms, conditions or privileges of sale or rental of a dwelling, or in the provision of services or facilities in connection with sales or rentals, because of race, color, religion, sex, handicap, familial status, or national origin.

(3) Engage in any conduct relating to the provision of housing which otherwise makes unavailable or denies dwellings to persons because of race, color, religion, sex, handicap, familial status, or national origin.

(4) Make, print or publish, or cause to be made, printed or published, any notice, statement or advertisement with respect to the sale or rental of a dwelling that indicates any preference, limitation or discrimination because of race, color, religion, sex, handicap, familial status, or national origin, or an intention to make any such preference, limitation or discrimination.

(5) Represent to any person because of race, color, religion, sex, handicap, familial status, or national origin that a dwelling is not available for sale or rental when such dwelling is in fact available.

629

§ 100.60

(6) Engage in blockbusting practices in connection with the sale or rental of dwellings because of race, color, religion, sex, handicap, familial status, or national origin.

(7) Deny access to or membership or participation in, or to discriminate against any person in his or her access to or membership or participation in, any multiple-listing service, real estate brokers' association, or other service organization or facility relating to the business of selling or renting a dwelling or in the terms or conditions or membership or participation, because of race, color, religion, sex, handicap, familial status, or national origin.

(c) The application of the Fair Housing Act with respect to persons with handicaps is discussed in subpart D of this part.

§ 100.60 Unlawful refusal to sell or rent or to negotiate for the sale or rental.

(a) It shall be unlawful for a person to refuse to sell or rent a dwelling to a person who has made a *bona fide* offer, because of race, color, religion, sex, familial status, or national origin or to refuse to negotiate with a person for the sale or rental of a dwelling because of race, color, religion, sex, familial status, or national origin, or to discriminate against any person in the sale or rental of a dwelling because of handicap.

(b) Prohibited actions under this section include, but are not limited to:

(1) Failing to accept or consider a *bona fide* offer because of race, color, religion, sex, handicap, familial status, or national origin.

(2) Refusing to sell or rent a dwelling to, or to negotiate for the sale or rental of a dwelling with, any person because of race, color, religion, sex, handicap, familial status, or national origin.

(3) Imposing different sales prices or rental charges for the sale or rental of a dwelling upon any person because of race, color, religion, sex, handicap, familial status, or national origin.

(4) Using different qualification criteria or applications, or sale or rental standards or procedures, such as income standards, application require-

24 CFR Subtitle B, Ch. I (4-1-08 Edition)

ments, application fees, credit analysis or sale or rental approval procedures or other requirements, because of race, color, religion, sex, handicap, familial status, or national origin.

(5) Evicting tenants because of their race, color, religion, sex, handicap, familial status, or national origin or because of the race, color, religion, sex, handicap, familial status, or national origin of a tenant's guest.

§ 100.65 Discrimination in terms, conditions and privileges and in services and facilities.

(a) It shall be unlawful, because of race, color, religion, sex, handicap, familial status, or national origin, to impose different terms, conditions or privileges relating to the sale or rental of a dwelling or to deny or limit services or facilities in connection with the sale or rental of a dwelling.

(b) Prohibited actions under this section include, but are not limited to:

(1) Using different provisions in leases or contracts of sale, such as those relating to rental charges, security deposits and the terms of a lease and those relating to down payment and closing requirements, because of race, color, religion, sex, handicap, familial status, or national origin.

(2) Failing or delaying maintenance or repairs of sale or rental dwellings because of race, color, religion, sex, handicap, familial status, or national origin.

(3) Failing to process an offer for the sale or rental of a dwelling or to communicate an offer accurately because of race, color, religion, sex, handicap, familial status, or national origin.

(4) Limiting the use of privileges, services or facilities associated with a dwelling because of race, color, religion, sex, handicap, familial status, or national origin of an owner, tenant or a person associated with him or her.

(5) Denying or limiting services or facilities in connection with the sale or rental of a dwelling, because a person failed or refused to provide sexual favors.

Office of Asst. Secy., Equal Opportunity, HUD § 100.75

§ 100.70 Other prohibited sale and rental conduct.

(a) It shall be unlawful, because of race, color, religion, sex, handicap, familial status, or national origin, to restrict or attempt to restrict the choices of a person by word or conduct in connection with seeking, negotiating for, buying or renting a dwelling so as to perpetuate, or tend to perpetuate, segregated housing patterns, or to discourage or obstruct choices in a community, neighborhood or development.

(b) It shall be unlawful, because of race, color, religion, sex, handicap, familial status, or national origin, to engage in any conduct relating to the provision of housing or of services and facilities in connection therewith that otherwise makes unavailable or denies dwellings to persons.

(c) Prohibited actions under paragraph (a) of this section, which are generally referred to as unlawful steering practices, include, but are not limited to:

(1) Discouraging any person from inspecting, purchasing or renting a dwelling because of race, color, religion, sex, handicap, familial status, or national origin, or because of the race, color, religion, sex, handicap, familial status, or national origin of persons in a community, neighborhood or development.

(2) Discouraging the purchase or rental of a dwelling because of race, color, religion, sex, handicap, familial status, or national origin, by exaggerating drawbacks or failing to inform any person of desirable features of a dwelling or of a community, neighborhood, or development.

(3) Communicating to any prospective purchaser that he or she would not be comfortable or compatible with existing residents of a community, neighborhood or development because of race, color, religion, sex, handicap, familial status, or national origin.

(4) Assigning any person to a particular section of a community, neighborhood or development, or to a particular floor of a building, because of race, color, religion, sex, handicap, familial status, or national origin.

(d) Prohibited activities relating to dwellings under paragraph (b) of this section include, but are not limited to:

(1) Discharging or taking other adverse action against an employee, broker or agent because he or she refused to participate in a discriminatory housing practice.

(2) Employing codes or other devices to segregate or reject applicants, purchasers or renters, refusing to take or to show listings of dwellings in certain areas because of race, color, religion, sex, handicap, familial status, or national origin, or refusing to deal with certain brokers or agents because they or one or more of their clients are of a particular race, color, religion, sex, handicap, familial status, or national origin.

(3) Denying or delaying the processing of an application made by a purchaser or renter or refusing to approve such a person for occupancy in a cooperative or condominium dwelling because of race, color, religion, sex, handicap, familial status, or national origin.

(4) Refusing to provide municipal services or property or hazard insurance for dwellings or providing such services or insurance differently because of race, color, religion, sex, handicap, familial status, or national origin.

§ 100.75 Discriminatory advertisements, statements and notices.

(a) It shall be unlawful to make, print or publish, or cause to be made, printed or published, any notice, statement or advertisement with respect to the sale or rental of a dwelling which indicates any preference, limitation or discrimination because of race, color, religion, sex, handicap, familial status, or national origin, or an intention to make any such preference, limitation or discrimination.

(b) The prohibitions in this section shall apply to all written or oral notices or statements by a person engaged in the sale or rental of a dwelling. Written notices and statements include any applications, flyers, brochures, deeds, signs, banners, posters, billboards or any documents used with respect to the sale or rental of a dwelling.

§ 100.80

(c) Discriminatory notices, statements and advertisements include, but are not limited to:

(1) Using words, phrases, photographs, illustrations, symbols or forms which convey that dwellings are available or not available to a particular group of persons because of race, color, religion, sex, handicap, familial status, or national origin.

(2) Expressing to agents, brokers, employees, prospective sellers or renters or any other persons a preference for or limitation on any purchaser or renter because of race, color, religion, sex, handicap, familial status, or national origin of such persons.

(3) Selecting media or locations for advertising the sale or rental of dwellings which deny particular segments of the housing market information about housing opportunities because of race, color, religion, sex, handicap, familial status, or national origin.

(4) Refusing to publish advertising for the sale or rental of dwellings or requiring different charges or terms for such advertising because of race, color, religion, sex, handicap, familial status, or national origin.

(d) 24 CFR part 109 provides information to assist persons to advertise dwellings in a nondiscriminatory manner and describes the matters the Department will review in evaluating compliance with the Fair Housing Act and in investigating complaints alleging discriminatory housing practices involving advertising.

§ 100.80 **Discriminatory representations on the availability of dwellings.**

(a) It shall be unlawful, because of race, color, religion, sex, handicap, familial status, or national origin, to provide inaccurate or untrue information about the availability of dwellings for sale or rental.

(b) Prohibited actions under this section include, but are not limited to:

(1) Indicating through words or conduct that a dwelling which is available for inspection, sale, or rental has been sold or rented, because of race, color, religion, sex, handicap, familial status, or national origin.

(2) Representing that covenants or other deed, trust or lease provisions

which purport to restrict the sale or rental of dwellings because of race, color, religion, sex, handicap, familial status, or national origin preclude the sale of rental of a dwelling to a person.

(3) Enforcing covenants or other deed, trust, or lease provisions which preclude the sale or rental of a dwelling to any person because of race, color, religion, sex, handicap, familial status, or national origin.

(4) Limiting information, by word or conduct, regarding suitably priced dwellings available for inspection, sale or rental, because of race, color, religion, sex, handicap, familial status, or national origin.

(5) Providing false or inaccurate information regarding the availability of a dwelling for sale or rental to any person, including testers, regardless of whether such person is actually seeking housing, because of race, color, religion, sex, handicap, familial status, or national origin.

§ 100.85 **Blockbusting.**

(a) It shall be unlawful, for profit, to induce or attempt to induce a person to sell or rent a dwelling by representations regarding the entry or prospective entry into the neighborhood of a person or persons of a particular race, color, religion, sex, familial status, or national origin or with a handicap.

(b) In establishing a discriminatory housing practice under this section it is not necessary that there was in fact profit as long as profit was a factor for engaging in the blockbusting activity.

(c) Prohibited actions under this section include, but are not limited to:

(1) Engaging, for profit, in conduct (including uninvited solicitations for listings) which conveys to a person that a neighborhood is undergoing or is about to undergo a change in the race, color, religion, sex, handicap, familial status, or national origin of persons residing in it, in order to encourage the person to offer a dwelling for sale or rental.

(2) Encouraging, for profit, any person to sell or rent a dwelling through assertions that the entry or prospective entry of persons of a particular race, color, religion, sex, familial status, or national origin, or with handicaps, can or will result in undesirable

consequences for the project, neighborhood or community, such as a lowering of property values, an increase in criminal or antisocial behavior, or a decline in the quality of schools or other services or facilities.

§ 100.90 Discrimination in the provision of brokerage services.

(a) It shall be unlawful to deny any person access to or membership or participation in any multiple listing service, real estate brokers' organization or other service, organization, or facility relating to the business of selling or renting dwellings, or to discriminate against any person in the terms or conditions of such access, membership or participation, because of race, color, religion, sex, handicap, familial status, or national origin.

(b) Prohibited actions under this section include, but are not limited to:

(1) Setting different fees for access to or membership in a multiple listing service because of race, color, religion, sex, handicap, familial status, or national origin.

(2) Denying or limiting benefits accruing to members in a real estate brokers' organization because of race, color, religion, sex, handicap, familial status, or national origin.

(3) Imposing different standards or criteria for membership in a real estate sales or rental organization because of race, color, religion, sex, handicap, familial status, or national origin.

(4) Establishing geographic boundaries or office location or residence requirements for access to or membership or participation in any multiple listing service, real estate brokers' organization or other service, organization or facility relating to the business of selling or renting dwellings, because of race, color, religion, sex, handicap, familial status, or national origin.

Subpart C—Discrimination in Residential Real Estate-Related Transactions

§ 100.110 Discriminatory practices in residential real estate-related transactions.

(a) This subpart provides the Department's interpretation of the conduct that is unlawful housing discrimination under section 805 of the Fair Housing Act.

(b) It shall be unlawful for any person or other entity whose business includes engaging in residential real estate-related transactions to discriminate against any person in making available such a transaction, or in the terms or conditions of such a transaction, because of race, color, religion, sex, handicap, familial status, or national origin.

§ 100.115 Residential real estate-related transactions.

The term residential *real estate-related transactions* means:

(a) The making or purchasing of loans or providing other financial assistance—

(1) For purchasing, constructing, improving, repairing or maintaining a dwelling; or

(2) Secured by residential real estate; or

(b) The selling, brokering or appraising of residential real property.

§ 100.120 Discrimination in the making of loans and in the provision of other financial assistance.

(a) It shall be unlawful for any person or entity whose business includes engaging in residential real estate-related transactions to discriminate against any person in making available loans or other financial assistance for a dwelling, or which is or is to be secured by a dwelling, because of race, color, religion, sex, handicap, familial status, or national origin.

(b) Prohibited practices under this section include, but are not limited to, failing or refusing to provide to any person, in connection with a residential real estate-related transaction, information regarding the availability of loans or other financial assistance, application requirements, procedures or standards for the review and approval of loans or financial assistance, or providing information which is inaccurate or different from that provided others, because of race, color, religion, sex, handicap, familial status, or national origin.

§ 100.125 Discrimination in the purchasing of loans.

(a) It shall be unlawful for any person or entity engaged in the purchasing of loans or other debts or securities which support the purchase, construction, improvement, repair or maintenance of a dwelling, or which are secured by residential real estate, to refuse to purchase such loans, debts, or securities, or to impose different terms or conditions for such purchases, because of race, color, religion, sex, handicap, familial status, or national origin.

(b) Unlawful conduct under this section includes, but is not limited to:

(1) Purchasing loans or other debts or securities which relate to, or which are secured by dwellings in certain communities or neighborhoods but not in others because of the race, color, religion, sex, handicap, familial status, or national origin of persons in such neighborhoods or communities.

(2) Pooling or packaging loans or other debts or securities which relate to, or which are secured by, dwellings differently because of race, color, religion, sex, handicap, familial status, or national origin.

(3) Imposing or using different terms or conditions on the marketing or sale of securities issued on the basis of loans or other debts or securities which relate to, or which are secured by, dwellings because of race, color, religion, sex, handicap, familial status, or national origin.

(c) This section does not prevent consideration, in the purchasing of loans, of factors justified by business necessity, including requirements of Federal law, relating to a transaction's financial security or to protection against default or reduction of the value of the security. Thus, this provision would not preclude considerations employed in normal and prudent transactions, provided that no such factor may in any way relate to race, color, religion, sex, handicap, familial status or national origin.

§ 100.130 Discrimination in the terms and conditions for making available loans or other financial assistance.

(a) It shall be unlawful for any person or entity engaged in the making of loans or in the provision of other finan-

cial assistance relating to the purchase, construction, improvement, repair or maintenance of dwellings or which are secured by residential real estate to impose different terms or conditions for the availability of such loans or other financial assistance because of race, color, religion, sex, handicap, familial status, or national origin.

(b) Unlawful conduct under this section includes, but is not limited to:

(1) Using different policies, practices or procedures in evaluating or in determining creditworthiness of any person in connection with the provision of any loan or other financial assistance for a dwelling or for any loan or other financial assistance which is secured by residential real estate because of race, color, religion, sex, handicap, familial status, or national origin.

(2) Determining the type of loan or other financial assistance to be provided with respect to a dwelling, or fixing the amount, interest rate, duration or other terms for a loan or other financial assistance for a dwelling or which is secured by residential real estate, because of race, color, religion, sex, handicap, familial status, or national origin.

§ 100.135 Unlawful practices in the selling, brokering, or appraising of residential real property.

(a) It shall be unlawful for any person or other entity whose business includes engaging in the selling, brokering or appraising of residential real property to discriminate against any person in making available such services, or in the performance of such services, because of race, color, religion, sex, handicap, familial status, or national origin.

(b) For the purposes of this section, the term appraisal means an estimate or opinion of the value of a specified residential real property made in a business context in connection with the sale, rental, financing or refinancing of a dwelling or in connection with any activity that otherwise affects the availability of a residential real estate-related transaction, whether the appraisal is oral or written, or transmitted formally or informally.

Office of Asst. Secy., Equal Opportunity, HUD § 100.143

The appraisal includes all written comments and other documents submitted as support for the estimate or opinion of value.

(c) Nothing in this section prohibits a person engaged in the business of making or furnishing appraisals of residential real property from taking into consideration factors other than race, color, religion, sex, handicap, familial status, or national origin.

(d) Practices which are unlawful under this section include, but are not limited to, using an appraisal of residential real property in connection with the sale, rental, or financing of any dwelling where the person knows or reasonably should know that the appraisal improperly takes into consideration race, color, religion, sex, handicap, familial status or national origin.

§ 100.140   General rules.

(a) *Voluntary self-testing and correction.* The report or results of a self-test a lender voluntarily conducts or authorizes are privileged as provided in this subpart if the lender has taken or is taking appropriate corrective action to address likely violations identified by the self-test. Data collection required by law or any governmental authority (federal, state, or local) is not voluntary.

(b) *Other privileges.* This subpart does not abrogate any evidentiary privilege otherwise provided by law.

[62 FR 66432, Dec. 18, 1997]

§ 100.141   Definitions.

As used in this subpart:

Lender means a person who engages in a residential real estate-related lending transaction.

Residential real estate-related lending transaction means the making of a loan:

(1) For purchasing, constructing, improving, repairing, or maintaining a dwelling; or

(2) Secured by residential real estate.

Self-test means any program, practice or study a lender voluntarily conducts or authorizes which is designed and used specifically to determine the extent or effectiveness of compliance with the Fair Housing Act. The self-test must create data or factual information that is not available and cannot be derived from loan files, applica-

tion files, or other residential real estate-related lending transaction records. Self-testing includes, but is not limited to, using fictitious credit applicants (testers) or conducting surveys of applicants or customers, nor is it limited to the pre-application stage of loan processing.

[62 FR 66432, Dec. 18, 1997]

§ 100.142   Types of information.

(a) The privilege under this subpart covers:

(1) The report or results of the self-test;

(2) Data or factual information created by the self-test;

(3) Workpapers, draft documents and final documents;

(4) Analyses, opinions, and conclusions if they directly result from the self-test report or results.

(b) The privilege does not cover:

(1) Information about whether a lender conducted a self-test, the methodology used or scope of the self-test, the time period covered by the self-test or the dates it was conducted;

(2) Loan files and application files, or other residential real estate-related lending transaction records (e.g., property appraisal reports, loan committee meeting minutes or other documents reflecting the basis for a decision to approve or deny a loan application, loan policies or procedures, underwriting standards, compensation records) and information or data derived from such files and records, even if such data has been aggregated, summarized or reorganized to facilitate analysis.

[62 FR 66432, Dec. 18, 1997]

§ 100.143   Appropriate   corrective action.

(a) The report or results of a self-test are privileged as provided in this subpart if the lender has taken or is taking appropriate corrective action to address likely violations identified by the self-test. Appropriate corrective action is required when a self-test shows it is more likely than not that a violation occurred even though no violation was adjudicated formally.

(b) A lender must take action reasonably likely to remedy the cause and effect of the likely violation and must:

(1) Identify the policies or practices that are the likely cause of the violation, such as inadequate or improper lending policies, failure to implement established policies, employee conduct, or other causes; and

(2) Assess the extent and scope of any likely violation, by determining which areas of operation are likely to be affected by those policies and practices, such as stages of the loan application process, types of loans, or the particular branch where the likely violation has occurred. Generally, the scope of the self-test governs the scope of the appropriate corrective action.

(c) Appropriate corrective action may include both prospective and remedial relief, except that to establish a privilege under this subpart:

(1) A lender is not required to provide remedial relief to a tester in a self-test;

(2) A lender is only required to provide remedial relief to an applicant identified by the self-test as one whose rights were more likely than not violated;

(3) A lender is not required to provide remedial relief to a particular applicant if the statute of limitations applicable to the violation expired before the lender obtained the results of the self-test or the applicant is otherwise ineligible for such relief.

(d) Depending on the facts involved, appropriate corrective action may include, but is not limited to, one or more of the following:

(1) If the self-test identifies individuals whose applications were inappropriately processed, offering to extend credit if the applications were improperly denied; compensating such persons for any damages, both out-of-pocket and compensatory;

(2) Correcting any institutional policies or procedures that may have contributed to the likely violation, and adopting new policies as appropriate;

(3) Identifying, and then training and/or disciplining the employees involved;

(4) Developing outreach programs, marketing strategies, or loan products to serve more effectively the segments of the lender's market that may have

been affected by the likely violation; and

(5) Improving audit and oversight systems to avoid a recurrence of the likely violations.

(e) Determination of appropriate corrective action is fact-based. Not every corrective measure listed in paragraph (d) of this section need be taken for each likely violation.

(f) Taking appropriate corrective action is not an admission by a lender that a violation occurred.

[62 FR 66432, Dec. 18, 1997]

§ 100.144 Scope of privilege.

The report or results of a self-test may not be obtained or used by an aggrieved person, complainant, department or agency in any:

(a) Proceeding or civil action in which a violation of the Fair Housing Act is alleged; or

(b) Examination or investigation relating to compliance with the Fair Housing Act.

[62 FR 66432, Dec. 18, 1997]

§ 100.145 Loss of privilege.

(a) The self-test report or results are not privileged under this subpart if the lender or person with lawful access to the report or results:

(1) Voluntarily discloses any part of the report or results or any other information privileged under this subpart to any aggrieved person, complainant, department, agency, or to the public; or

(2) Discloses the report or results or any other information privileged under this subpart as a defense to charges that a lender violated the Fair Housing Act; or

(3) Fails or is unable to produce self-test records or information needed to determine whether the privilege applies.

(b) Disclosures or other actions undertaken to carry out appropriate corrective action do not cause the lender to lose the privilege.

[62 FR 66432, Dec. 18, 1997]

§ 100.146 Limited use of privileged information.

Notwithstanding § 100.145, the self-test report or results may be obtained

Office of Asst. Secy., Equal Opportunity, HUD   **§ 100.201**

and used by an aggrieved person, applicant, department or agency solely to determine a penalty or remedy after the violation of the Fair Housing Act has been adjudicated or admitted. Disclosures for this limited purpose may be used only for the particular proceeding in which the adjudication or admission is made. Information disclosed under this section remains otherwise privileged under this subpart.

[62 FR 66433, Dec. 18, 1997]

§ 100.147 Adjudication.

An aggrieved person, complainant, department or agency that challenges a privilege asserted under § 100.144 may seek a determination of the existence and application of that privilege in:

(a) A court of competent jurisdiction; or

(b) An administrative law proceeding with appropriate jurisdiction.

[62 FR 66433, Dec. 18, 1997]

§ 100.148 Effective date.

The privilege under this subpart applies to self-tests conducted both before and after January 30, 1998, except that a self-test conducted before January 30, 1998 is not privileged:

(a) If there was a court action or administrative proceeding before January 30, 1998, including the filing of a complaint alleging a violation of the Fair Housing Act with the Department or a substantially equivalent state or local agency; or

(b) If any part of the report or results were disclosed before January 30, 1998 to any aggrieved person, complainant, department or agency, or to the general public.

[62 FR 66433, Dec. 18, 1997]

Subpart D—Prohibition Against Discrimination Because of Handicap

§ 100.200 Purpose.

The purpose of this subpart is to effectuate sections 6 (a) and (b) and 15 of the Fair Housing Amendments Act of 1988.

§ 100.201 Definitions.

As used in this subpart:

Accessible, when used with respect to the public and common use areas of a building containing covered multifamily dwellings, means that the public or common use areas of the building can be approached, entered, and used by individuals with physical handicaps. The phrase *readily accessible to and usable by* is synonymous with accessible. A public or common use area that complies with the appropriate requirements of ANSI A117.1–1986 or a comparable standard is *accessible* within the meaning of this paragraph.

Accessible route means a continuous unobstructed path connecting accessible elements and spaces in a building or within a site that can be negotiated by a person with a severe disability using a wheelchair and that is also safe for and usable by people with other disabilities. Interior accessible routes may include corridors, floors, ramps, elevators and lifts. Exterior accessible routes may include parking access aisles, curb ramps, walks, ramps and lifts. A route that complies with the appropriate requirements of ANSI A117.1–1986 or a comparable standard is an *accessible route.*

ANSI A117.1–1986 means the 1986 edition of the American National Standard for buildings and facilities providing accessibility and usability for physically handicapped people. This incorporation by reference was approved by the Director of the Federal Register in accordance with 5 U.S.C. 552(a) and 1 CFR part 51. Copies may be obtained from American National Standards Institute, Inc., 1430 Broadway, New York, NY 10018. Copies may be inspected at the Department of Housing and Urban Development, 451 Seventh Street, SW., room 10276, Washington, DC, or at the National Archives and Records Administration (NARA). For information on the availability of this material at NARA, call 202–741–6030, or go to: *http://www.archives.gov/federal_register/code_of_federal_regulations/ibr_locations.html.*

Building means a structure, facility or portion thereof that contains or serves one or more dwelling units.

Building entrance on an accessible route means an accessible entrance to a building that is connected by an accessible route to public transportation

637

stops, to accessible parking and passenger loading zones, or to public streets or sidewalks, if available. A building entrance that complies with ANSI A117.1–1986 or a comparable standard complies with the requirements of this paragraph.

Common use areas means rooms, spaces or elements inside or outside of a building that are made available for the use of residents of a building or the guests thereof. These areas include hallways, lounges, lobbies, laundry rooms, refuse rooms, mail rooms, recreational areas and passageways among and between buildings.

Controlled substance means any drug or other substance, or immediate precursor included in the definition in section 102 of the Controlled Substances Act (21 U.S.C. 802).

Covered multifamily dwellings means buildings consisting of 4 or more dwelling units if such buildings have one or more elevators; and ground floor dwelling units in other buildings consisting of 4 or more dwelling units.

Dwelling unit means a single unit of residence for a family or one or more persons. Examples of dwelling units include: a single family home; an apartment unit within an apartment building; and in other types of dwellings in which sleeping accommodations are provided but toileting or cooking facilities are shared by occupants of more than one room or portion of the dwelling, rooms in which people sleep. Examples of the latter include dormitory rooms and sleeping accommodations in shelters intended for occupancy as a residence for homeless persons.

Entrance means any access point to a building or portion of a building used by residents for the purpose of entering.

Exterior means all areas of the premises outside of an individual dwelling unit.

First occupancy means a building that has never before been used for any purpose.

Ground floor means a floor of a building with a building entrance on an accessible route. A building may have more than one ground floor.

Handicap means, with respect to a person, a physical or mental impairment which substantially limits one or more major life activities; a record of such an impairment; or being regarded as having such an impairment. This term does not include current, illegal use of or addiction to a controlled substance. For purposes of this part, an individual shall not be considered to have a handicap solely because that individual is a transvestite. As used in this definition:

(a) *Physical or mental impairment* includes:

(1) Any physiological disorder or condition, cosmetic disfigurement, or anatomical loss affecting one or more of the following body systems: Neurological; musculoskeletal; special sense organs; respiratory, including speech organs; cardiovascular; reproductive; digestive; genito-urinary; hemic and lymphatic; skin; and endocrine; or

(2) Any mental or psychological disorder, such as mental retardation, organic brain syndrome, emotional or mental illness, and specific learning disabilities. The term *physical or mental impairment* includes, but is not limited to, such diseases and conditions as orthopedic, visual, speech and hearing impairments, cerebral palsy, autism, epilepsy, muscular dystrophy, multiple sclerosis, cancer, heart disease, diabetes, Human Immunodeficiency Virus infection, mental retardation, emotional illness, drug addiction (other than addiction caused by current, illegal use of a controlled substance) and alcoholism.

(b) *Major life activities* means functions such as caring for one's self, performing manual tasks, walking, seeing, hearing, speaking, breathing, learning and working.

(c) *Has a record of such an impairment* means has a history of, or has been misclassified as having, a mental or physical impairment that substantially limits one or more major life activities.

(d) *Is regarded as having an impairment* means:

(1) Has a physical or mental impairment that does not substantially limit one or more major life activities but that is treated by another person as constituting such a limitation;

(2) Has a physical or mental impairment that substantially limits one or

Office of Asst. Secy., Equal Opportunity, HUD　　　　　　**§ 100.203**

more major life activities only as a result of the attitudes of other toward such impairment; or

(3) Has none of the impairments defined in paragraph (a) of this definition but is treated by another person as having such an impairment.

Interior means the spaces, parts, components or elements of an individual dwelling unit.

Modification means any change to the public or common use areas of a building or any change to a dwelling unit.

Premises means the interior or exterior spaces, parts, components or elements of a building, including individual dwelling units and the public and common use areas of a building.

Public use areas means interior or exterior rooms or spaces of a building that are made available to the general public. Public use may be provided at a building that is privately or publicly owned.

Site means a parcel of land bounded by a property line or a designated portion of a public right or way.

[54 FR 3283, Jan. 23, 1989, as amended at 69 FR 18803, Apr. 9, 2004]

§ 100.202　General prohibitions against discrimination because of handicap.

(a) It shall be unlawful to discriminate in the sale or rental, or to otherwise make unavailable or deny, a dwelling to any buyer or renter because of a handicap of—

(1) That buyer or renter;

(2) A person residing in or intending to reside in that dwelling after it is so sold, rented, or made available; or

(3) Any person associated with that person.

(b) It shall be unlawful to discriminate against any person in the terms, conditions, or privileges of the sale or rental of a dwelling, or in the provision of services or facilities in connection with such dwelling, because of a handicap of—

(1) That buyer or renter;

(2) A person residing in or intending to reside in that dwelling after it is so sold, rented, or made available; or

(3) Any person associated with that person.

(c) It shall be unlawful to make an inquiry to determine whether an applicant for a dwelling, a person intending to reside in that dwelling after it is so sold, rented or made available, or any person associated with that person, has a handicap or to make inquiry as to the nature or severity of a handicap of such a person. However, this paragraph does not prohibit the following inquiries, provided these inquiries are made of all applicants, whether or not they have handicaps:

(1) Inquiry into an applicant's ability to meet the requirements of ownership or tenancy;

(2) Inquiry to determine whether an applicant is qualified for a dwelling available only to persons with handicaps or to persons with a particular type of handicap;

(3) Inquiry to determine whether an applicant for a dwelling is qualified for a priority available to persons with handicaps or to persons with a particular type of handicap;

(4) Inquiring whether an applicant for a dwelling is a current illegal abuser or addict of a controlled substance;

(5) Inquiring whether an applicant has been convicted of the illegal manufacture or distribution of a controlled substance.

(d) Nothing in this subpart requires that a dwelling be made available to an individual whose tenancy would constitute a direct threat to the health or safety of other individuals or whose tenancy would result in substantial physical damage to the property of others.

§ 100.203　Reasonable modifications of existing premises.

(a) It shall be unlawful for any person to refuse to permit, at the expense of a handicapped person, reasonable modifications of existing premises, occupied or to be occupied by a handicapped person, if the proposed modifications may be necessary to afford the handicapped person full enjoyment of the premises of a dwelling. In the case of a rental, the landlord may, where it is reasonable to do so, condition permission for a modification on the renter agreeing to restore the interior of the premises to the condition that existed before the modification, reasonable wear and tear excepted. The landlord may not increase for handicapped persons any customarily required security deposit.

323

§ 100.204

However, where it is necessary in order to ensure with reasonable certainty that funds will be available to pay for the restorations at the end of the tenancy, the landlord may negotiate as part of such a restoration agreement a provision requiring that the tenant pay into an interest bearing escrow account, over a reasonable period, a reasonable amount of money not to exceed the cost of the restorations. The interest in any such account shall accrue to the benefit of the tenant.

(b) A landlord may condition permission for a modification on the renter providing a reasonable description of the proposed modifications as well as reasonable assurances that the work will be done in a workmanlike manner and that any required building permits will be obtained.

(c) The application of paragraph (a) of this section may be illustrated by the following examples:

Example (1): A tenant with a handicap asks his or her landlord for permission to install grab bars in the bathroom at his or her own expense. It is necessary to reinforce the walls with blocking between studs in order to affix the grab bars. It is unlawful for the landlord to refuse to permit the tenant, at the tenant's own expense, from making the modifications necessary to add the grab bars. However, the landlord may condition permission for the modification on the tenant agreeing to restore the bathroom to the condition that existed before the modification, reasonable wear and tear excepted. It would be reasonable for the landlord to require the tenant to remove the grab bars at the end of the tenancy. The landlord may also reasonably require that the wall to which the grab bars are to be attached be repaired and restored to its original condition, reasonable wear and tear excepted. However, it would be unreasonable for the landlord to require the tenant to remove the blocking, since the reinforced walls will not interfere in any way with the landlord's or the next tenant's use and enjoyment of the premises and may be needed by some future tenant.

Example (2): An applicant for rental housing has a child who uses a wheelchair. The bathroom door in the dwelling unit is too narrow to permit the wheelchair to pass. The applicant asks the landlord for permission to widen the doorway at the applicant's own expense. It is unlawful for the landlord to refuse to permit the applicant to make the modification. Further, the landlord may *not*, in usual circumstances, condition permission for the modification on the applicant paying for the doorway to be narrowed at the end of

the lease because a wider doorway will not interfere with the landlord's or the next tenant's use and enjoyment of the premises.

§ 100.204 **Reasonable accommodations.**

(a) It shall be unlawful for any person to refuse to make reasonable accommodations in rules, policies, practices, or services, when such accommodations may be necessary to afford a handicapped person equal opportunity to use and enjoy a dwelling unit, including public and common use areas.

(b) The application of this section may be illustrated by the following examples:

Example (1): A blind applicant for rental housing wants live in a dwelling unit with a seeing eye dog. The building has a *no pets* policy. It is a violation of § 100.204 for the owner or manager of the apartment complex to refuse to permit the applicant to live in the apartment with a seeing eye dog because, without the seeing eye dog, the blind person will not have an equal opportunity to use and enjoy a dwelling.

Example (2): Progress Gardens is a 300 unit apartment complex with 450 parking spaces which are available to tenants and guests of Progress Gardens on a *first come first served* basis. John applies for housing in Progress Gardens. John is mobility impaired and is unable to walk more than a short distance and therefore requests that a parking space near his unit be reserved for him so he will not have to walk very far to get to his apartment. It is a violation of § 100.204 for the owner or manager of Progress Gardens to refuse to make this accommodation. Without a reserved space, John might be unable to live in Progress Gardens at all or, when he has to park in a space far from his unit, might have great difficulty getting from his car to his apartment unit. The accommodation therefore is necessary to afford John an equal opportunity to use and enjoy a dwelling. The accommodation is reasonable because it is feasible and practical under the circumstances.

§ 100.205 **Design and construction requirements.**

(a) Covered multifamily dwellings for first occupancy after March 13, 1991 shall be designed and constructed to have at least one building entrance on an accessible route unless it is impractical to do so because of the terrain or unusual characteristics of the site. For purposes of this section, a covered multifamily dwelling shall be deemed to be designed and constructed for first occupancy on or before March 13, 1991, if the

640

Fair Housing

A Guidebook for Owners and Managers of Apartments

Office of Asst. Secy., Equal Opportunity, HUD § 100.205

dwelling is occupied by that date, or if the last building permit or renewal thereof for the dwelling is issued by a State, County or local government on or before June 15, 1990. The burden of establishing impracticality because of terrain or unusual site characteristics is on the person or persons who designed or constructed the housing facility.

(b) The application of paragraph (a) of this section may be illustrated by the following examples:

Example (1): A real estate developer plans to construct six covered multifamily dwelling units on a site with a hilly terrain. Because of the terrain, it will be necessary to climb a long and steep stairway in order to enter the dwellings. Since there is no practical way to provide an accessible route to any of the dwellings, one need not be provided.

Example (2): A real estate developer plans to construct a building consisting of 10 units of multifamily housing on a waterfront site that floods frequently. Because of this unusual characteristic of the site, the builder plans to construct the building on stilts. It is customary for housing in the geographic area where the site is located to be built on stilts. The housing may lawfully be constructed on the proposed site on stilts even though this means that there will be no practical way to provide an accessible route to the building entrance.

Example (3): A real estate developer plans to construct a multifamily housing facility on a particular site. The developer would like the facility to be built on the site to contain as many units as possible. Because of the configuration and terrain of the site, it is possible to construct a building with 105 units on the site provided the site does not have an accessible route leading to the building entrance. It is also possible to construct a building on the site with an accessible route leading to the building entrance. However, such a building would have no more than 100 dwelling units. The building to be constructed on the site must have a building entrance on an accessible route because it is not impractical to provide such an entrance because of the terrain or unusual characteristics of the site.

(c) All covered multifamily dwellings for first occupancy after March 13, 1991 with a building entrance on an accessible route shall be designed and constructed in such a manner that—

(1) The public and common use areas are readily accessible to and usable by handicapped persons;

(2) All the doors designed to allow passage into and within all premises are sufficiently wide to allow passage by handicapped persons in wheelchairs; and

(3) All premises within covered multifamily dwelling units contain the following features of adaptable design:

(i) An accessible route into and through the covered dwelling unit;

(ii) Light switches, electrical outlets, thermostats, and other environmental controls in accessible locations;

(iii) Reinforcements in bathroom walls to allow later installation of grab bars around the toilet, tub, shower, stall and shower seat, where such facilities are provided; and

(iv) Usable kitchens and bathrooms such that an individual in a wheelchair can maneuver about the space.

(d) The application of paragraph (c) of this section may be illustrated by the following examples:

Example (1): A developer plans to construct a 100 unit condominium apartment building with one elevator. In accordance with paragraph (a), the building has at least one accessible route leading to an accessible entrance. All 100 units are covered multifamily dwelling units and they all must be designed and constructed so that they comply with the accessibility requirements of paragraph (c) of this section.

Example (2): A developer plans to construct 30 garden apartments in a three story building. The building will not have an elevator. The building will have one accessible entrance which will be on the first floor. Since the building does not have an elevator, only the *ground floor* units are covered multifamily units. The *ground floor* is the first floor because that is the floor that has an accessible entrance. All of the dwelling units on the first floor must meet the accessibility requirements of paragraph (c) of this section and must have access to at least one of each type of public or common use area available for residents in the building.

(e) Compliance with the appropriate requirements of ANSI A117.1–1986 suffices to satisfy the requirements of paragraph (c)(3) of this section.

(f) Compliance with a duly enacted law of a State or unit of general local government that includes the requirements of paragraphs (a) and (c) of this section satisfies the requirements of paragraphs (a) and (c) of this section.

(g)(1) It is the policy of HUD to encourage States and units of general local government to include, in their existing procedures for the review and approval of newly constructed covered multifamily dwellings, determinations as to whether the design and construction of such dwellings are consistent with paragraphs (a) and (c) of this section.

(2) A State or unit of general local government may review and approve newly constructed multifamily dwellings for the purpose of making determinations as to whether the requirements of paragraphs (a) and (c) of this section are met.

(h) Determinations of compliance or noncompliance by a State or a unit of general local government under paragraph (f) or (g) of this section are not conclusive in enforcement proceedings under the Fair Housing Amendments Act.

(i) This subpart does not invalidate or limit any law of a State or political subdivision of a State that requires dwellings to be designed and constructed in a manner that affords handicapped persons greater access than is required by this subpart.

[54 FR 3283, Jan. 23, 1989, as amended at 56 FR 11665, Mar. 20, 1991]

Subpart E—Housing for Older Persons

§ 100.300 Purpose.

The purpose of this subpart is to effectuate the exemption in the Fair Housing Amendments Act of 1988 that relates to housing for older persons.

§ 100.301 Exemption.

(a) The provisions regarding familial status in this part do not apply to housing which satisfies the requirements of §§ 100.302, 100.303 or § 100.304.

(b) Nothing in this part limits the applicability of any reasonable local, State, or Federal restrictions regarding the maximum number of occupants permitted to occupy a dwelling.

§ 100.302 State and Federal elderly housing programs.

The provisions regarding familial status in this part shall not apply to housing provided under any Federal or State program that the Secretary de-

termines is specifically designed and operated to assist elderly persons, as defined in the State or Federal program.

§ 100.303 62 or over housing.

(a) The provisions regarding familial status in this part shall not apply to housing intended for, and solely occupied by, persons 62 years of age or older. Housing satisfies the requirements of this section even though:

(1) There are persons residing in such housing on September 13, 1988 who are under 62 years of age, provided that all new occupants are persons 62 years of age or older;

(2) There are unoccupied units, provided that such units are reserved for occupancy by persons 62 years of age or over;

(3) There are units occupied by employees of the housing (and family members residing in the same unit) who are under 62 years of age provided they perform substantial duties directly related to the management or maintenance of the housing.

(b) The following examples illustrate the application of paragraph (a) of this section:

Example (1): John and Mary apply for housing at the Vista Heights apartment complex which is an elderly housing complex operated for persons 62 years of age or older. John is 62 years of age. Mary is 59 years of age. If Vista Heights wishes to retain its "62 or over" exemption it must refuse to rent to John and Mary because Mary is under 62 years of age. However, if Vista Heights does rent to John and Mary, it might qualify for the "55 or over" exemption in § 100.304.

Example (2): The Blueberry Hill retirement community has 100 dwelling units. On September 13, 1988, 15 units were vacant and 35 units were occupied with at least one person who is under 62 years of age. The remaining 50 units were occupied by persons who were all 62 years of age or older. Blueberry Hill can qualify for the "62 or over" exemption as long as all units that were occupied after September 13, 1988 are occupied by persons who were 62 years of age or older. The people under 62 in the 35 units previously described need not be required to leave for Blueberry Hill to qualify for the "62 or over" exemption.

Office of Asst. Secy., Equal Opportunity, HUD §100.305

§100.304 Housing for persons who are 55 years of age or older.

(a) The provisions regarding familial status in this part shall not apply to housing intended and operated for persons 55 years of age or older. Housing qualifies for this exemption if:

(1) The alleged violation occurred before December 28, 1995 and the housing community or facility complied with the HUD regulations in effect at the time of the alleged violation; or

(2) The alleged violation occurred on or after December 28, 1995 and the housing community or facility complies with:

(i) Section 807(b)(2)(C) (42 U.S.C. 3607(b)) of the Fair Housing Act as amended; and

(ii) 24 CFR 100.305, 100.306, and 100.307.

(b) For purposes of this subpart, *housing facility or community* means any dwelling or group of dwelling units governed by a common set of rules, regulations or restrictions. A portion or portions of a single building shall not constitute a housing facility or community. Examples of a housing facility or community include, but are not limited to:

(1) A condominium association;

(2) A cooperative;

(3) A property governed by a home-owners' or resident association;

(4) A municipally zoned area;

(5) A leased property under common private ownership;

(6) A mobile home park; and

(7) A manufactured housing community.

(c) For purposes of this subpart, *older person* means a person 55 years of age or older.

[64 FR 16329, Apr. 2, 1999]

§100.305 80 percent occupancy.

(a) In order for a housing facility or community to qualify as housing for older persons under §100.304, at least 80 percent of its occupied units must be occupied by at least one person 55 years of age or older.

(b) For purposes of this subpart, *occupied unit* means:

(1) A dwelling unit that is actually occupied by one or more persons on the date that the exemption is claimed; or

(2) A temporarily vacant unit, if the primary occupant has resided in the unit during the past year and intends to return on a periodic basis.

(c) For purposes of this subpart, *occupied by at least one person 55 years of age or older* means that on the date the exemption for housing designed for persons who are 55 years of age or older is claimed:

(1) At least one occupant of the dwelling unit is 55 years of age or older; or

(2) If the dwelling unit is temporarily vacant, at least one of the occupants immediately prior to the date on which the unit was temporarily vacated was 55 years of age or older.

(d) Newly constructed housing for first occupancy after March 12, 1989 need not comply with the requirements of this section until at least 25 percent of the units are occupied. For purposes of this section, newly constructed housing includes a facility or community that has been wholly unoccupied for at least 90 days prior to re-occupancy due to renovation or rehabilitation.

(e) Housing satisfies the requirements of this section even though:

(1) On September 13, 1988, under 80 percent of the occupied units in the housing facility or community were occupied by at least one person 55 years of age or older, provided that at least 80 percent of the units occupied by new occupants after September 13, 1988 are occupied by at least one person 55 years of age or older.

(2) There are unoccupied units, provided that at least 80 percent of the occupied units are occupied by at least one person 55 years of age or older.

(3) There are units occupied by employees of the housing facility or community (and family members residing in the same unit) who are under 55 years of age, provided the employees perform substantial duties related to the management or maintenance of the facility or community.

(4) There are units occupied by persons who are necessary to provide a reasonable accommodation to disabled residents as required by §100.204 and who are under the age of 55.

(5) For a period expiring one year from the effective date of this final

70982 Federal Register / Vol. 63, No. 245 / Tuesday, December 22, 1998 / Notices

DEPARTMENT OF HOUSING AND URBAN DEVELOPMENT

[Docket No. FR–4405–N–01]

Fair Housing Enforcement— Occupancy Standards; Notice of Statement of Policy

Note: This document, FR Doc. 98–33568, was originally published on December 18, 1998 at 63 FR 70256–70257. It is being republished to reproduce the camera copy of the appendix furnished by the agency.

AGENCY: Office of the Assistant Secretary for Fair Housing and Equal Opportunity, HUD.

ACTION: Notice of Statement of Policy.

SUMMARY: This statement of policy advises the public of the factors that HUD will consider when evaluating a housing provider's occupancy policies to determine whether actions under the provider's policies may constitute discriminatory conduct under the Fair Housing Act on the basis of familial status (the presence of children in a family). Publication of this notice meets the requirements of the Quality Housing and Work Responsibility Act of 1998.

DATES: Effective date: December 18, 1998.

FOR FURTHER INFORMATION CONTACT: Sara Pratt, Director, Office of Investigations, Office of Fair Housing and Equal Opportunity, Room 5204, 451 Seventh Street, SW, Washington, DC 20410, telephone (202) 708–2290 (not a toll-free number). For hearing- and speech-impaired persons, this telephone number may be accessed via TTY (text telephone) by calling the Federal Information Relay Service at 1–800–877–8339 (toll-free).

SUPPLEMENTARY INFORMATION:

Statutory and Regulatory Background

Section 589 of the Quality Housing and Work Responsibility Act of 1998 (Pub. L. 105–276, 112 Stat. 2461, approved October 21, 1998, "QHWRA") requires HUD to publish a notice in the **Federal Register** that advises the public of the occupancy standards that HUD uses for enforcement purposes under the Fair Housing Act (42 U.S.C. 3601–3619). Section 589 requires HUD to publish this notice within 60 days of enactment of the QHWRA, and states that the notice will be effective upon publication. Specifically, section 589 states, in relevant part, that:

[T]he specific and unmodified standards provided in the March 20, 1991, Memorandum from the General Counsel of [HUD] to all Regional Counsel shall be the policy of [HUD] with respect to complaints of discrimination under the Fair Housing Act * * * on the basis of familial status which involve an occupancy standard established by a housing provider.

The Fair Housing Act prohibits discrimination in any aspect of the sale, rental, financing or advertising of dwellings on the basis of race, color, religion, national origin, sex or familial status (the presence of children in the family). The Fair Housing Act also provides that nothing in the Act "limits the applicability of any reasonable local, State or Federal restrictions regarding the maximum number of occupants permitted to occupy a dwelling." The Fair Housing Act gave HUD responsibility for implementation and enforcement of the Act's requirements. The Fair Housing Act authorizes HUD to receive complaints alleging discrimination in violation of the Act, to investigate these complaints, and to engage in efforts to resolve informally matters raised in the complaint. In cases where the complaint is not resolved, the Fair Housing Act authorizes HUD to make a determination of whether or not there is reasonable cause to believe that discrimination has occurred. HUD's regulations, implementing the Fair Housing Act (42 U.S.C. 3614) are found in 24 CFR part 100.

In 1991, HUD's General Counsel, Frank Keating, determined that some confusion existed because of the absence of more detailed guidance regarding what occupancy restrictions are reasonable under the Act. To address this confusion, General Counsel Keating issued internal guidance to HUD Regional Counsel on factors that they should consider when examining complaints filed with HUD under the Fair Housing Act, to determine whether or not there is reasonable cause to believe discrimination has occurred.

This Notice

Through this notice HUD implements section 589 of the QHWRA by adopting as its policy on occupancy standards, for purposes of enforcement actions under the Fair Housing Act, the standards provided in the Memorandum of General Counsel Frank Keating to Regional Counsel dated March 20, 1991, attached as Appendix A.

Authority: 42 U.S.C. 3535(d), 112 Stat. 2461.

Dated: December 14, 1998.

Eva M. Plaza,

Assistant Secretary for Fair Housing and Equal Opportunity.

BILLING CODE 4210–28–P

Federal Register/Vol. 63, No. 245/Tuesday, December 22, 1998/Notices   70983

U. S. Department of Housing and Urban Development
Washington, D.C. 20410-0500

APPENDIX A

March 20, 1991

OFFICE OF GENERAL COUNSEL

MEMORANDUM FOR: All Regional Counsel

FROM: Frank Keating, G

SUBJECT: Fair Housing Enforcement Policy: Occupancy Cases

    On February 21, 1991, I issued a memorandum designed to facilitate your review of cases involving occupancy policies under the Fair Housing Act. The memorandum was based on my review of a significant number of such cases and was intended to constitute internal guidance to be used by Regional Counsel in reviewing cases involving occupancy restrictions. It was not intended to create a definitive test for whether a landlord or manager would be liable in a particular case, nor was it intended to establish occupancy policies or requirements for any particular type of housing.

    However, in discussions within the Department, and with the Department of Justice and the public, it is clear that the February 21 memorandum has resulted in a significant misunderstanding of the Department's position on the question of occupancy policies which would be reasonable under the Fair Housing Act. In this respect, many people mistakenly viewed the February 21 memorandum as indicating that the Department was establishing an occupancy policy which it would consider reasonable in any fair housing case, rather than providing guidance to Regional Counsel on the evaluation of evidence in familial status cases which involve the use of an occupancy policy adopted by a housing provider.

    For example, there is a HUD Handbook provision regarding the size of the unit needed for public housing tenants. See Handbook 7465.1 REV-2, Public Housing Occupancy Handbook: Admission, revised section 5-1 (issued February 12, 1991). While that Handbook provision states that HUD does not specify the number of persons who may live in public housing units of various sizes, it provides guidance about the factors public housing agencies may consider in establishing reasonable occupancy policies. Neither this memorandum nor the memorandum of February 21, 1991 overrides the guidance that Handbook provides about program requirements.

70984   Federal Register / Vol. 63, No. 245 / Tuesday, December 22, 1998 / Notices

As you know, assuring Fair Housing for all is one of Secretary Kemp's top priorities. Prompt and vigorous enforcement of all the provisions of the Fair Housing Act, including the protections in the Act for families with children, is a critical responsibility of mine and every person in the Office of General Counsel. I expect Headquarters and Regional Office staff to continue their vigilant efforts to proceed to formal enforcement in all cases in which there is reasonable cause to believe that a discriminatory housing practice under the Act has occurred or is about to occur. This is particularly important in cases where occupancy restrictions are used to exclude families with children or to unreasonably limit the ability of families with children to obtain housing.

In order to assure that the Department's position in the area of occupancy policies is fully understood, I believe that it is imperative to articulate more fully the Department's position on reasonable occupancy policies and to describe the approach that the Department takes in its review of occupancy cases.

Specifically, the Department believes that an occupancy policy of two persons in a bedroom, as a general rule, is reasonable under the Fair Housing Act. The Department of Justice has advised us that this is the general policy it has incorporated in consent decrees and proposed orders, and such a general policy also is consistent with the guidance provided to housing providers in the HUD handbook referenced above. However, the reasonableness of any occupancy policy is rebuttable, and neither the February 21 memorandum nor this memorandum implies that the Department will determine compliance with the Fair Housing Act based solely on the number of people permitted in each bedroom. Indeed, as we stated in the final rule implementing the Fair Housing Amendments Act of 1988, the Department's position is as follows:

> [T]here is nothing in the legislative history which indicates any intent on the part of Congress to provide for the development of a national occupancy code. . . .

> On the other hand, there is no basis to conclude that Congress intended that an owner or manager of dwellings would be unable to restrict the number of occupants who could reside in a dwelling. Thus, the Department believes that in appropriate circumstances, owners and managers may develop and implement reasonable occupancy requirements based on factors such as the number and size of sleeping areas or bedrooms and the overall size of the dwelling unit. In this regard, it must be noted that, in connection with a complaint alleging discrimination on the basis of familial status, the Department will carefully examine any such

Federal Register / Vol. 63, No. 245 / Tuesday, December 22, 1998 / Notices   70985

nongovernmental restriction to determine whether it operates
unreasonably to limit or exclude families with children.

24 C.F.R. Chapter I, Subchapter A. Appendix I at 566-67 (1990).

Thus, in reviewing occupancy cases, HUD will consider the
size and number of bedrooms and other special circumstances. The
following principles and hypothetical examples should assist you
in determining whether the size of the bedrooms or special
circumstances would make an occupancy policy unreasonable.

Size of bedrooms and unit

Consider two theoretical situations in which a housing
provider refused to permit a family of five to rent a two-bedroom
dwelling based on a "two people per bedroom" policy. In the
first, the complainants are a family of five who applied to rent
an apartment with two large bedrooms and spacious living areas.
In the second, the complainants are a family of five who applied
to rent a mobile home space on which they planned to live in a
small two-bedroom mobile home. Depending on the other facts,
issuance of a charge might be warranted in the first situation,
but not in the second.

The size of the bedrooms also can be a factor suggesting
that a determination of no reasonable cause is appropriate. For
example, if a mobile home is advertised as a "two-bedroom" home,
but one bedroom is extremely small, depending on all the facts,
it could be reasonable for the park manager to limit occupancy of
the home to two people.

Age of children

The following hypotheticals involving two housing providers
who refused to permit three people to share a bedroom illustrate
this principle. In the first, the complainants are two adult
parents who applied to rent a one-bedroom apartment with their
infant child, and both the bedroom and the apartment were large.
In the second, the complainants are a family of two adult parents
and one teenager who applied to rent a one-bedroom apartment.
Depending on the other facts, issuance of a charge might be
warranted in the first hypothetical, but not in the second.

Configuration of unit

The following imaginary situations illustrate special
circumstances involving unit configuration. Two condominium
associations each reject a purchase by a family of two adults and
three children based on a rule limiting sales to buyers who
satisfy a "two people per bedroom" occupancy policy. The first
association manages a building in which the family of the five sought
to purchase a unit consisting of two bedrooms plus a den or

70986   Federal Register/Vol. 63, No. 245/Tuesday, December 22, 1998/Notices

study. The second manages a building in which the family of five sought to purchase a two-bedroom unit which did not have a study or den. Depending on the other facts, a charge might be warranted in the first situation, but not in the second.

Other physical limitations of housing

In addition to physical considerations such as the size of each bedroom and the overall size and configuration of the dwelling, the Department will consider limiting factors identified by housing providers, such as the capacity of the septic, sewer, or other building systems.

State and local law

If a dwelling is governed by State or local governmental occupancy requirements, and the housing provider's occupancy policies reflect those requirements, HUD would consider the governmental requirements as a special circumstance tending to indicate that the housing provider's occupancy policies are reasonable.

Other relevant factors

Other relevant factors supporting a reasonable cause recommendation based on the conclusion that the occupancy policies are pretextual would include evidence that the housing provider has: (1) made discriminatory statements; (2) adopted discriminatory rules governing the use of common facilities; (3) taken other steps to discourage families with children from living in its housing; or (4) enforced its occupancy policies only against families with children. For example, the fact that a development was previously marketed as an "adults only" development would militate in favor of issuing a charge. This is an especially strong factor if there is other evidence suggesting that the occupancy policies are a pretext for excluding families with children.

An occupancy policy which limits the number of <u>children</u> per unit is less likely to be reasonable than one which limits the number of <u>people</u> per unit.

Special circumstances also may be found where the housing provider limits the total number of dwellings he or she is willing to rent to families with children. For example, assume a landlord owns a building of two-bedroom units, in which a policy of four people per unit is reasonable. If the landlord adopts a four person per unit policy, but refuses to rent to a family of two adults and two children because twenty of the thirty units already are occupied by families with children, a reasonable cause recommendation would be warranted.

Federal Register / Vol. 63, No. 245 / Tuesday, December 22, 1998 / Notices   70987

If your review of the evidence indicates that these or other special circumstances are present, making application of a "two people per bedroom" policy unreasonably restrictive, you should prepare a reasonable cause determination. The Executive Summary should explain the special circumstances which support your recommendation.

[FR Doc. 98–33568 Filed 12–17–98; 8:45 am]
BILLING CODE BILLING CODE 4210–28–C

Appendix C: Sources for Regulations and Information

The U.S. Department of Justice offers technical assistance on the ADA Standards for Accessible Design and other ADA provisions applying to businesses, non-profit service agencies, and state and local government programs.

Homepage:
www.usdoj.gov

ADA Information Line for documents and questions
(800) 514-0301 (voice)
(800) 514-0383 (TDD)

Publications and Downloads
www.usdoj.gov/crt/ada/publicat.htm

The Access Board is an independent Federal agency that develops accessibility guidelines and provides technical assistance.

Homepage
www.access-board.gov

Telephone
(800) 872-2253 (voice)
(800) 993-2822 (TDD)

Publications and Downloads
Americans With Disabilities Act Accessibility Guidelines:
www.access-board.gov/adaag/html/adaag.htm
Uniform Federal Accessibility Standards (UFAS):
www.access-board.gov/ufas/ufas-html/ufas.htm

The U.S. Department of Housing and Urban Development, Office of Fair Housing and Equal Opportunity is responsible for enforcement of the Fair Housing Act and other civil rights laws.

Homepage:
http://www.hud.gov/offices/fheo/index.cfm

Telephone
(800) 347-3739 (voice)

Publications and Downloads
www.hudclips.org

INDEX

W

The Compass Group, LLC

Compass is a consulting firm specializing in affordable housing policy, finance and management. Our expertise is most valuable to those with portfolios facing change. Public and private clients include apartment owners, not-for-profits, trade associations, and government agencies.

Compass works in all facets of the multifamily affordable housing challenge, from transactions to regulations. Please contact us if you are interested in learning more about who we are and what we do.

The Compass Group, LLC
927 15th Street, N.W., Suite 600
Washington, DC 20005
www.compassgroup.net

NAHMA

NAHMA is the leading voice for affordable housing management, advocating on behalf of multifamily property managers and owners whose mission is to provide quality affordable housing. NAHMA supports legislative and regulatory policy that promotes the development and preservation of decent and safe affordable housing, is a vital resource for technical education and information, fosters strategic relations between government and industry, and recognizes those who exemplify the best in affordable housing. Founded in 1990, NAHMA's membership today includes the industry's most distinguished multifamily management companies, owners and other industry stakeholders. To learn more about NAHMA, contact us at:

National Affordable Housing Management Association
400 N. Columbus St., Suite 203
Alexandria, VA 22314
(703) 683-8630
www.nahma.org

To order
additional copies
of this book:

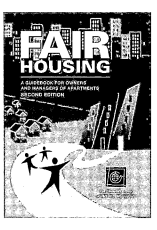

Fair Housing

A Guidebook for Owners and Managers of Apartments, Second Edition

Published by the Compass Group, LLC

ISBN: 978-0-615-2291-4

This invaluable reference work should be in the hands of everyone concerned with the professional management of apartments—from leasing agents to policy analysts.

Thorough research, extensive cross-referencing and indexing, clean and straightforward writing, and a quick-access question and answer format makes this the only reference of its kind on the subject.

Substantially updated in 2008.

To Order Call 877-563-4605 (toll free)

Discounts for volume purchasers. In addition, NAHMA members enjoy a discounted price.

CD-ROM Edition

The Fair Housing Guidebook, Second Edition is also available in CD-ROM format, for ease of use. Word-search the material, or follow the extensive hyperlinks to explore the facets of a complex issue.

Electronic Copy Licensing

The Fair Housing Guidebook, Second Edition is available as a site-license, for corporate users who wish to ensure broad access within an organization. Please contact anker@compassgroup.net to inquire about this option.